"Amid it all, Glidden the storyteller exudes intimacy and warm… her sometimes confessional persona. And Glidden the knowledge-… she paints: forever toward the light."—MICHAEL CAVNA, THE *WASHINGTON*…

"A memoir of a trip this left-leaning Jew takes to Israel, determined to have her ideas about the Israeli-Palestinian conflict confirmed. Of course, things turn out more complicated than Glidden had imagined. So do her deceptively simple line drawings, their delicate watercolor shadings, and the thinking that informs the vivid dialogue in a graphic nonfiction novel of subtlety and understated wit." —KEN TUCKER, *ENTERTAINMENT WEEKLY*

"Glidden, a progressive American Jew who is sharply critical of Israeli policies vis-à-vis the Occupied Territories, went on an all-expense paid "birthright" trip to Israel in an attempt to discover some grand truths at the heart of the Arab-Israeli conflict. This graphic memoir tells the touching and often funny story of her utter failure to do so."—*PUBLISHERS WEEKLY*

"Beautiful watercolors and well-chosen viewpoints detail the land and architecture, and a richly individuated cast of characters carries the reader into and beyond the Israel Glidden experiences as she comes to the realization that others don't need to agree with her in order for her to feel heard by them."—*BOOKLIST*

"Glidden's book is a serious discussion, but one which is carried out with humor and imagination." —NIRIT ANDERMAN, *HAARETZ*

"[Glidden] turns her own misconceptions into a whimsical but cutting memoir of a Birthright Israel trip, replete with sharp-eyed observations about Holy-Land quirks."—MICHAEL KAMINER, *FORWARD*

"The book is part travelogue, part coming-of-age memoir, and part intrepid if relentless quest for cultural understanding."—DEBORAH VANKIN, *LOS ANGELES TIMES HERO COMPLEX*

"Glidden should be commended for taking on this heated topic and treating it with honesty, self-reflection, and humor."—JUDY BATALION, *JEWISH QUARTERLY*

"Sarah's pre-conceived notions were sometimes confirmed, sometimes challenged, and she emerges from the whole experience perhaps more confused but definitely more enlightened. Welcome to the Middle East where nothing is black and white."—CK, *JEWLICIOUS*

"Israel tugs at her heart, and when [Glidden] feels an unexpected connection to the land and the people, her emotions are palpable to readers."—WENDY WASMAN, *JEWISH BOOK COUNCIL*

"This is a book for anyone who has sought to understand the world around them and realized how much more there is to learn."—DAVID WOLKIN, *COMICS ALLIANCE*

"Glidden took a Birthright Israel tour to try to understand better what drives all the tension, hatred, and conflict between Israel and Palestine. She turned her experiences into this, one of the best graphic novels of the last few years."—JASON DIAMOND, *FLAVORWIRE*

"Glidden's art is perfect for this book. [Her] figures are simple and expressive, and the watercolor artwork makes the backdrop and scenery feel realistic but slightly tinged with a shadow of memory, like a postcard."—PAUL CONSTANT, THE *STRANGER*

"*How To Understand Israel* lays out a fairly comprehensive history of the country and its conflicts, but what gives the book its spark is the way Glidden nests the history in her own prejudices—while understanding that they are prejudices…the result is a surprisingly disarming book—easy to read, and rewarding to contemplate."—THE *AV CLUB*

"Religiously non-observant and sympathetic to Palestinians at the start, Glidden has an emotional trip, trying to separate one person's truth from another's…This is one of the best graphic stories of 2010." —MIKE RHODE, *WASHINGTON CITY PAPER*

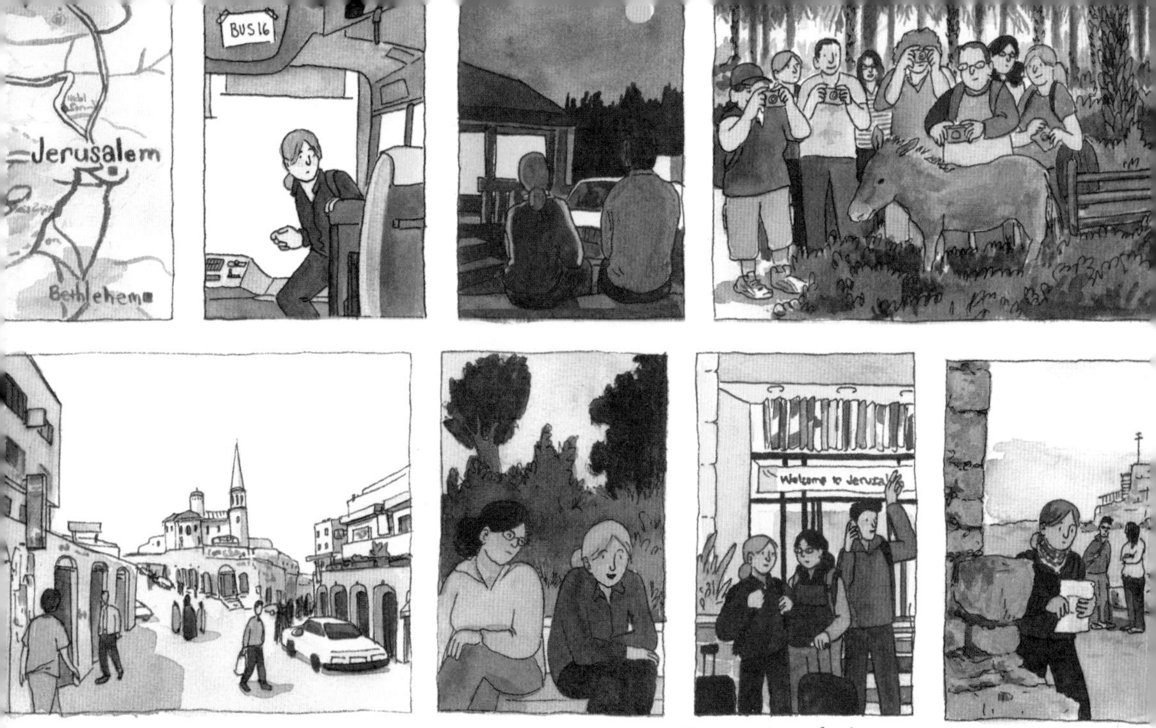

Jerusalem
Bethlehem
BUS 16

For Renée!

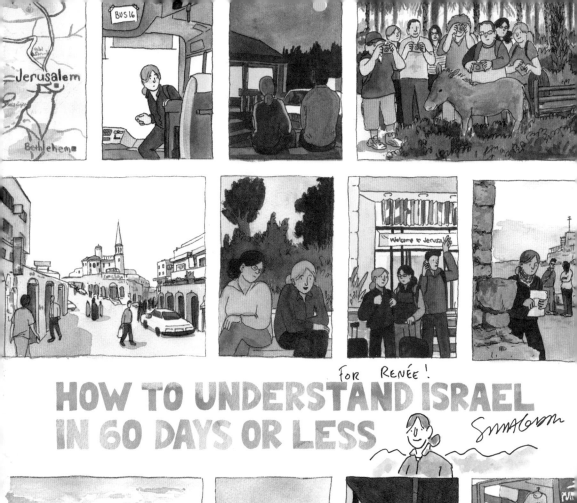

HOW TO UNDERSTAND ISRAEL IN 60 DAYS OR LESS

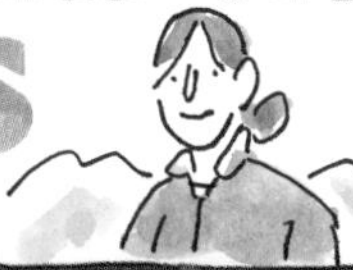

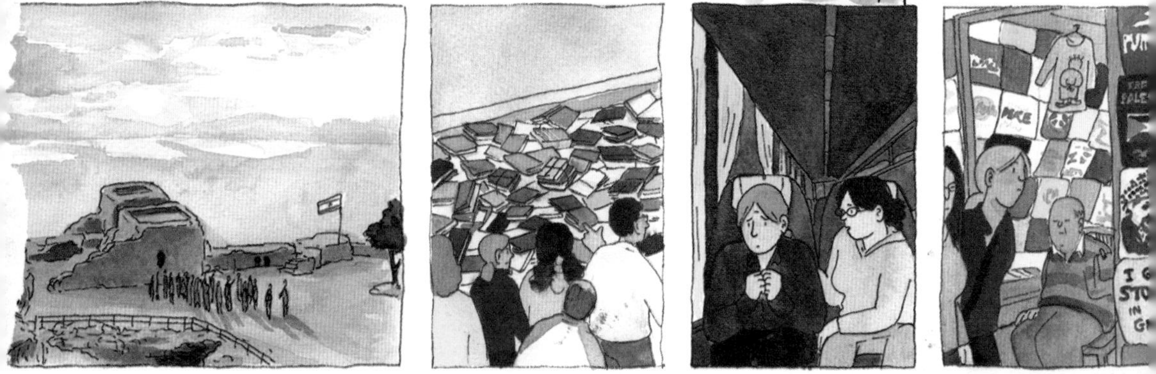

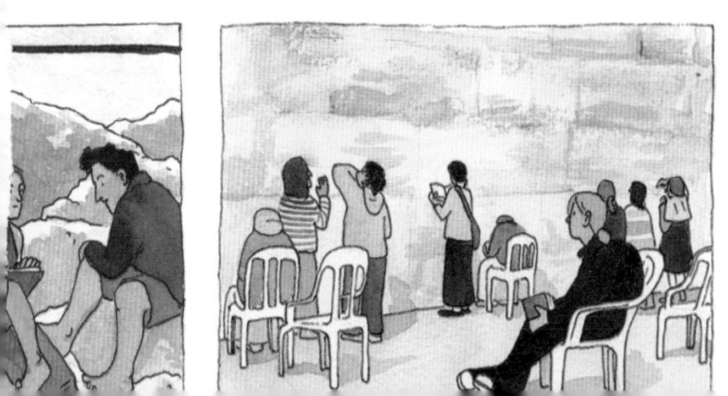

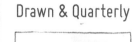

Drawn & Quarterly

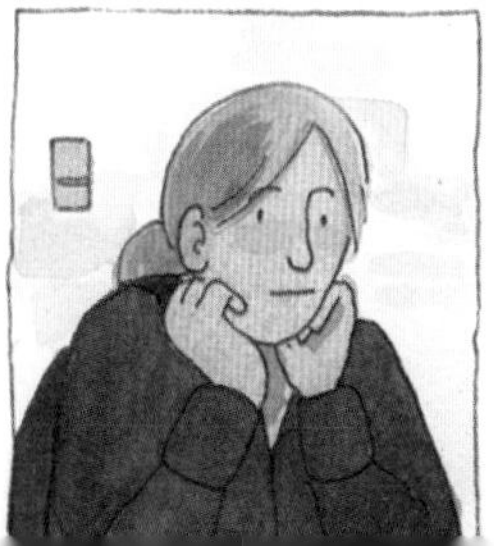

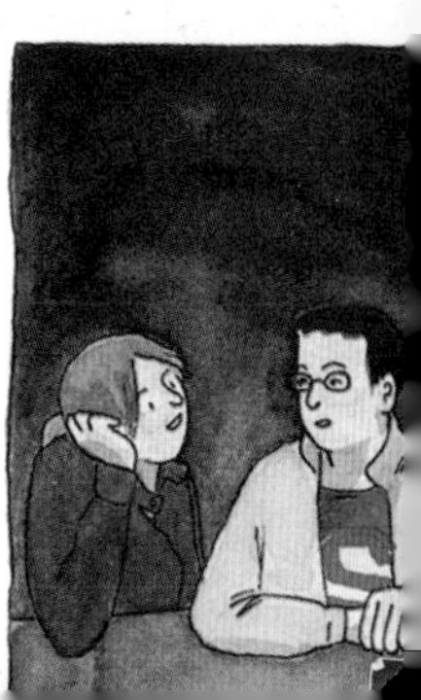

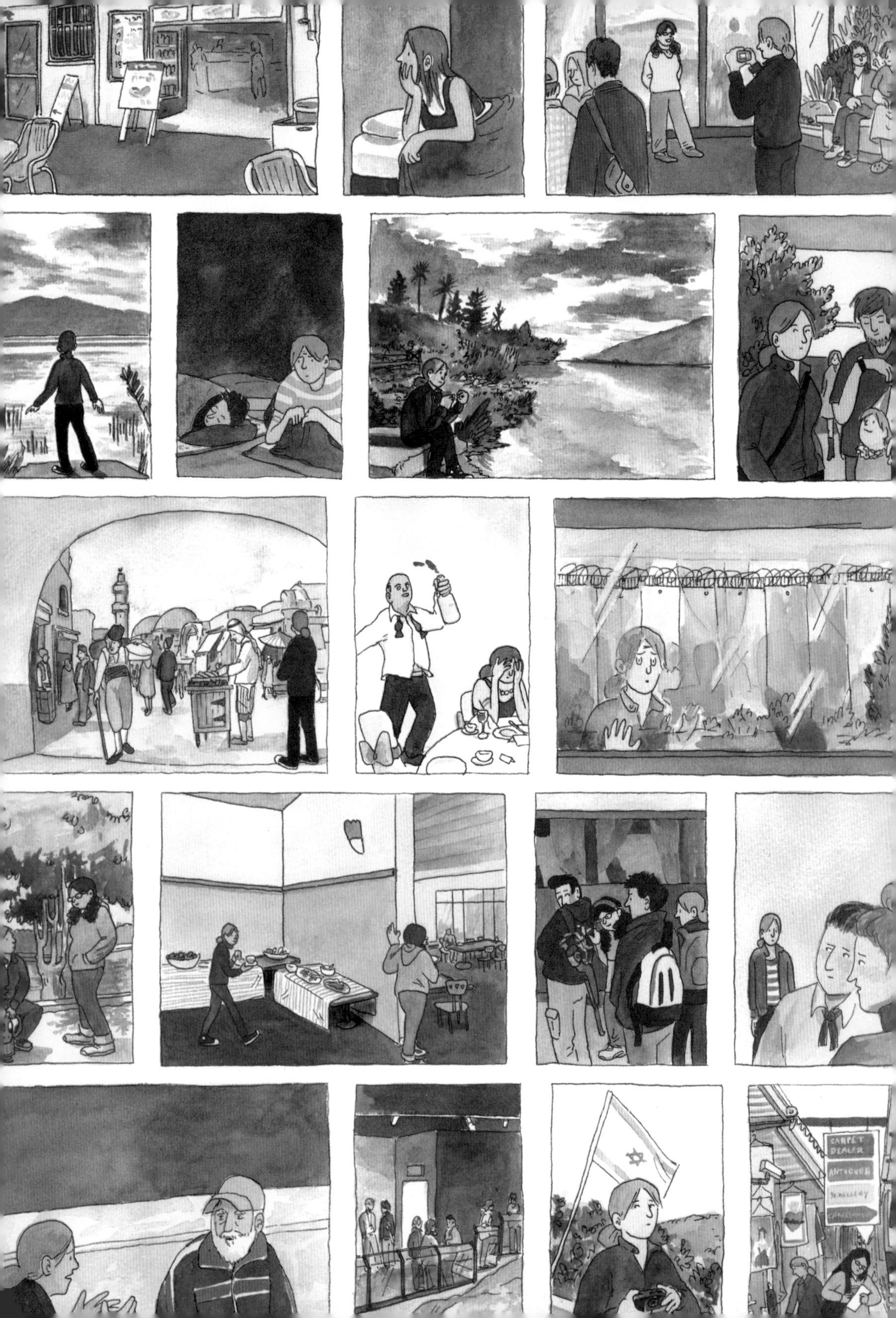
CARPET DEALER
ANTIQUES

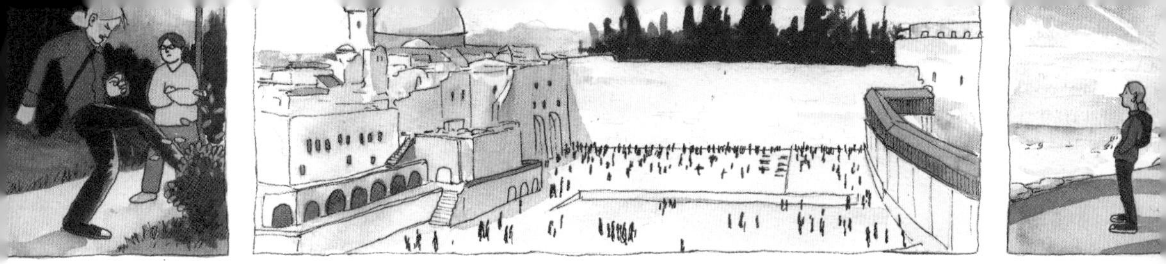

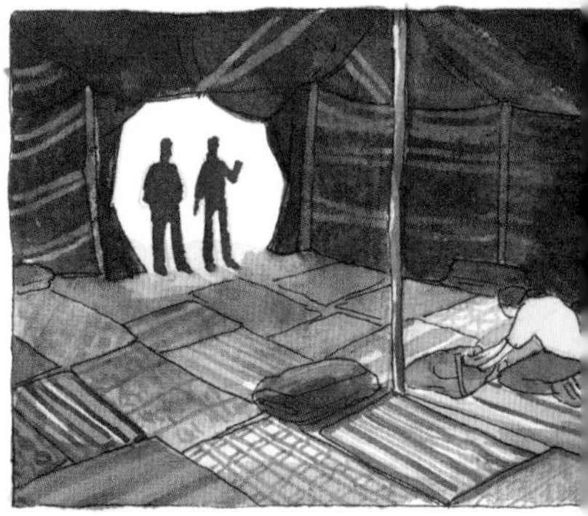

HOW TO UNDERSTAND ISRAEL IN 60 DAYS OR LESS

SARAH GLIDDEN

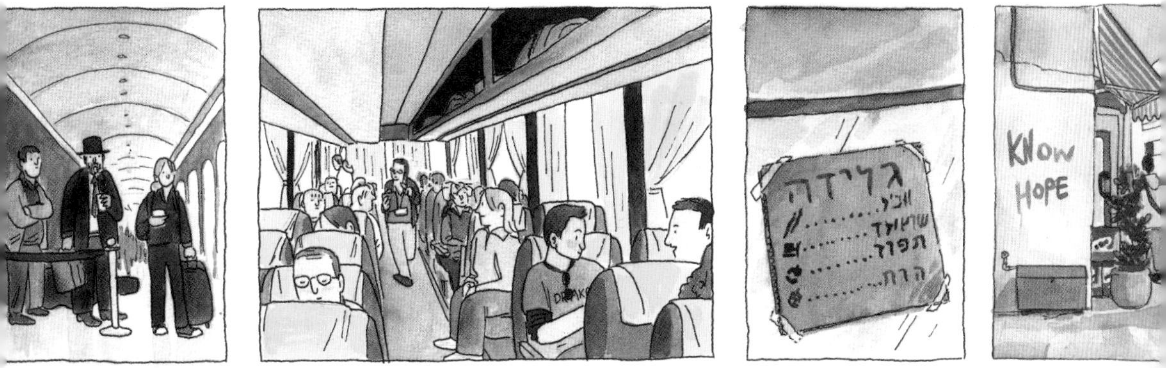
KNOW
HOPE

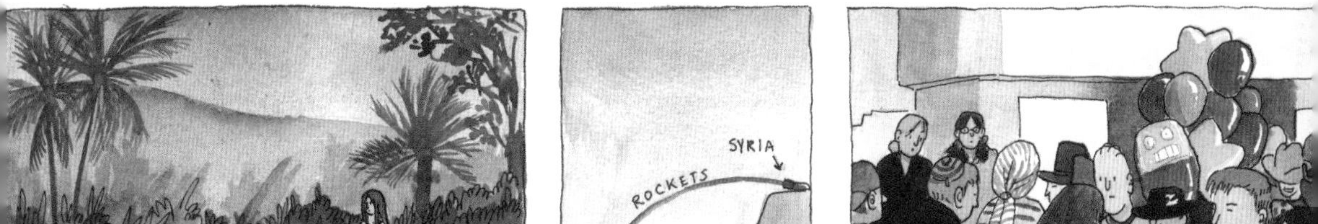
SYRIA
ROCKETS
ISRAEL

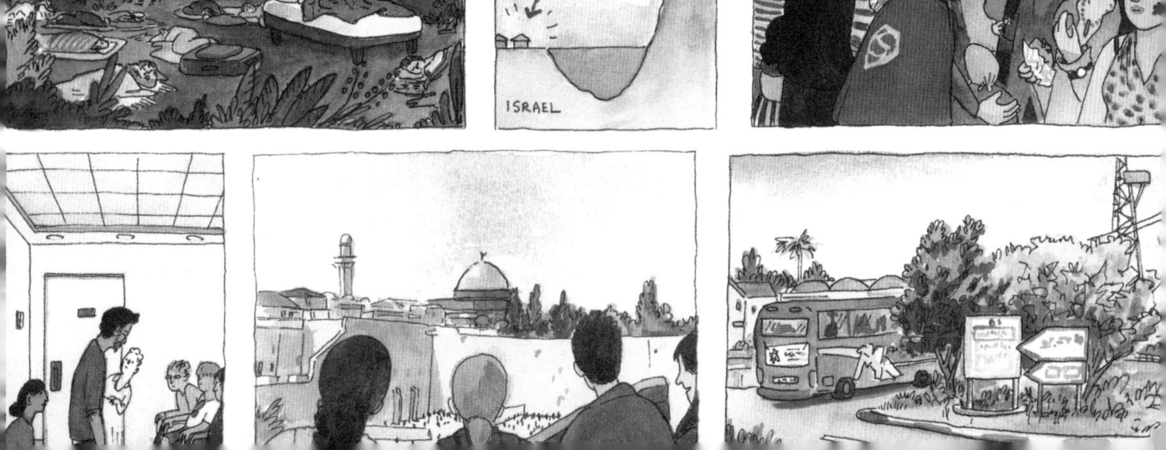

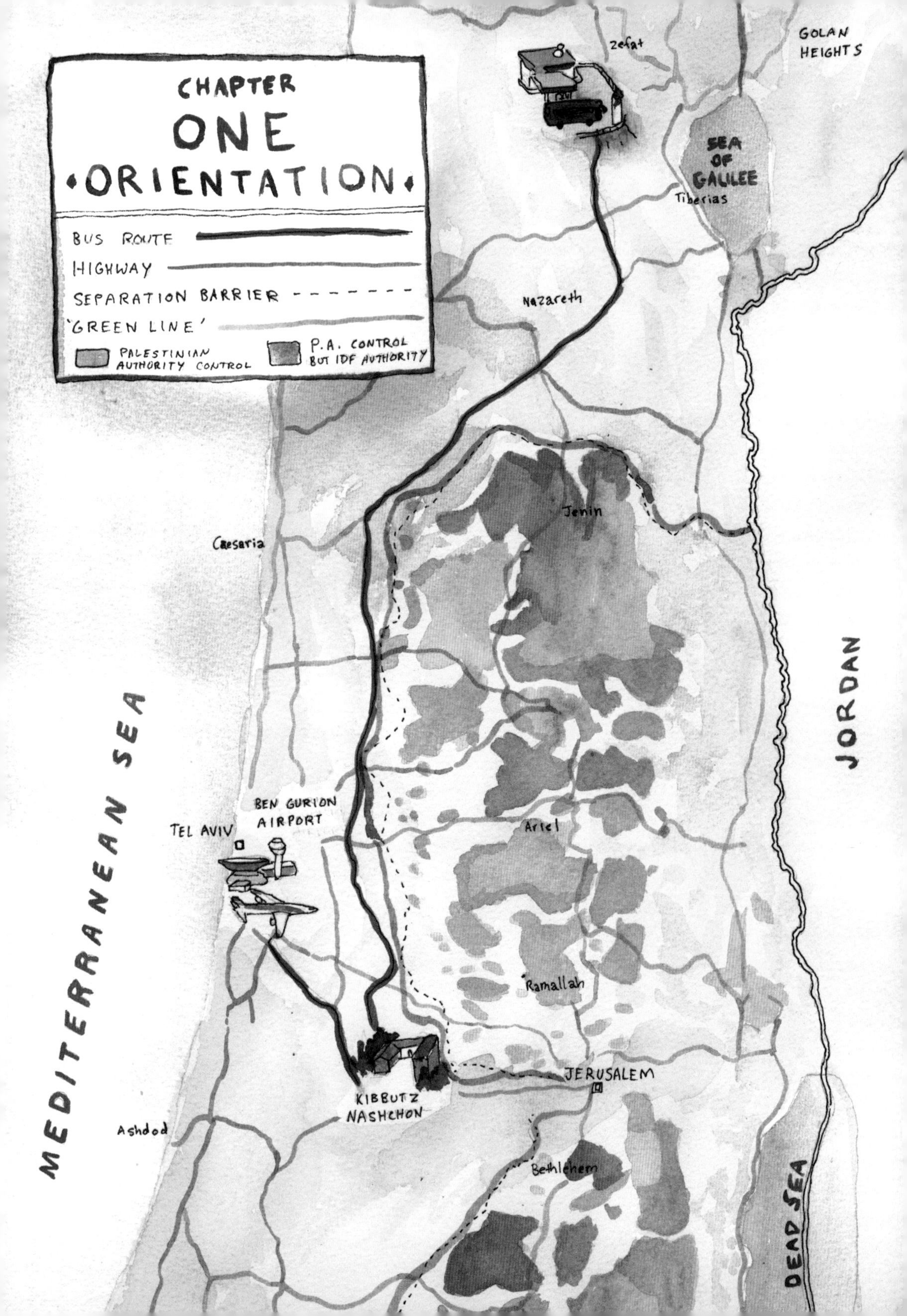
CHAPTER
ONE
ORIENTATION
BUS ROUTE
HIGHWAY
SEPARATION BARRIER
'GREEN LINE'
PALESTINIAN AUTHORITY CONTROL
P.A. CONTROL BUT IDF AUTHORITY
Zefat
GOLAN HEIGHTS
SEA OF GALILEE
Tiberias
Nazareth
Jenin
Caesaria
JORDAN
MEDITERRANEAN SEA
BEN GURION AIRPORT
TEL AVIV
Ariel
Ramallah
JERUSALEM
KIBBUTZ NASHCHON
Ashdod
Bethlehem
DEAD SEA

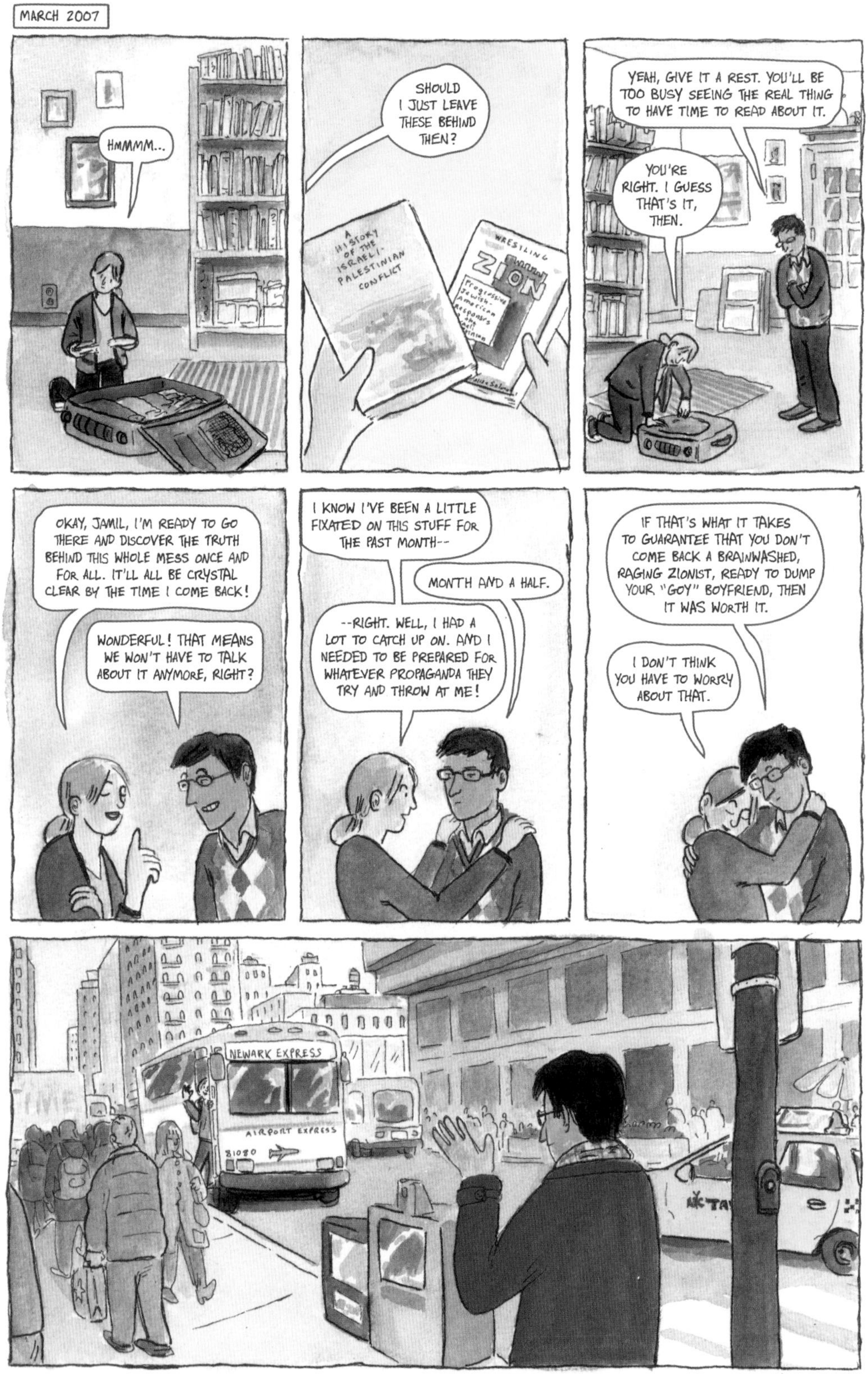
MARCH 2007
HMMMM...
SHOULD I JUST LEAVE THESE BEHIND THEN?
A HISTORY OF THE ISRAELI-PALESTINIAN CONFLICT
WRESTLING ZION
YEAH, GIVE IT A REST. YOU'LL BE TOO BUSY SEEING THE REAL THING TO HAVE TIME TO READ ABOUT IT.
YOU'RE RIGHT. I GUESS THAT'S IT, THEN.
OKAY, JAMIL, I'M READY TO GO THERE AND DISCOVER THE TRUTH BEHIND THIS WHOLE MESS ONCE AND FOR ALL. IT'LL ALL BE CRYSTAL CLEAR BY THE TIME I COME BACK!
WONDERFUL! THAT MEANS WE WON'T HAVE TO TALK ABOUT IT ANYMORE, RIGHT?
I KNOW I'VE BEEN A LITTLE FIXATED ON THIS STUFF FOR THE PAST MONTH--
MONTH AND A HALF.
--RIGHT. WELL, I HAD A LOT TO CATCH UP ON. AND I NEEDED TO BE PREPARED FOR WHATEVER PROPAGANDA THEY TRY AND THROW AT ME!
IF THAT'S WHAT IT TAKES TO GUARANTEE THAT YOU DON'T COME BACK A BRAINWASHED, RAGING ZIONIST, READY TO DUMP YOUR "GOY" BOYFRIEND, THEN IT WAS WORTH IT.
I DON'T THINK YOU HAVE TO WORRY ABOUT THAT.
NEWARK EXPRESS
AIRPORT EXPRESS
81080

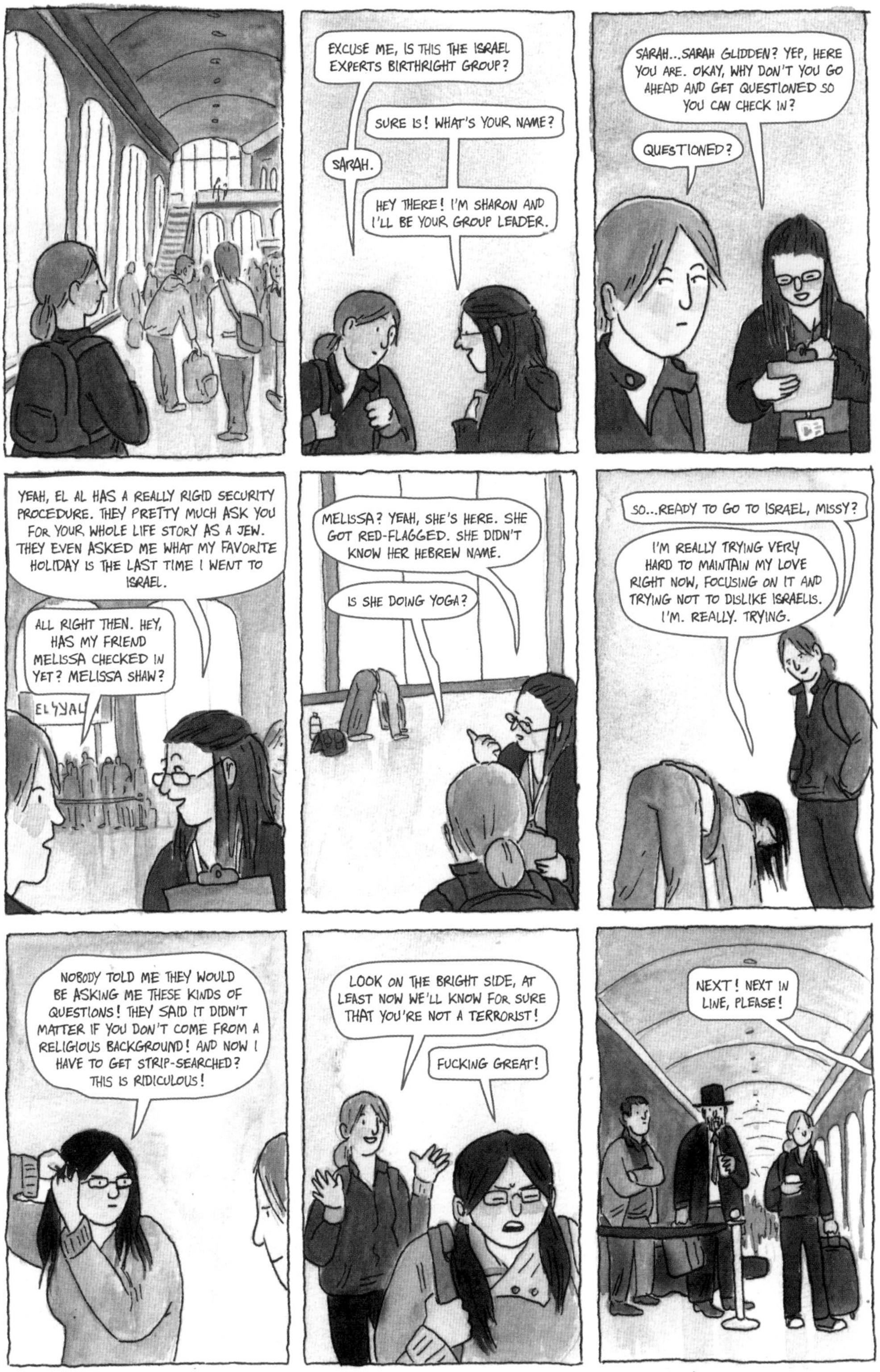
EXCUSE ME, IS THIS THE ISRAEL EXPERTS BIRTHRIGHT GROUP?
SURE IS! WHAT'S YOUR NAME?
SARAH.
HEY THERE! I'M SHARON AND I'LL BE YOUR GROUP LEADER.
SARAH...SARAH GLIDDEN? YEP, HERE YOU ARE. OKAY, WHY DON'T YOU GO AHEAD AND GET QUESTIONED SO YOU CAN CHECK IN?
QUESTIONED?
YEAH, EL AL HAS A REALLY RIGID SECURITY PROCEDURE. THEY PRETTY MUCH ASK YOU FOR YOUR WHOLE LIFE STORY AS A JEW. THEY EVEN ASKED ME WHAT MY FAVORITE HOLIDAY IS THE LAST TIME I WENT TO ISRAEL.
ALL RIGHT THEN. HEY, HAS MY FRIEND MELISSA CHECKED IN YET? MELISSA SHAW?
MELISSA? YEAH, SHE'S HERE. SHE GOT RED-FLAGGED. SHE DIDN'T KNOW HER HEBREW NAME.
IS SHE DOING YOGA?
SO...READY TO GO TO ISRAEL, MISSY?
I'M REALLY TRYING VERY HARD TO MAINTAIN MY LOVE RIGHT NOW, FOCUSING ON IT AND TRYING NOT TO DISLIKE ISRAELIS. I'M. REALLY. TRYING.
NOBODY TOLD ME THEY WOULD BE ASKING ME THESE KINDS OF QUESTIONS! THEY SAID IT DIDN'T MATTER IF YOU DON'T COME FROM A RELIGIOUS BACKGROUND! AND NOW I HAVE TO GET STRIP-SEARCHED? THIS IS RIDICULOUS!
LOOK ON THE BRIGHT SIDE, AT LEAST NOW WE'LL KNOW FOR SURE THAT YOU'RE NOT A TERRORIST!
FUCKING GREAT!
NEXT! NEXT IN LINE, PLEASE!

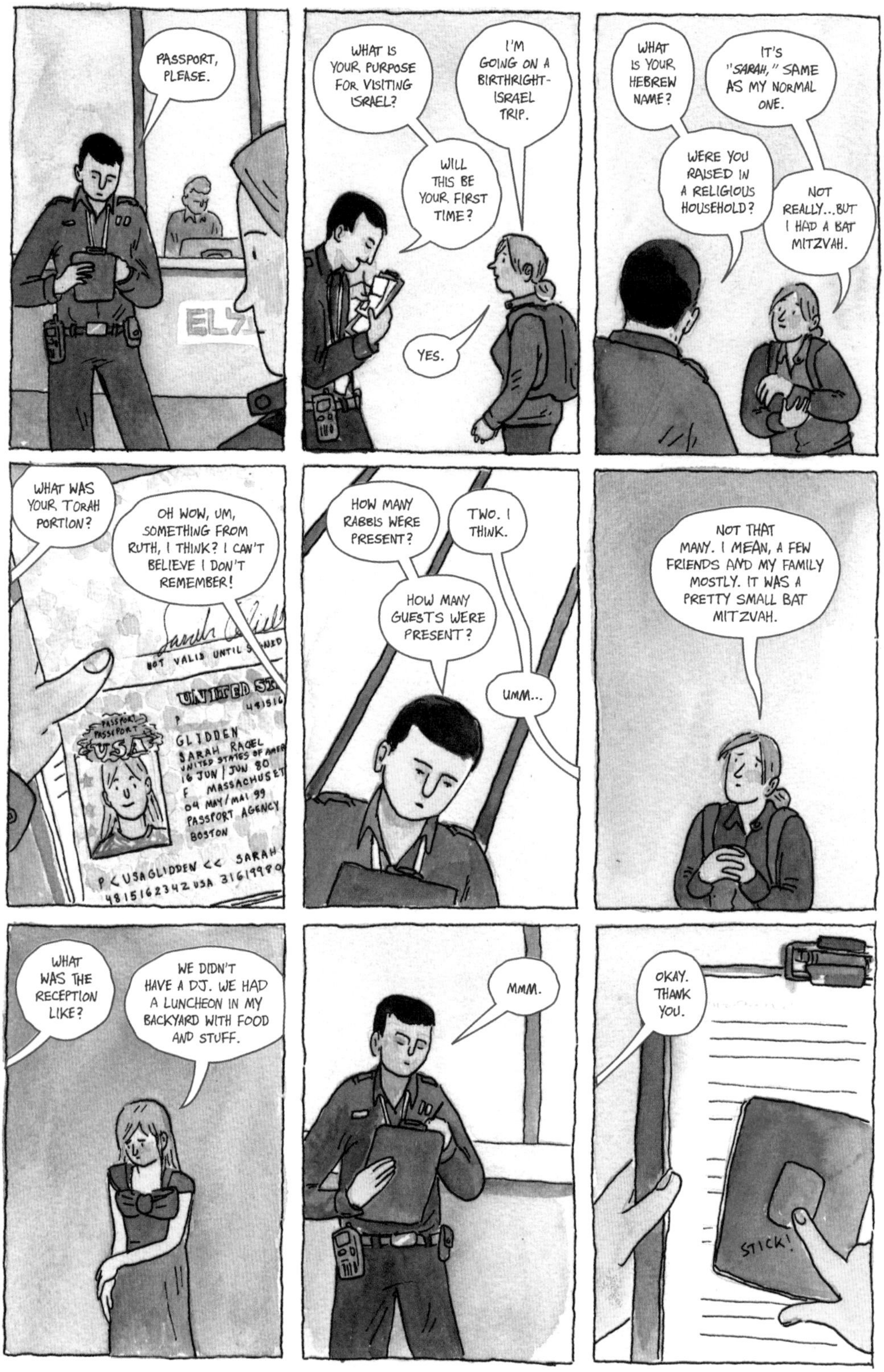
PASSPORT, PLEASE.
WHAT IS YOUR PURPOSE FOR VISITING ISRAEL?
I'M GOING ON A BIRTHRIGHT-ISRAEL TRIP.
WILL THIS BE YOUR FIRST TIME?
YES.
WHAT IS YOUR HEBREW NAME?
IT'S "SARAH," SAME AS MY NORMAL ONE.
WERE YOU RAISED IN A RELIGIOUS HOUSEHOLD?
NOT REALLY...BUT I HAD A BAT MITZVAH.
WHAT WAS YOUR TORAH PORTION?
OH WOW, UM, SOMETHING FROM RUTH, I THINK? I CAN'T BELIEVE I DON'T REMEMBER!
NOT VALID UNTIL SIGNED
GLIDDEN
SARAH RACEL
UNITED STATES OF AMER
16 JUN / JUN 80
F MASSACHUSET
04 MAY/MAI 99
PASSPORT AGENCY
BOSTON
P<USAGLIDDEN<< SARAH
4815162342USA 31619980
HOW MANY RABBIS WERE PRESENT?
TWO. I THINK.
HOW MANY GUESTS WERE PRESENT?
UMM...
NOT THAT MANY. I MEAN, A FEW FRIENDS AND MY FAMILY MOSTLY. IT WAS A PRETTY SMALL BAT MITZVAH.
WHAT WAS THE RECEPTION LIKE?
WE DIDN'T HAVE A DJ. WE HAD A LUNCHEON IN MY BACKYARD WITH FOOD AND STUFF.
MMM.
OKAY. THANK YOU.
STICK!

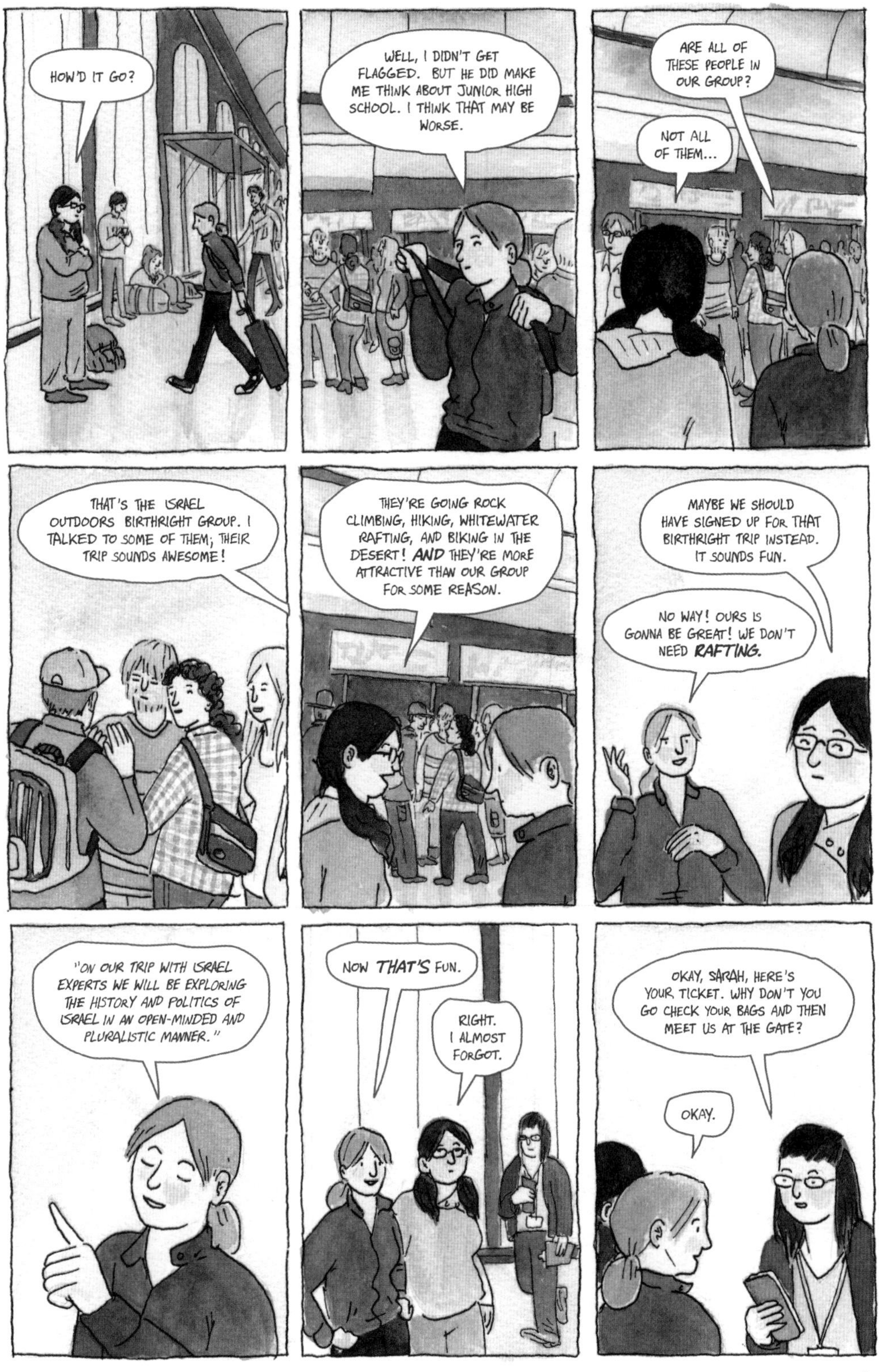
HOW'D IT GO?
WELL, I DIDN'T GET FLAGGED. BUT HE DID MAKE ME THINK ABOUT JUNIOR HIGH SCHOOL. I THINK THAT MAY BE WORSE.
ARE ALL OF THESE PEOPLE IN OUR GROUP?
NOT ALL OF THEM...
THAT'S THE ISRAEL OUTDOORS BIRTHRIGHT GROUP. I TALKED TO SOME OF THEM; THEIR TRIP SOUNDS AWESOME!
THEY'RE GOING ROCK CLIMBING, HIKING, WHITEWATER RAFTING, AND BIKING IN THE DESERT! AND THEY'RE MORE ATTRACTIVE THAN OUR GROUP FOR SOME REASON.
MAYBE WE SHOULD HAVE SIGNED UP FOR THAT BIRTHRIGHT TRIP INSTEAD. IT SOUNDS FUN.
NO WAY! OURS IS GONNA BE GREAT! WE DON'T NEED RAFTING.
"ON OUR TRIP WITH ISRAEL EXPERTS WE WILL BE EXPLORING THE HISTORY AND POLITICS OF ISRAEL IN AN OPEN-MINDED AND PLURALISTIC MANNER."
NOW THAT'S FUN.
RIGHT. I ALMOST FORGOT.
OKAY, SARAH, HERE'S YOUR TICKET. WHY DON'T YOU GO CHECK YOUR BAGS AND THEN MEET US AT THE GATE?
OKAY.

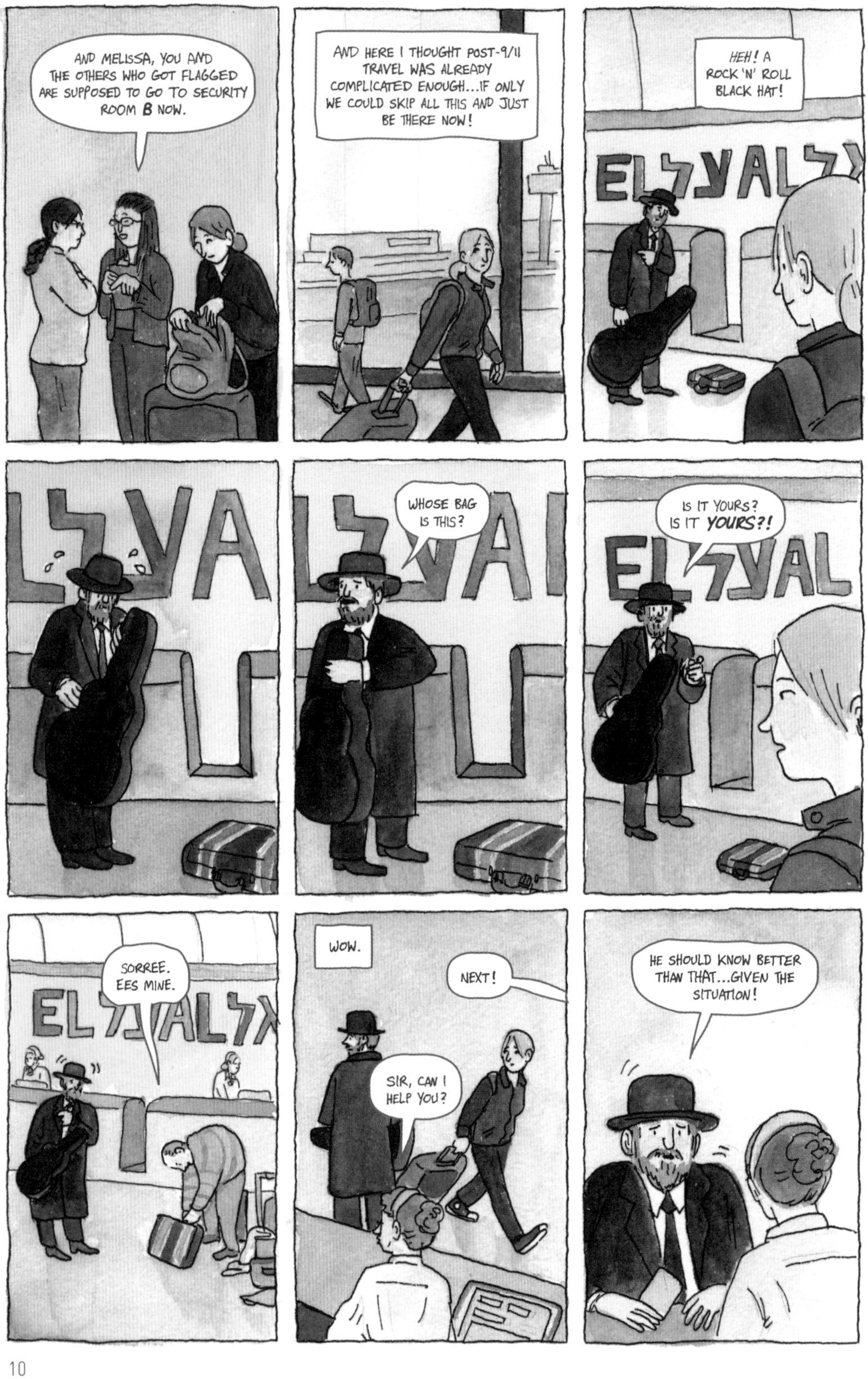
AND MELISSA, YOU AND THE OTHERS WHO GOT FLAGGED ARE SUPPOSED TO GO TO SECURITY ROOM B NOW.
AND HERE I THOUGHT POST-9/11 TRAVEL WAS ALREADY COMPLICATED ENOUGH...IF ONLY WE COULD SKIP ALL THIS AND JUST BE THERE NOW!
HEH! A ROCK 'N' ROLL BLACK HAT!
EL AL
WHOSE BAG IS THIS?
IS IT YOURS? IS IT ***YOURS?!***
SORREE. EES MINE.
WOW.
NEXT!
SIR, CAN I HELP YOU?
HE SHOULD KNOW BETTER THAN THAT...GIVEN THE SITUATION!

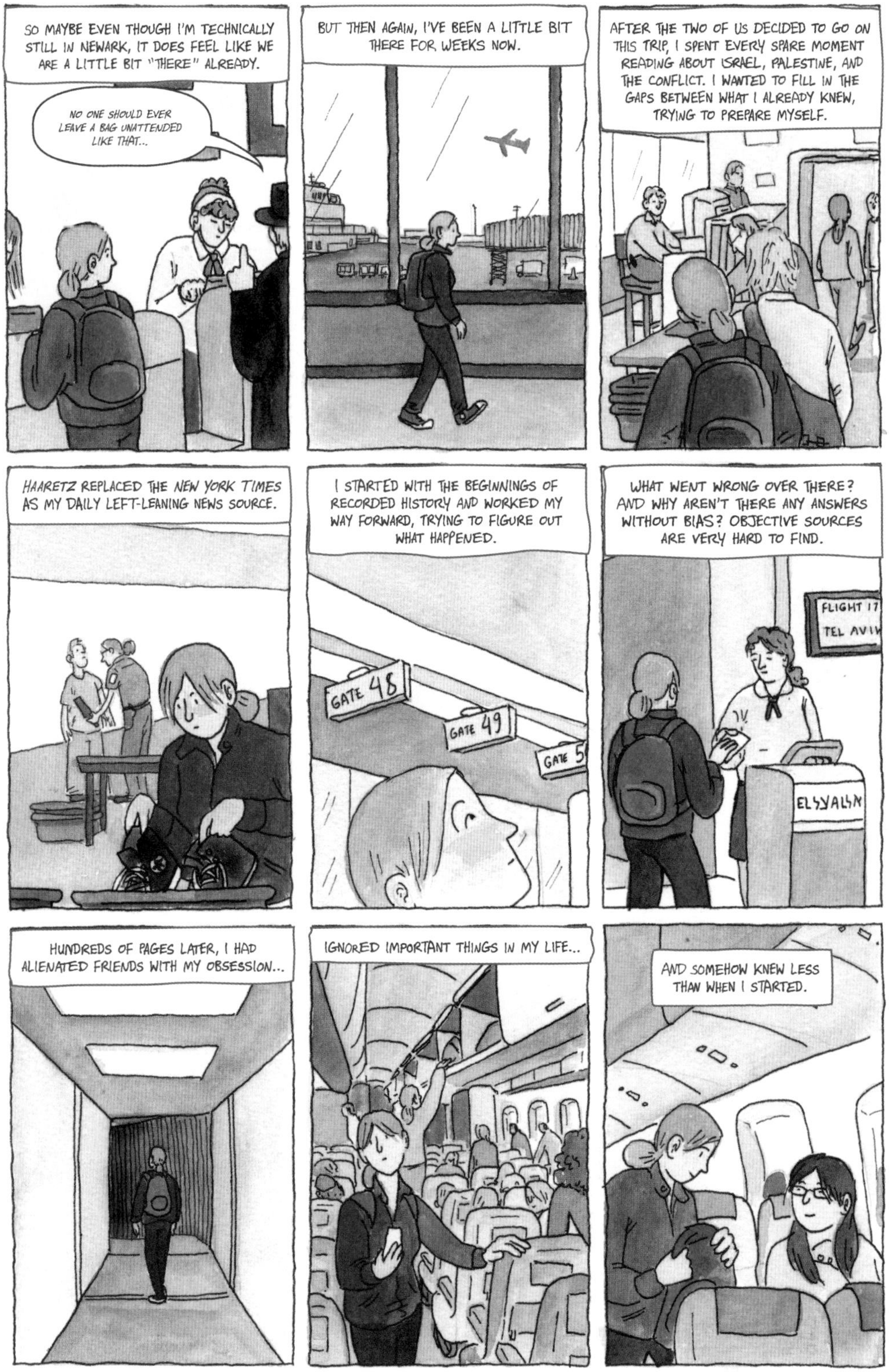
SO MAYBE EVEN THOUGH I'M TECHNICALLY STILL IN NEWARK, IT DOES FEEL LIKE WE ARE A LITTLE BIT "THERE" ALREADY.
NO ONE SHOULD EVER LEAVE A BAG UNATTENDED LIKE THAT...
BUT THEN AGAIN, I'VE BEEN A LITTLE BIT THERE FOR WEEKS NOW.
AFTER THE TWO OF US DECIDED TO GO ON THIS TRIP, I SPENT EVERY SPARE MOMENT READING ABOUT ISRAEL, PALESTINE, AND THE CONFLICT. I WANTED TO FILL IN THE GAPS BETWEEN WHAT I ALREADY KNEW, TRYING TO PREPARE MYSELF.
HAARETZ REPLACED THE *NEW YORK TIMES* AS MY DAILY LEFT-LEANING NEWS SOURCE.
I STARTED WITH THE BEGINNINGS OF RECORDED HISTORY AND WORKED MY WAY FORWARD, TRYING TO FIGURE OUT WHAT HAPPENED.
GATE 48
GATE 49
WHAT WENT WRONG OVER THERE? AND WHY AREN'T THERE ANY ANSWERS WITHOUT BIAS? OBJECTIVE SOURCES ARE VERY HARD TO FIND.
HUNDREDS OF PAGES LATER, I HAD ALIENATED FRIENDS WITH MY OBSESSION...
IGNORED IMPORTANT THINGS IN MY LIFE...
AND SOMEHOW KNEW LESS THAN WHEN I STARTED.

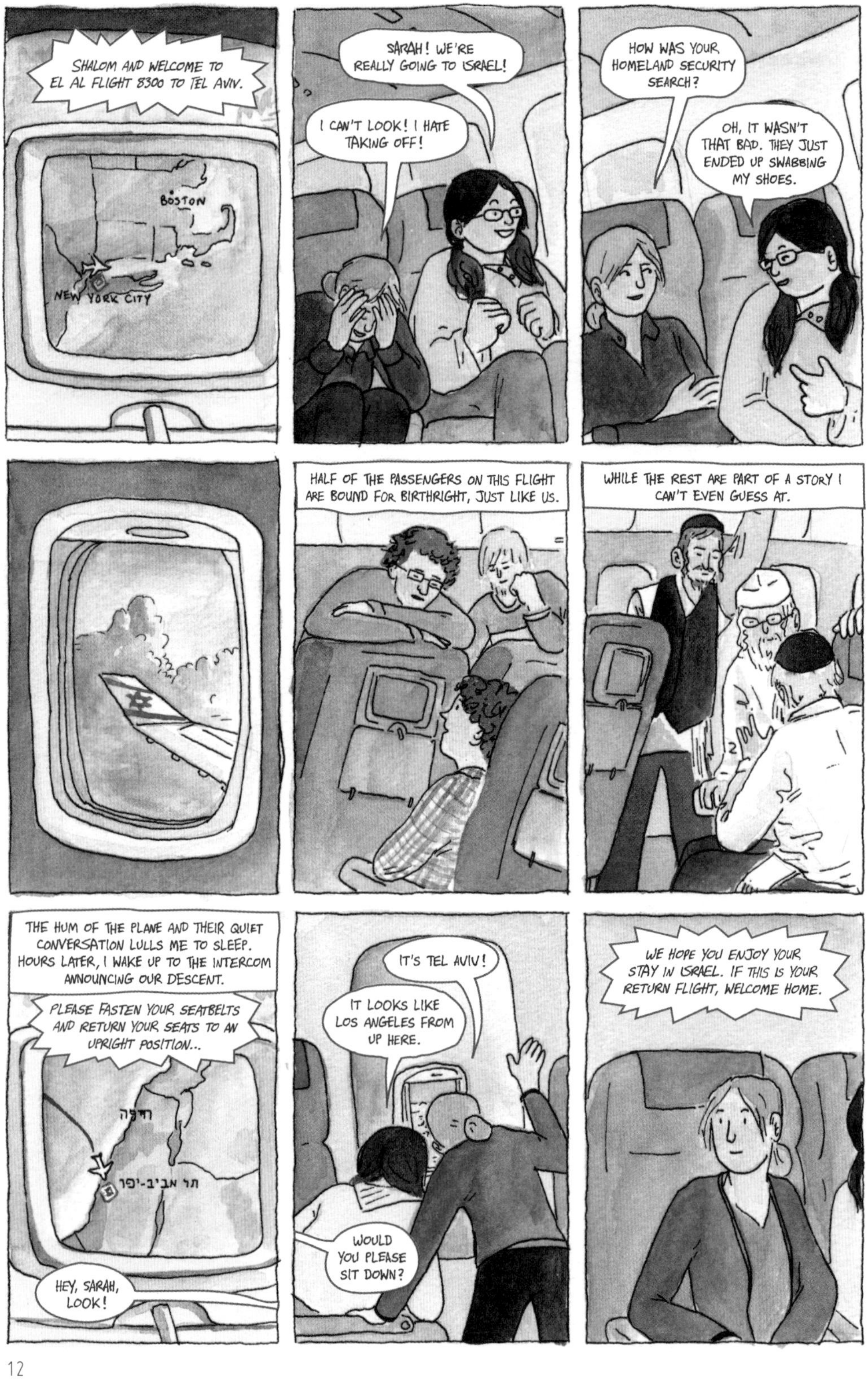
SHALOM AND WELCOME TO EL AL FLIGHT 8300 TO TEL AVIV.
BOSTON
NEW YORK CITY
SARAH! WE'RE REALLY GOING TO ISRAEL!
I CAN'T LOOK! I HATE TAKING OFF!
HOW WAS YOUR HOMELAND SECURITY SEARCH?
OH, IT WASN'T THAT BAD. THEY JUST ENDED UP SWABBING MY SHOES.
HALF OF THE PASSENGERS ON THIS FLIGHT ARE BOUND FOR BIRTHRIGHT, JUST LIKE US.
WHILE THE REST ARE PART OF A STORY I CAN'T EVEN GUESS AT.
THE HUM OF THE PLANE AND THEIR QUIET CONVERSATION LULLS ME TO SLEEP. HOURS LATER, I WAKE UP TO THE INTERCOM ANNOUNCING OUR DESCENT.
PLEASE FASTEN YOUR SEATBELTS AND RETURN YOUR SEATS TO AN UPRIGHT POSITION...
תל אביב-יפו
HEY, SARAH, LOOK!
IT'S TEL AVIV!
IT LOOKS LIKE LOS ANGELES FROM UP HERE.
WOULD YOU PLEASE SIT DOWN?
WE HOPE YOU ENJOY YOUR STAY IN ISRAEL. IF THIS IS YOUR RETURN FLIGHT, WELCOME HOME.

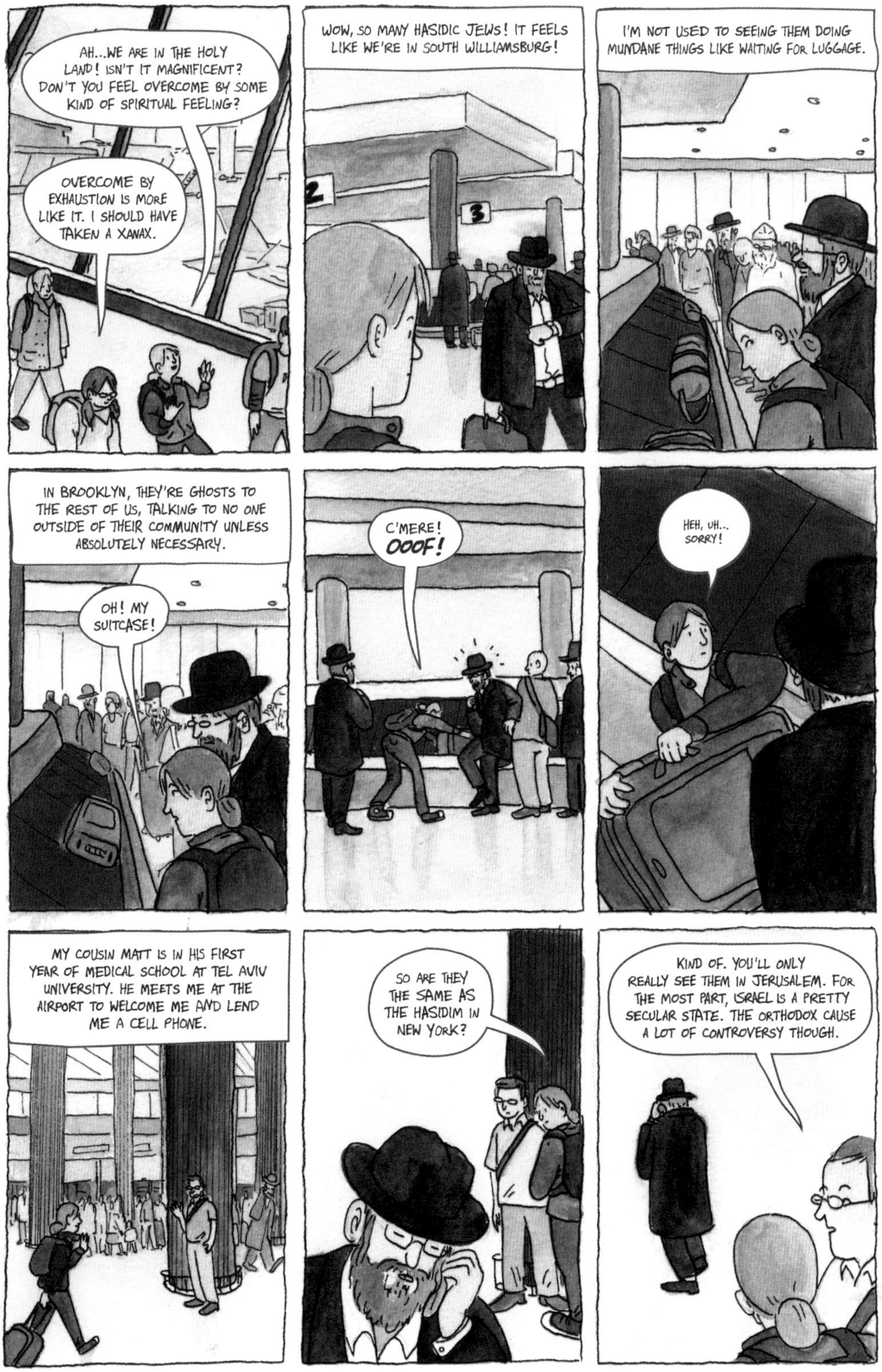
AH...WE ARE IN THE HOLY LAND! ISN'T IT MAGNIFICENT? DON'T YOU FEEL OVERCOME BY SOME KIND OF SPIRITUAL FEELING?
OVERCOME BY EXHAUSTION IS MORE LIKE IT. I SHOULD HAVE TAKEN A XANAX.
WOW, SO MANY HASIDIC JEWS! IT FEELS LIKE WE'RE IN SOUTH WILLIAMSBURG!
2
3
I'M NOT USED TO SEEING THEM DOING MUNDANE THINGS LIKE WAITING FOR LUGGAGE.
IN BROOKLYN, THEY'RE GHOSTS TO THE REST OF US, TALKING TO NO ONE OUTSIDE OF THEIR COMMUNITY UNLESS ABSOLUTELY NECESSARY.
OH! MY SUITCASE!
C'MERE! OOOF!
HEH, UH... SORRY!
MY COUSIN MATT IS IN HIS FIRST YEAR OF MEDICAL SCHOOL AT TEL AVIV UNIVERSITY. HE MEETS ME AT THE AIRPORT TO WELCOME ME AND LEND ME A CELL PHONE.
SO ARE THEY THE SAME AS THE HASIDIM IN NEW YORK?
KIND OF. YOU'LL ONLY REALLY SEE THEM IN JERUSALEM. FOR THE MOST PART, ISRAEL IS A PRETTY SECULAR STATE. THE ORTHODOX CAUSE A LOT OF CONTROVERSY THOUGH.

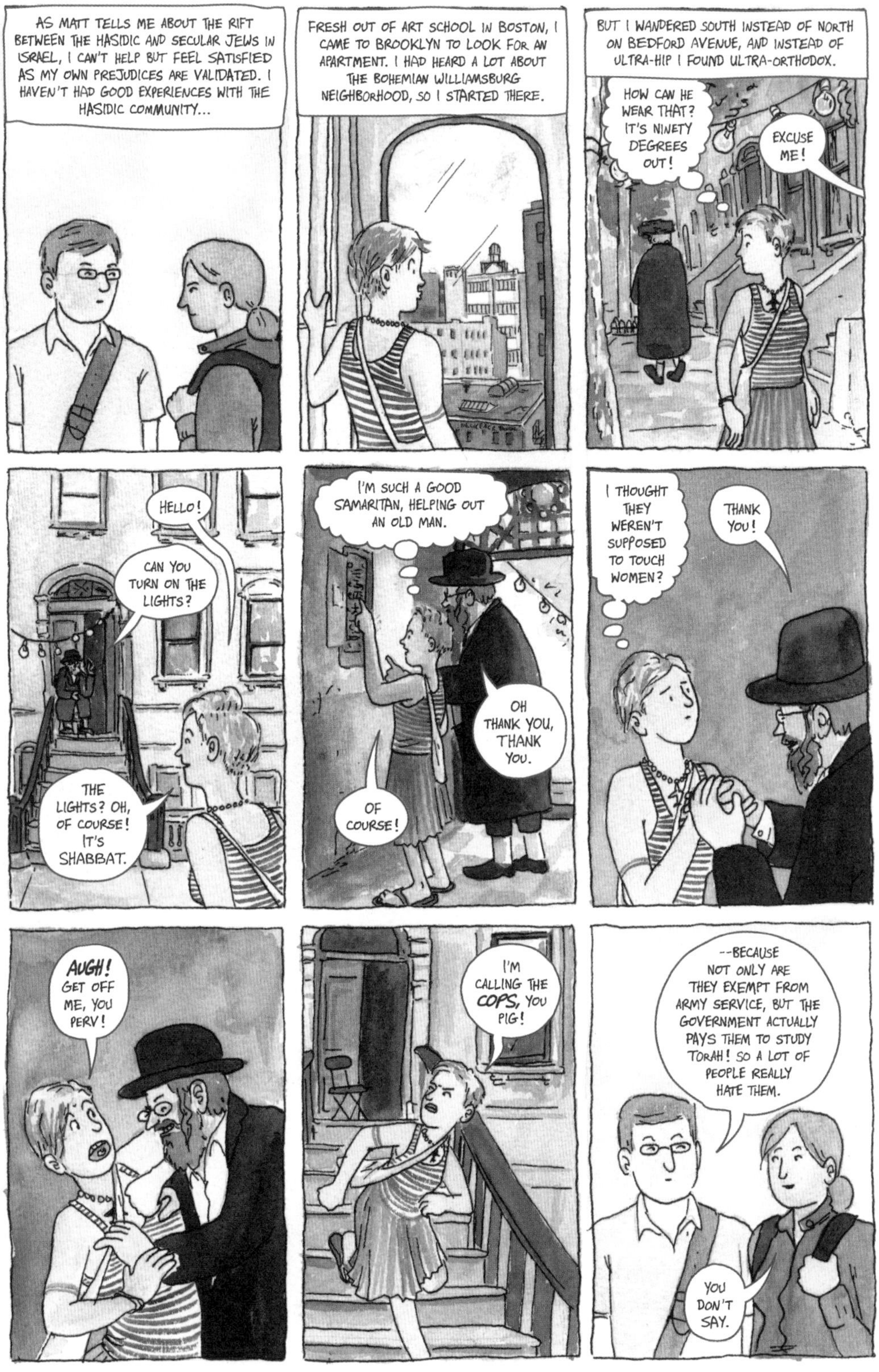

AS MATT TELLS ME ABOUT THE RIFT BETWEEN THE HASIDIC AND SECULAR JEWS IN ISRAEL, I CAN'T HELP BUT FEEL SATISFIED AS MY OWN PREJUDICES ARE VALIDATED. I HAVEN'T HAD GOOD EXPERIENCES WITH THE HASIDIC COMMUNITY...
FRESH OUT OF ART SCHOOL IN BOSTON, I CAME TO BROOKLYN TO LOOK FOR AN APARTMENT. I HAD HEARD A LOT ABOUT THE BOHEMIAN WILLIAMSBURG NEIGHBORHOOD, SO I STARTED THERE.
BUT I WANDERED SOUTH INSTEAD OF NORTH ON BEDFORD AVENUE, AND INSTEAD OF ULTRA-HIP I FOUND ULTRA-ORTHODOX.
HOW CAN HE WEAR THAT? IT'S NINETY DEGREES OUT!
EXCUSE ME!
HELLO!
CAN YOU TURN ON THE LIGHTS?
THE LIGHTS? OH, OF COURSE! IT'S SHABBAT.
I'M SUCH A GOOD SAMARITAN, HELPING OUT AN OLD MAN.
OH THANK YOU, THANK YOU.
OF COURSE!
I THOUGHT THEY WEREN'T SUPPOSED TO TOUCH WOMEN?
THANK YOU!
AUGH! GET OFF ME, YOU PERV!
I'M CALLING THE COPS, YOU PIG!
--BECAUSE NOT ONLY ARE THEY EXEMPT FROM ARMY SERVICE, BUT THE GOVERNMENT ACTUALLY PAYS THEM TO STUDY TORAH! SO A LOT OF PEOPLE REALLY HATE THEM.
YOU DON'T SAY.

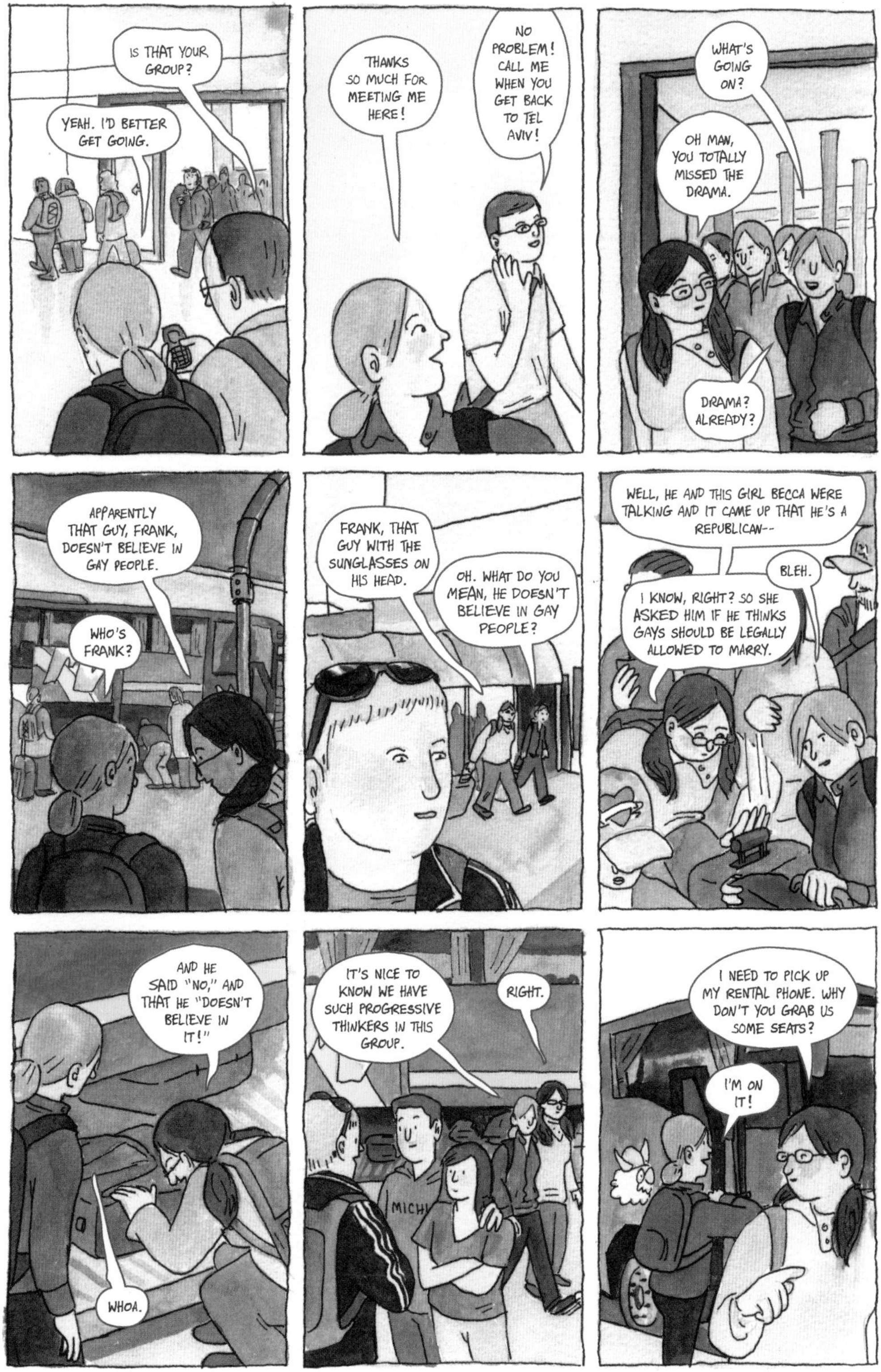
IS THAT YOUR GROUP?
YEAH. I'D BETTER GET GOING.
THANKS SO MUCH FOR MEETING ME HERE!
NO PROBLEM! CALL ME WHEN YOU GET BACK TO TEL AVIV!
WHAT'S GOING ON?
OH MAN, YOU TOTALLY MISSED THE DRAMA.
DRAMA? ALREADY?
APPARENTLY THAT GUY, FRANK, DOESN'T BELIEVE IN GAY PEOPLE.
WHO'S FRANK?
FRANK, THAT GUY WITH THE SUNGLASSES ON HIS HEAD.
OH. WHAT DO YOU MEAN, HE DOESN'T BELIEVE IN GAY PEOPLE?
WELL, HE AND THIS GIRL BECCA WERE TALKING AND IT CAME UP THAT HE'S A REPUBLICAN--
BLEH.
I KNOW, RIGHT? SO SHE ASKED HIM IF HE THINKS GAYS SHOULD BE LEGALLY ALLOWED TO MARRY.
AND HE SAID "NO," AND THAT HE "DOESN'T BELIEVE IN IT!"
WHOA.
IT'S NICE TO KNOW WE HAVE SUCH PROGRESSIVE THINKERS IN THIS GROUP.
RIGHT.
MICHI
I NEED TO PICK UP MY RENTAL PHONE. WHY DON'T YOU GRAB US SOME SEATS?
I'M ON IT!

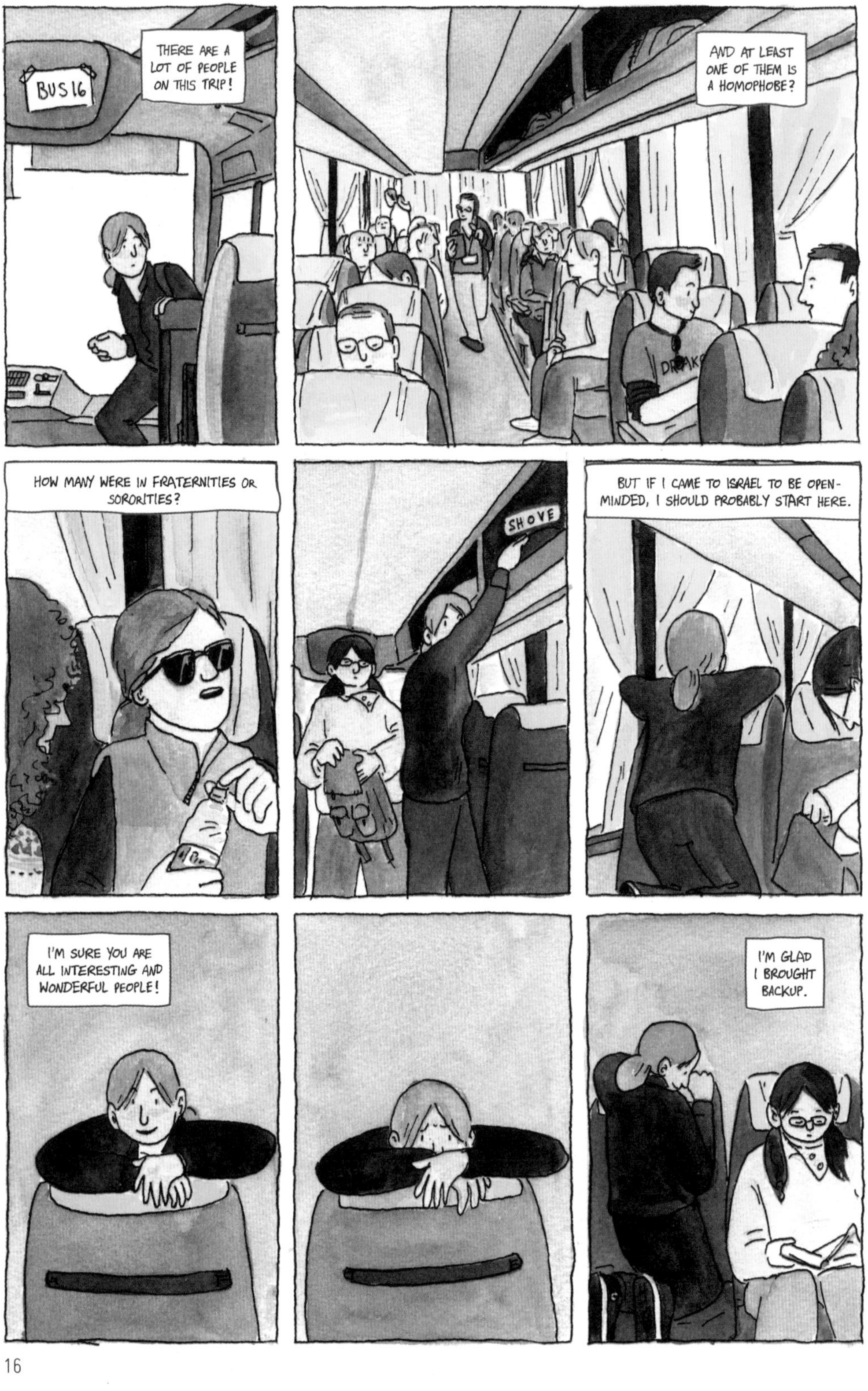
BUS 16
THERE ARE A LOT OF PEOPLE ON THIS TRIP!
AND AT LEAST ONE OF THEM IS A HOMOPHOBE?
DRAKE
HOW MANY WERE IN FRATERNITIES OR SORORITIES?
SHOVE
BUT IF I CAME TO ISRAEL TO BE OPEN-MINDED, I SHOULD PROBABLY START HERE.
I'M SURE YOU ARE ALL INTERESTING AND WONDERFUL PEOPLE!
I'M GLAD I BROUGHT BACKUP.

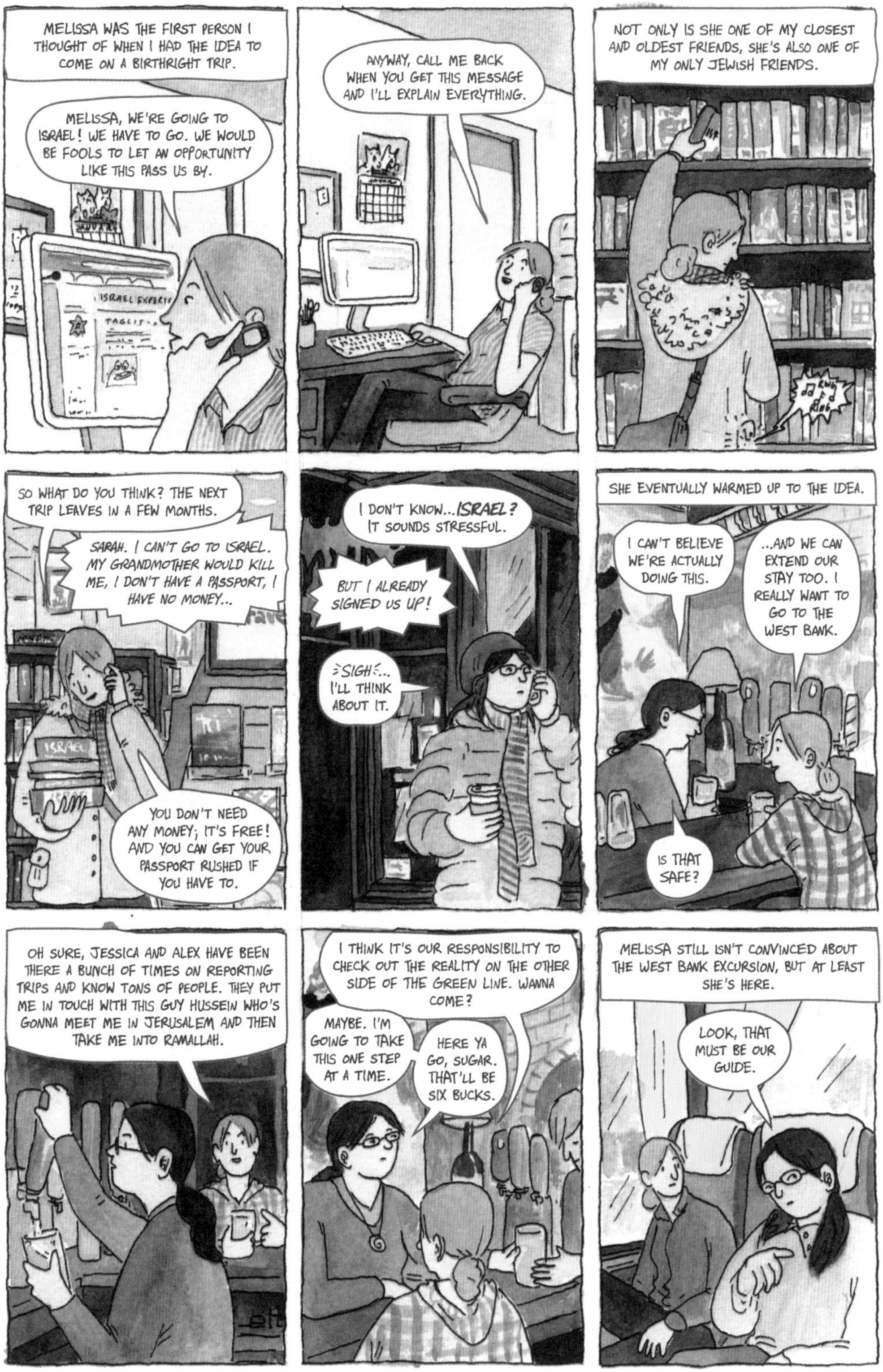
MELISSA WAS THE FIRST PERSON I THOUGHT OF WHEN I HAD THE IDEA TO COME ON A BIRTHRIGHT TRIP.
MELISSA, WE'RE GOING TO ISRAEL! WE HAVE TO GO. WE WOULD BE FOOLS TO LET AN OPPORTUNITY LIKE THIS PASS US BY.
ANYWAY, CALL ME BACK WHEN YOU GET THIS MESSAGE AND I'LL EXPLAIN EVERYTHING.
NOT ONLY IS SHE ONE OF MY CLOSEST AND OLDEST FRIENDS, SHE'S ALSO ONE OF MY ONLY JEWISH FRIENDS.
SO WHAT DO YOU THINK? THE NEXT TRIP LEAVES IN A FEW MONTHS.
SARAH. I CAN'T GO TO ISRAEL. MY GRANDMOTHER WOULD KILL ME, I DON'T HAVE A PASSPORT, I HAVE NO MONEY...
YOU DON'T NEED ANY MONEY; IT'S FREE! AND YOU CAN GET YOUR PASSPORT RUSHED IF YOU HAVE TO.
I DON'T KNOW... ISRAEL? IT SOUNDS STRESSFUL.
BUT I ALREADY SIGNED US UP!
SIGH... I'LL THINK ABOUT IT.
SHE EVENTUALLY WARMED UP TO THE IDEA.
I CAN'T BELIEVE WE'RE ACTUALLY DOING THIS.
...AND WE CAN EXTEND OUR STAY TOO. I REALLY WANT TO GO TO THE WEST BANK.
IS THAT SAFE?
OH SURE, JESSICA AND ALEX HAVE BEEN THERE A BUNCH OF TIMES ON REPORTING TRIPS AND KNOW TONS OF PEOPLE. THEY PUT ME IN TOUCH WITH THIS GUY HUSSEIN WHO'S GONNA MEET ME IN JERUSALEM AND THEN TAKE ME INTO RAMALLAH.
I THINK IT'S OUR RESPONSIBILITY TO CHECK OUT THE REALITY ON THE OTHER SIDE OF THE GREEN LINE. WANNA COME?
MAYBE. I'M GOING TO TAKE THIS ONE STEP AT A TIME.
HERE YA GO, SUGAR. THAT'LL BE SIX BUCKS.
MELISSA STILL ISN'T CONVINCED ABOUT THE WEST BANK EXCURSION, BUT AT LEAST SHE'S HERE.
LOOK, THAT MUST BE OUR GUIDE.

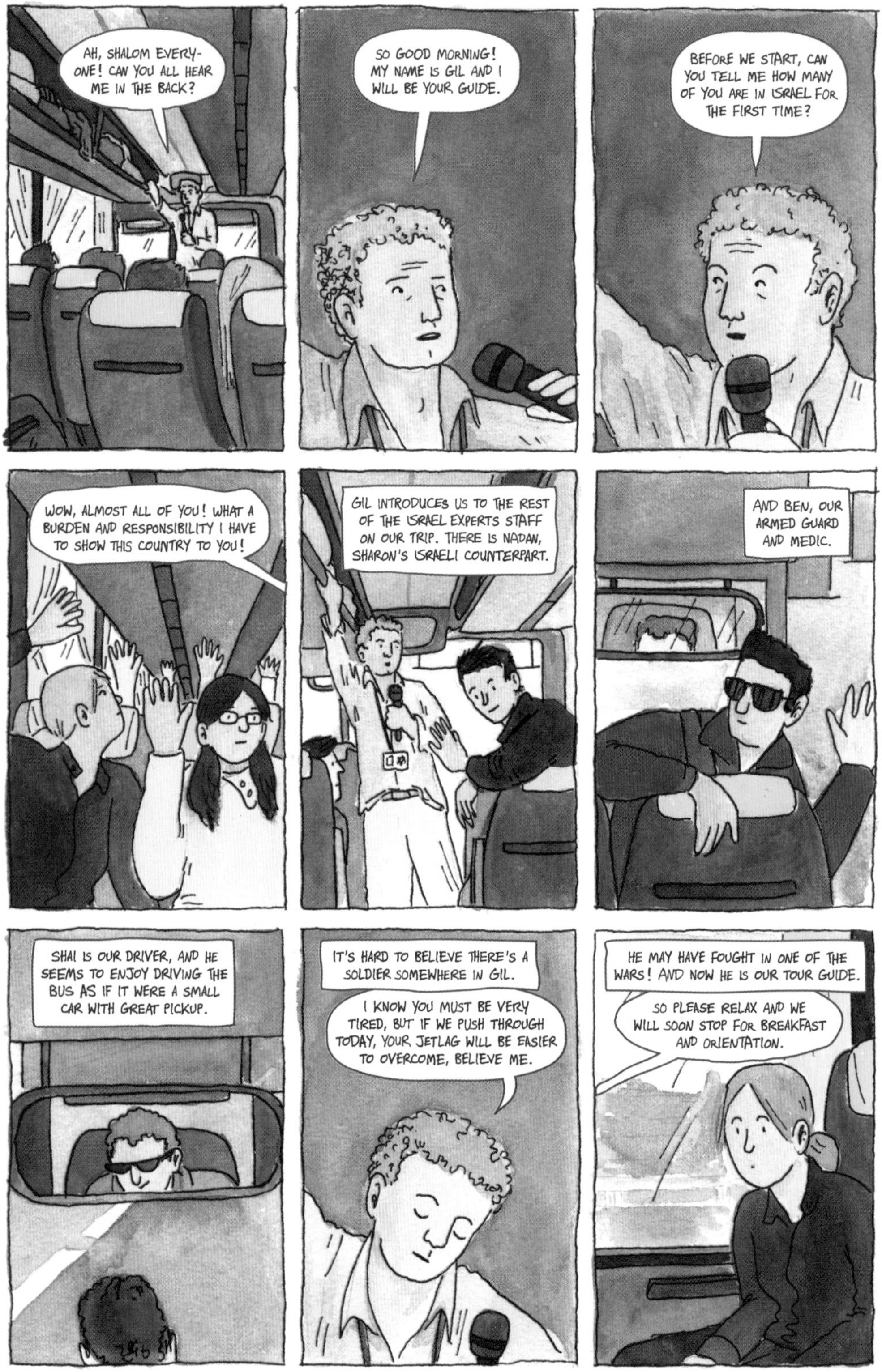

AH, SHALOM EVERY-ONE! CAN YOU ALL HEAR ME IN THE BACK?
SO GOOD MORNING! MY NAME IS GIL AND I WILL BE YOUR GUIDE.
BEFORE WE START, CAN YOU TELL ME HOW MANY OF YOU ARE IN ISRAEL FOR THE FIRST TIME?
WOW, ALMOST ALL OF YOU! WHAT A BURDEN AND RESPONSIBILITY I HAVE TO SHOW THIS COUNTRY TO YOU!
GIL INTRODUCES US TO THE REST OF THE ISRAEL EXPERTS STAFF ON OUR TRIP. THERE IS NADAN, SHARON'S ISRAELI COUNTERPART.
AND BEN, OUR ARMED GUARD AND MEDIC.
SHAI IS OUR DRIVER, AND HE SEEMS TO ENJOY DRIVING THE BUS AS IF IT WERE A SMALL CAR WITH GREAT PICKUP.
IT'S HARD TO BELIEVE THERE'S A SOLDIER SOMEWHERE IN GIL.
I KNOW YOU MUST BE VERY TIRED, BUT IF WE PUSH THROUGH TODAY, YOUR JETLAG WILL BE EASIER TO OVERCOME, BELIEVE ME.
HE MAY HAVE FOUGHT IN ONE OF THE WARS! AND NOW HE IS OUR TOUR GUIDE.
SO PLEASE RELAX AND WE WILL SOON STOP FOR BREAKFAST AND ORIENTATION.

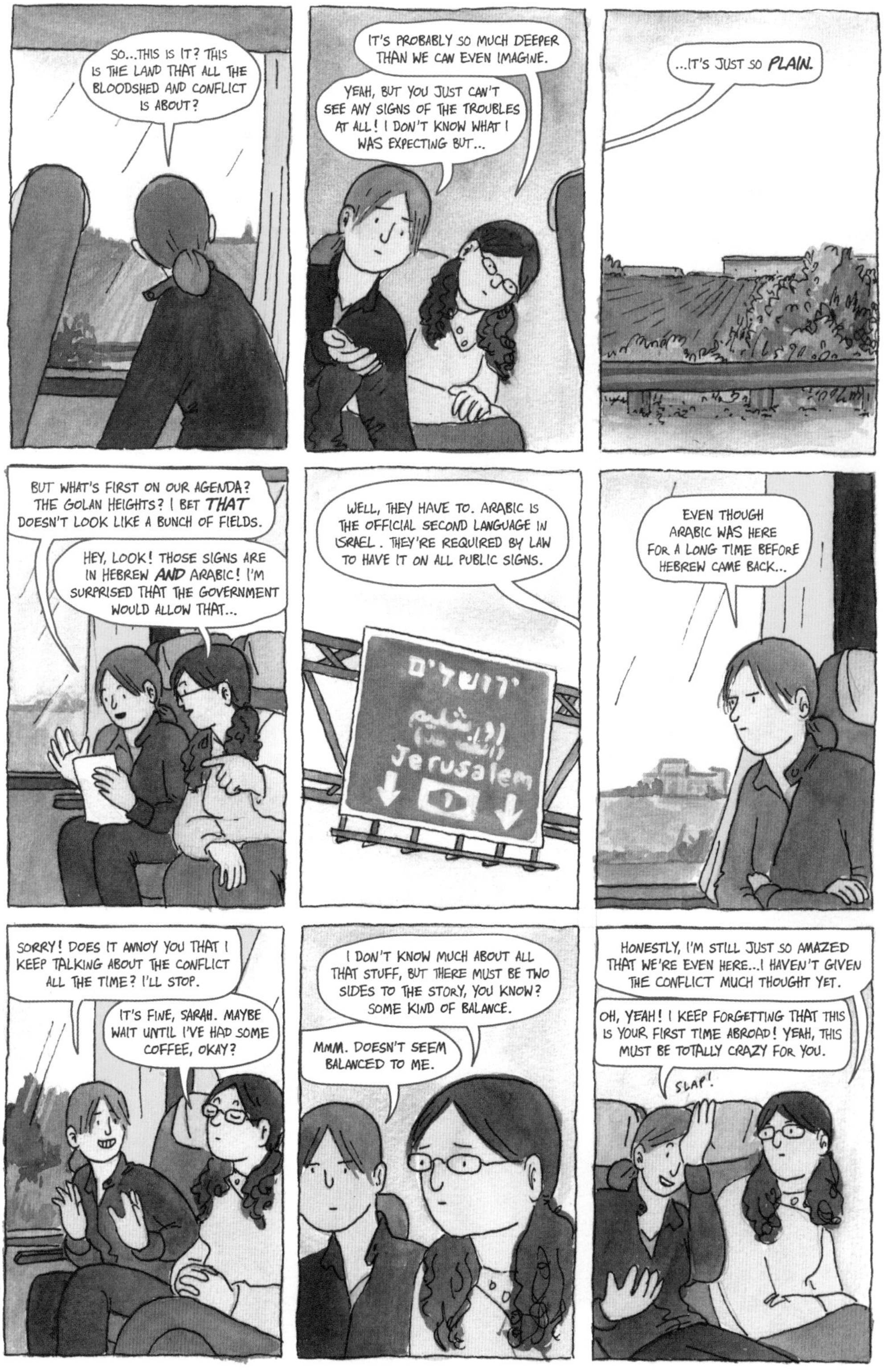
SO...THIS IS IT? THIS IS THE LAND THAT ALL THE BLOODSHED AND CONFLICT IS ABOUT?
IT'S PROBABLY SO MUCH DEEPER THAN WE CAN EVEN IMAGINE.
YEAH, BUT YOU JUST CAN'T SEE ANY SIGNS OF THE TROUBLES AT ALL! I DON'T KNOW WHAT I WAS EXPECTING BUT...
...IT'S JUST SO PLAIN.
BUT WHAT'S FIRST ON OUR AGENDA? THE GOLAN HEIGHTS? I BET THAT DOESN'T LOOK LIKE A BUNCH OF FIELDS.
HEY, LOOK! THOSE SIGNS ARE IN HEBREW AND ARABIC! I'M SURPRISED THAT THE GOVERNMENT WOULD ALLOW THAT...
WELL, THEY HAVE TO. ARABIC IS THE OFFICIAL SECOND LANGUAGE IN ISRAEL. THEY'RE REQUIRED BY LAW TO HAVE IT ON ALL PUBLIC SIGNS.
ירושלים
Jerusalem
1
EVEN THOUGH ARABIC WAS HERE FOR A LONG TIME BEFORE HEBREW CAME BACK...
SORRY! DOES IT ANNOY YOU THAT I KEEP TALKING ABOUT THE CONFLICT ALL THE TIME? I'LL STOP.
IT'S FINE, SARAH. MAYBE WAIT UNTIL I'VE HAD SOME COFFEE, OKAY?
I DON'T KNOW MUCH ABOUT ALL THAT STUFF, BUT THERE MUST BE TWO SIDES TO THE STORY, YOU KNOW? SOME KIND OF BALANCE.
MMM. DOESN'T SEEM BALANCED TO ME.
HONESTLY, I'M STILL JUST SO AMAZED THAT WE'RE EVEN HERE...I HAVEN'T GIVEN THE CONFLICT MUCH THOUGHT YET.
OH, YEAH! I KEEP FORGETTING THAT THIS IS YOUR FIRST TIME ABROAD! YEAH, THIS MUST BE TOTALLY CRAZY FOR YOU.
SLAP!

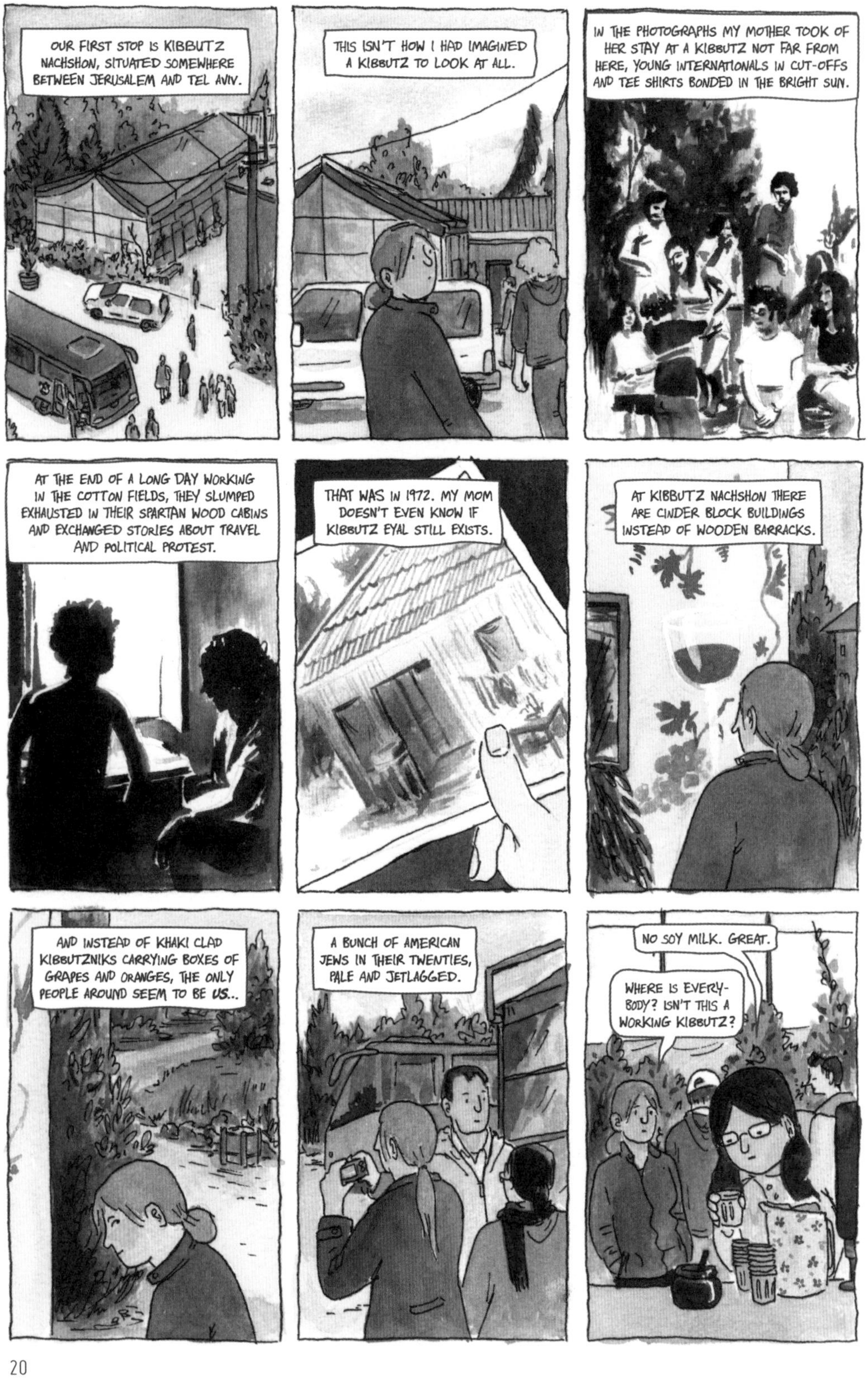
OUR FIRST STOP IS KIBBUTZ NACHSHON, SITUATED SOMEWHERE BETWEEN JERUSALEM AND TEL AVIV.
THIS ISN'T HOW I HAD IMAGINED A KIBBUTZ TO LOOK AT ALL.
IN THE PHOTOGRAPHS MY MOTHER TOOK OF HER STAY AT A KIBBUTZ NOT FAR FROM HERE, YOUNG INTERNATIONALS IN CUT-OFFS AND TEE SHIRTS BONDED IN THE BRIGHT SUN.
AT THE END OF A LONG DAY WORKING IN THE COTTON FIELDS, THEY SLUMPED EXHAUSTED IN THEIR SPARTAN WOOD CABINS AND EXCHANGED STORIES ABOUT TRAVEL AND POLITICAL PROTEST.
THAT WAS IN 1972. MY MOM DOESN'T EVEN KNOW IF KIBBUTZ EYAL STILL EXISTS.
AT KIBBUTZ NACHSHON THERE ARE CINDER BLOCK BUILDINGS INSTEAD OF WOODEN BARRACKS.
AND INSTEAD OF KHAKI CLAD KIBBUTZNIKS CARRYING BOXES OF GRAPES AND ORANGES, THE ONLY PEOPLE AROUND SEEM TO BE US..
A BUNCH OF AMERICAN JEWS IN THEIR TWENTIES, PALE AND JETLAGGED.
NO SOY MILK. GREAT.
WHERE IS EVERYBODY? ISN'T THIS A WORKING KIBBUTZ?

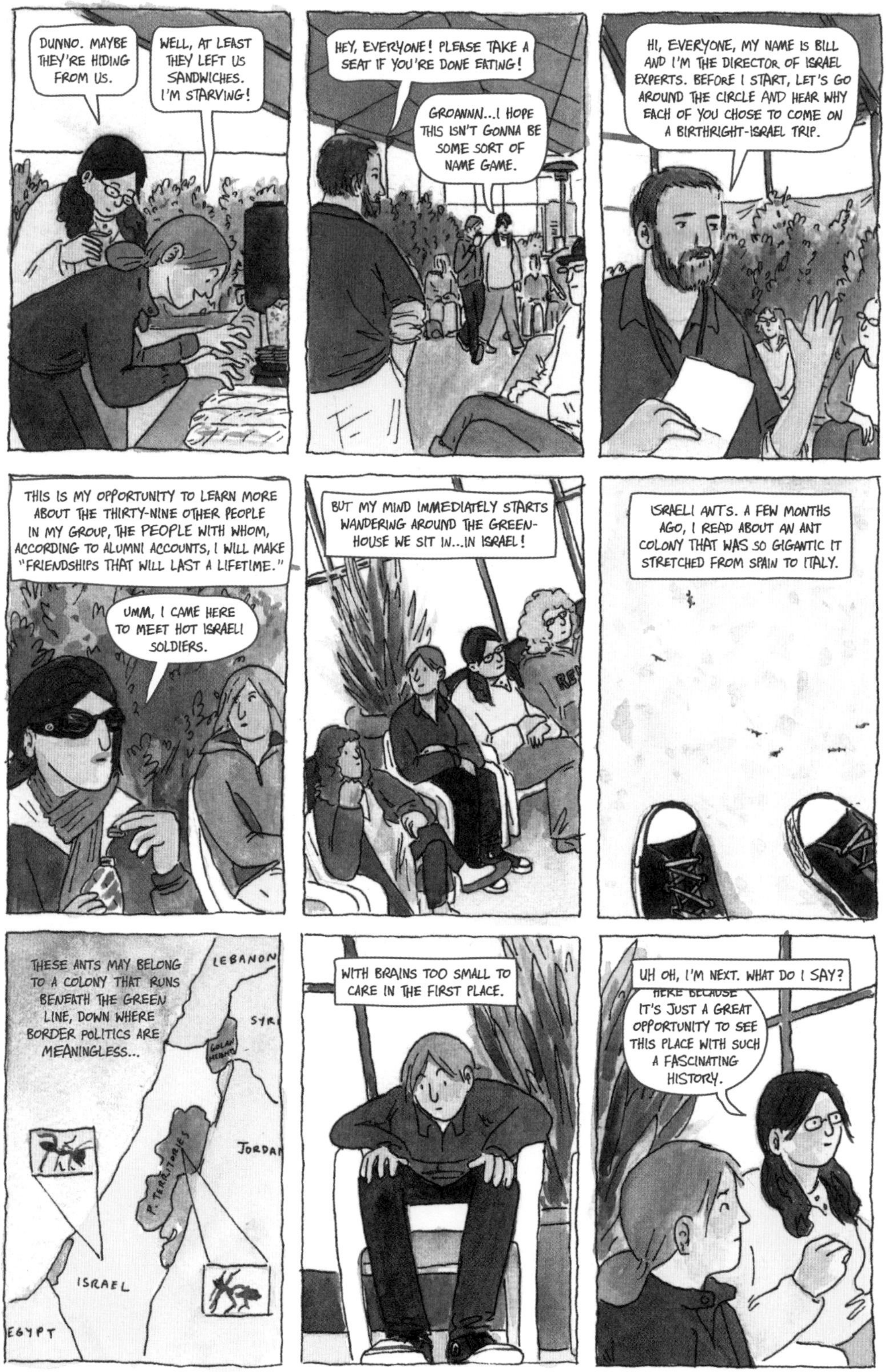
DUNNO. MAYBE THEY'RE HIDING FROM US.
WELL, AT LEAST THEY LEFT US SANDWICHES. I'M STARVING!
HEY, EVERYONE! PLEASE TAKE A SEAT IF YOU'RE DONE EATING!
GROANNN...I HOPE THIS ISN'T GONNA BE SOME SORT OF NAME GAME.
HI, EVERYONE, MY NAME IS BILL AND I'M THE DIRECTOR OF ISRAEL EXPERTS. BEFORE I START, LET'S GO AROUND THE CIRCLE AND HEAR WHY EACH OF YOU CHOSE TO COME ON A BIRTHRIGHT-ISRAEL TRIP.
THIS IS MY OPPORTUNITY TO LEARN MORE ABOUT THE THIRTY-NINE OTHER PEOPLE IN MY GROUP, THE PEOPLE WITH WHOM, ACCORDING TO ALUMNI ACCOUNTS, I WILL MAKE "FRIENDSHIPS THAT WILL LAST A LIFETIME."
UMM, I CAME HERE TO MEET HOT ISRAELI SOLDIERS.
BUT MY MIND IMMEDIATELY STARTS WANDERING AROUND THE GREEN-HOUSE WE SIT IN...IN ISRAEL!
ISRAELI ANTS. A FEW MONTHS AGO, I READ ABOUT AN ANT COLONY THAT WAS SO GIGANTIC IT STRETCHED FROM SPAIN TO ITALY.
THESE ANTS MAY BELONG TO A COLONY THAT RUNS BENEATH THE GREEN LINE, DOWN WHERE BORDER POLITICS ARE MEANINGLESS...
LEBANON
SYR
JORDA
P. TERRITORIES
ISRAEL
EGYPT
WITH BRAINS TOO SMALL TO CARE IN THE FIRST PLACE.
UH OH, I'M NEXT. WHAT DO I SAY?
HERE BECAUSE IT'S JUST A GREAT OPPORTUNITY TO SEE THIS PLACE WITH SUCH A FASCINATING HISTORY.

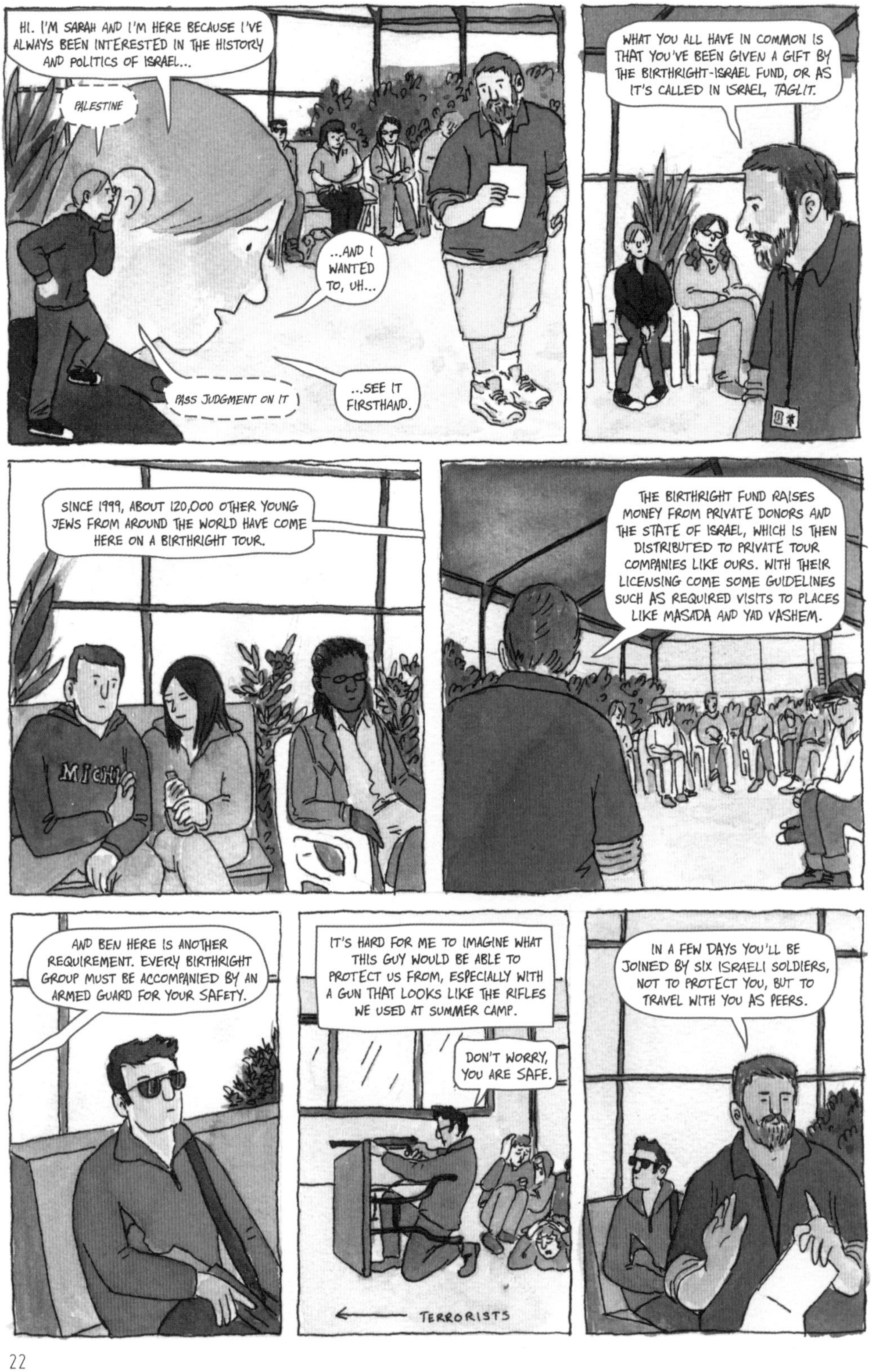
HI. I'M SARAH AND I'M HERE BECAUSE I'VE ALWAYS BEEN INTERESTED IN THE HISTORY AND POLITICS OF ISRAEL...
PALESTINE
...AND I WANTED TO, UH...
PASS JUDGMENT ON IT
...SEE IT FIRSTHAND.
WHAT YOU ALL HAVE IN COMMON IS THAT YOU'VE BEEN GIVEN A GIFT BY THE BIRTHRIGHT-ISRAEL FUND, OR AS IT'S CALLED IN ISRAEL, TAGLIT.
SINCE 1999, ABOUT 120,000 OTHER YOUNG JEWS FROM AROUND THE WORLD HAVE COME HERE ON A BIRTHRIGHT TOUR.
MICHI
THE BIRTHRIGHT FUND RAISES MONEY FROM PRIVATE DONORS AND THE STATE OF ISRAEL, WHICH IS THEN DISTRIBUTED TO PRIVATE TOUR COMPANIES LIKE OURS. WITH THEIR LICENSING COME SOME GUIDELINES SUCH AS REQUIRED VISITS TO PLACES LIKE MASADA AND YAD VASHEM.
AND BEN HERE IS ANOTHER REQUIREMENT. EVERY BIRTHRIGHT GROUP MUST BE ACCOMPANIED BY AN ARMED GUARD FOR YOUR SAFETY.
IT'S HARD FOR ME TO IMAGINE WHAT THIS GUY WOULD BE ABLE TO PROTECT US FROM, ESPECIALLY WITH A GUN THAT LOOKS LIKE THE RIFLES WE USED AT SUMMER CAMP.
DON'T WORRY, YOU ARE SAFE.
TERRORISTS
IN A FEW DAYS YOU'LL BE JOINED BY SIX ISRAELI SOLDIERS, NOT TO PROTECT YOU, BUT TO TRAVEL WITH YOU AS PEERS.

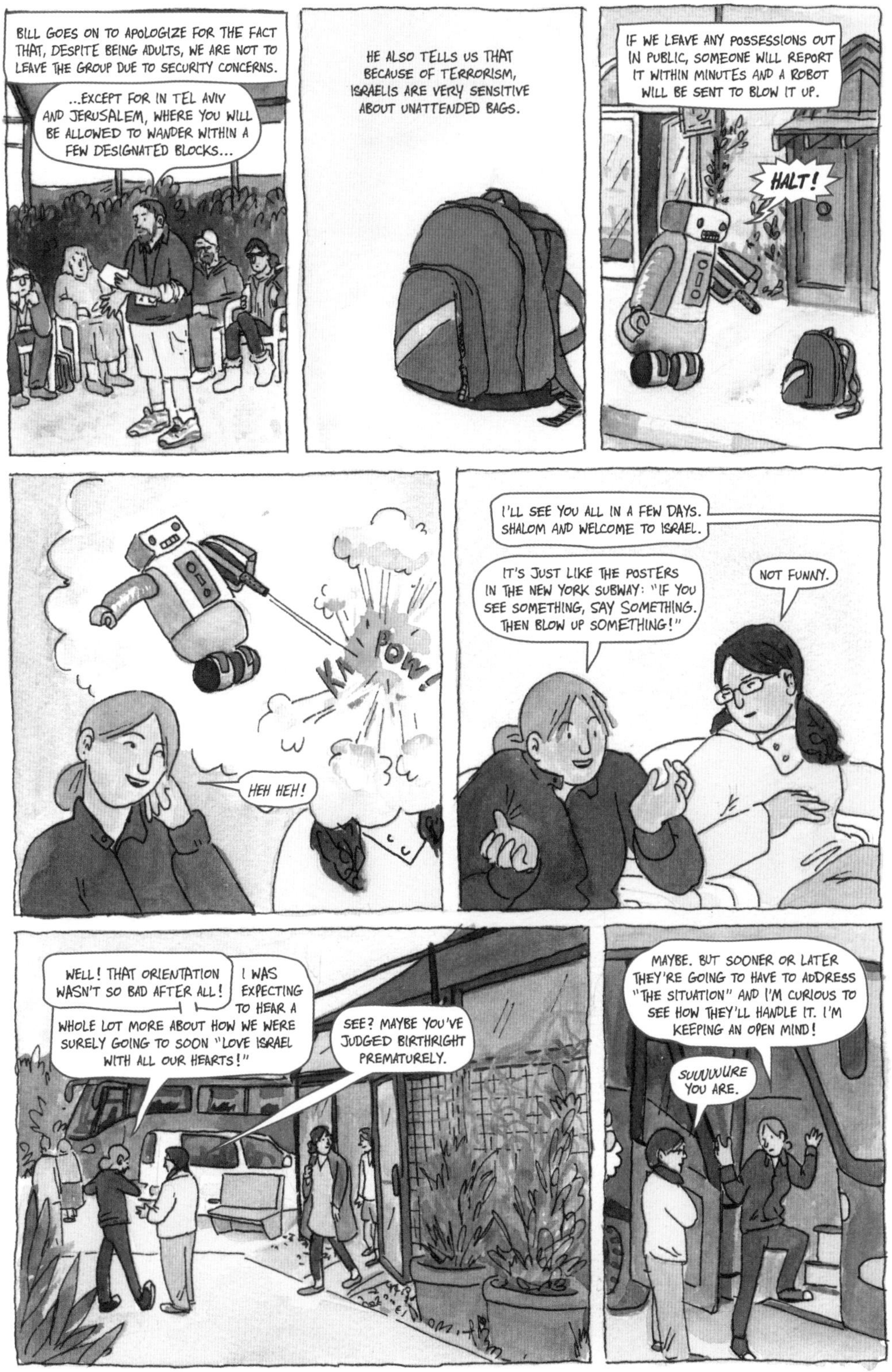
BILL GOES ON TO APOLOGIZE FOR THE FACT THAT, DESPITE BEING ADULTS, WE ARE NOT TO LEAVE THE GROUP DUE TO SECURITY CONCERNS.
...EXCEPT FOR IN TEL AVIV AND JERUSALEM, WHERE YOU WILL BE ALLOWED TO WANDER WITHIN A FEW DESIGNATED BLOCKS...
HE ALSO TELLS US THAT BECAUSE OF TERRORISM, ISRAELIS ARE VERY SENSITIVE ABOUT UNATTENDED BAGS.
IF WE LEAVE ANY POSSESSIONS OUT IN PUBLIC, SOMEONE WILL REPORT IT WITHIN MINUTES AND A ROBOT WILL BE SENT TO BLOW IT UP.
HALT!
KA POW!
HEH HEH!
I'LL SEE YOU ALL IN A FEW DAYS. SHALOM AND WELCOME TO ISRAEL.
IT'S JUST LIKE THE POSTERS IN THE NEW YORK SUBWAY: "IF YOU SEE SOMETHING, SAY SOMETHING. THEN BLOW UP SOMETHING!"
NOT FUNNY.
WELL! THAT ORIENTATION WASN'T SO BAD AFTER ALL!
I WAS EXPECTING TO HEAR A WHOLE LOT MORE ABOUT HOW WE WERE SURELY GOING TO SOON "LOVE ISRAEL WITH ALL OUR HEARTS!"
SEE? MAYBE YOU'VE JUDGED BIRTHRIGHT PREMATURELY.
MAYBE. BUT SOONER OR LATER THEY'RE GOING TO HAVE TO ADDRESS "THE SITUATION" AND I'M CURIOUS TO SEE HOW THEY'LL HANDLE IT. I'M KEEPING AN OPEN MIND!
SUUUUURE YOU ARE.

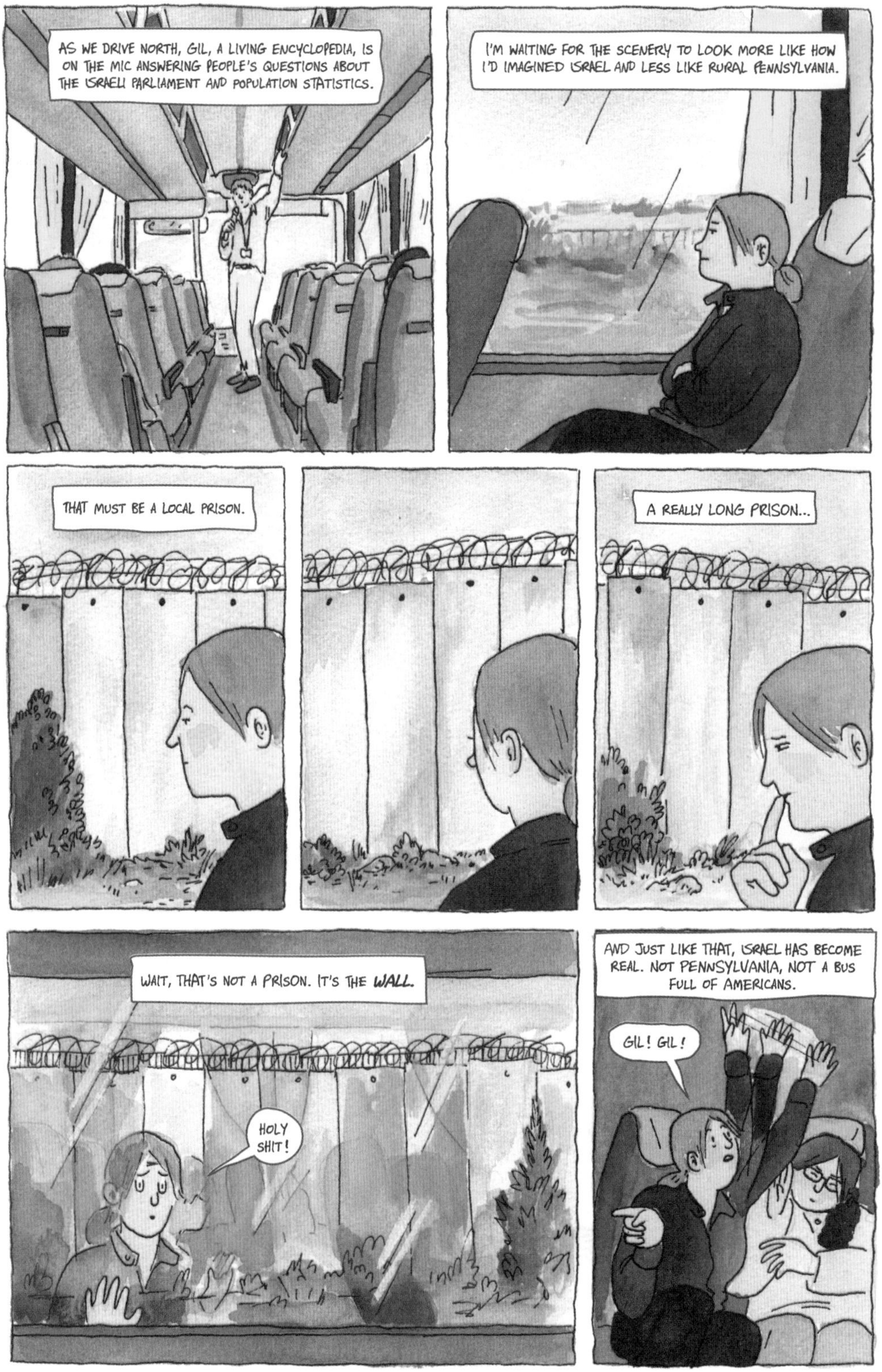
AS WE DRIVE NORTH, GIL, A LIVING ENCYCLOPEDIA, IS ON THE MIC ANSWERING PEOPLE'S QUESTIONS ABOUT THE ISRAELI PARLIAMENT AND POPULATION STATISTICS.
I'M WAITING FOR THE SCENERY TO LOOK MORE LIKE HOW I'D IMAGINED ISRAEL AND LESS LIKE RURAL PENNSYLVANIA.
THAT MUST BE A LOCAL PRISON.
A REALLY LONG PRISON...
WAIT, THAT'S NOT A PRISON. IT'S THE WALL.
HOLY SHIT!
AND JUST LIKE THAT, ISRAEL HAS BECOME REAL. NOT PENNSYLVANIA, NOT A BUS FULL OF AMERICANS.
GIL! GIL!

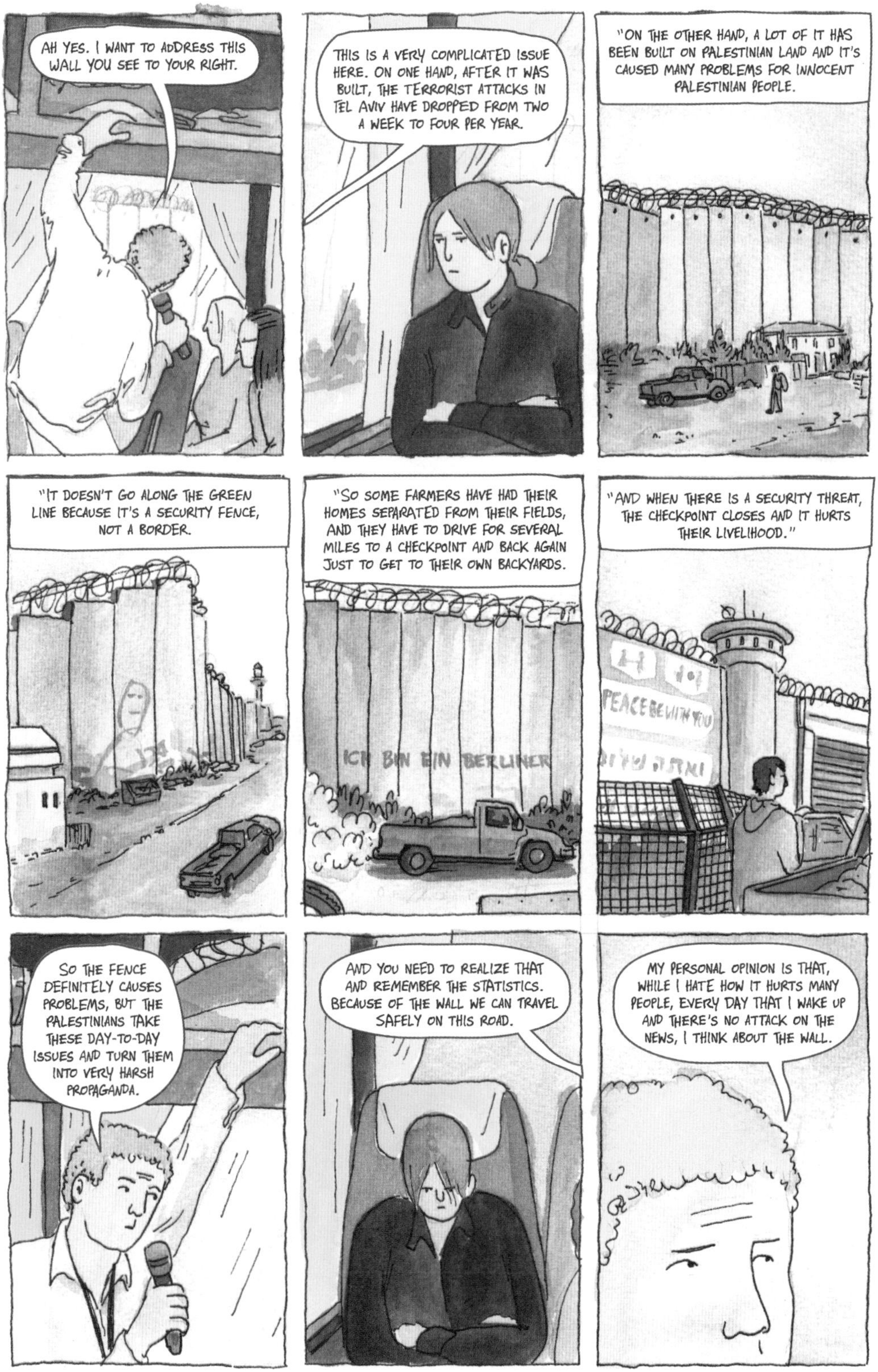
AH YES. I WANT TO ADDRESS THIS WALL YOU SEE TO YOUR RIGHT.
THIS IS A VERY COMPLICATED ISSUE HERE. ON ONE HAND, AFTER IT WAS BUILT, THE TERRORIST ATTACKS IN TEL AVIV HAVE DROPPED FROM TWO A WEEK TO FOUR PER YEAR.
"ON THE OTHER HAND, A LOT OF IT HAS BEEN BUILT ON PALESTINIAN LAND AND IT'S CAUSED MANY PROBLEMS FOR INNOCENT PALESTINIAN PEOPLE.
"IT DOESN'T GO ALONG THE GREEN LINE BECAUSE IT'S A SECURITY FENCE, NOT A BORDER.
"SO SOME FARMERS HAVE HAD THEIR HOMES SEPARATED FROM THEIR FIELDS, AND THEY HAVE TO DRIVE FOR SEVERAL MILES TO A CHECKPOINT AND BACK AGAIN JUST TO GET TO THEIR OWN BACKYARDS.
ICH BIN EIN BERLINER
"AND WHEN THERE IS A SECURITY THREAT, THE CHECKPOINT CLOSES AND IT HURTS THEIR LIVELIHOOD."
PEACE BE WITH YOU
SO THE FENCE DEFINITELY CAUSES PROBLEMS, BUT THE PALESTINIANS TAKE THESE DAY-TO-DAY ISSUES AND TURN THEM INTO VERY HARSH PROPAGANDA.
AND YOU NEED TO REALIZE THAT AND REMEMBER THE STATISTICS. BECAUSE OF THE WALL WE CAN TRAVEL SAFELY ON THIS ROAD.
MY PERSONAL OPINION IS THAT, WHILE I HATE HOW IT HURTS MANY PEOPLE, EVERY DAY THAT I WAKE UP AND THERE'S NO ATTACK ON THE NEWS, I THINK ABOUT THE WALL.

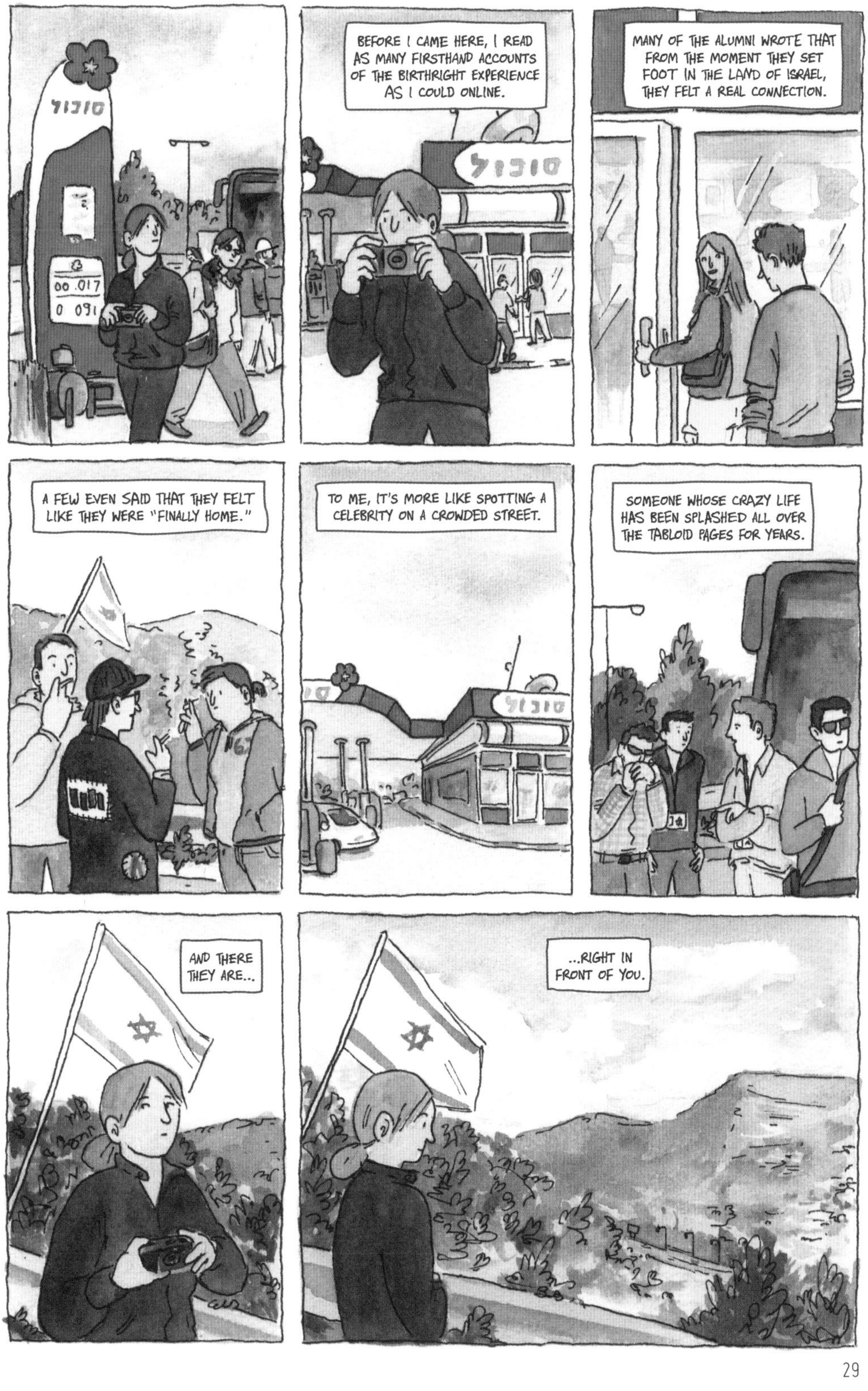
סונול
BEFORE I CAME HERE, I READ AS MANY FIRSTHAND ACCOUNTS OF THE BIRTHRIGHT EXPERIENCE AS I COULD ONLINE.
סונול
MANY OF THE ALUMNI WROTE THAT FROM THE MOMENT THEY SET FOOT IN THE LAND OF ISRAEL, THEY FELT A REAL CONNECTION.
A FEW EVEN SAID THAT THEY FELT LIKE THEY WERE "FINALLY HOME."
TO ME, IT'S MORE LIKE SPOTTING A CELEBRITY ON A CROWDED STREET.
סונול
SOMEONE WHOSE CRAZY LIFE HAS BEEN SPLASHED ALL OVER THE TABLOID PAGES FOR YEARS.
AND THERE THEY ARE...
...RIGHT IN FRONT OF YOU.

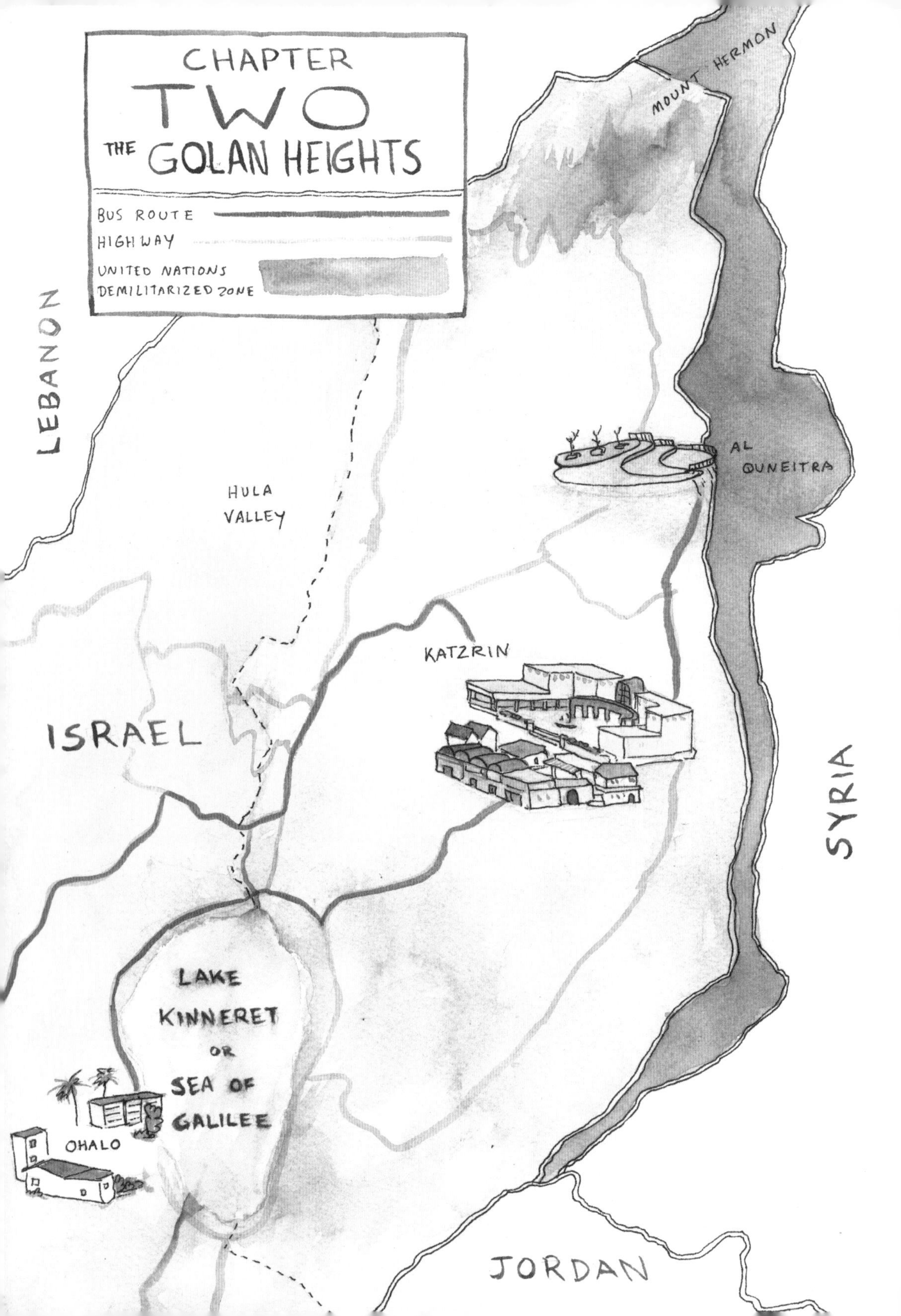
CHAPTER
TWO
THE GOLAN HEIGHTS
BUS ROUTE
HIGHWAY
UNITED NATIONS
DEMILITARIZED ZONE
MOUNT HERMON
LEBANON
AL QUNEITRA
HULA VALLEY
KATZRIN
ISRAEL
SYRIA
LAKE KINNERET OR SEA OF GALILEE
OHALO
JORDAN

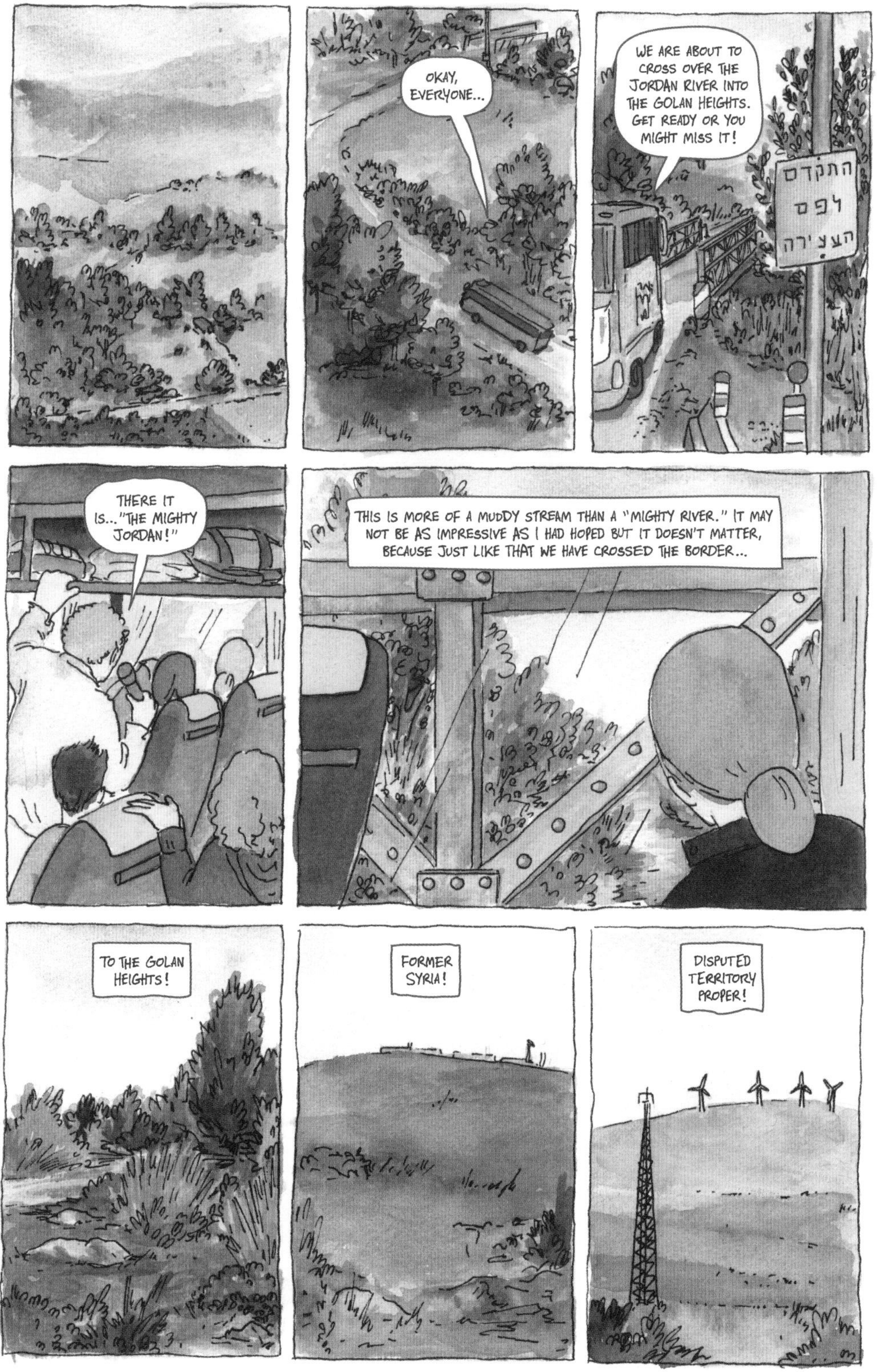
OKAY, EVERYONE...
WE ARE ABOUT TO CROSS OVER THE JORDAN RIVER INTO THE GOLAN HEIGHTS. GET READY OR YOU MIGHT MISS IT!
התקדם
לפס
THERE IT IS..."THE MIGHTY JORDAN!"
THIS IS MORE OF A MUDDY STREAM THAN A "MIGHTY RIVER." IT MAY NOT BE AS IMPRESSIVE AS I HAD HOPED BUT IT DOESN'T MATTER, BECAUSE JUST LIKE THAT WE HAVE CROSSED THE BORDER...
TO THE GOLAN HEIGHTS!
FORMER SYRIA!
DISPUTED TERRITORY PROPER!

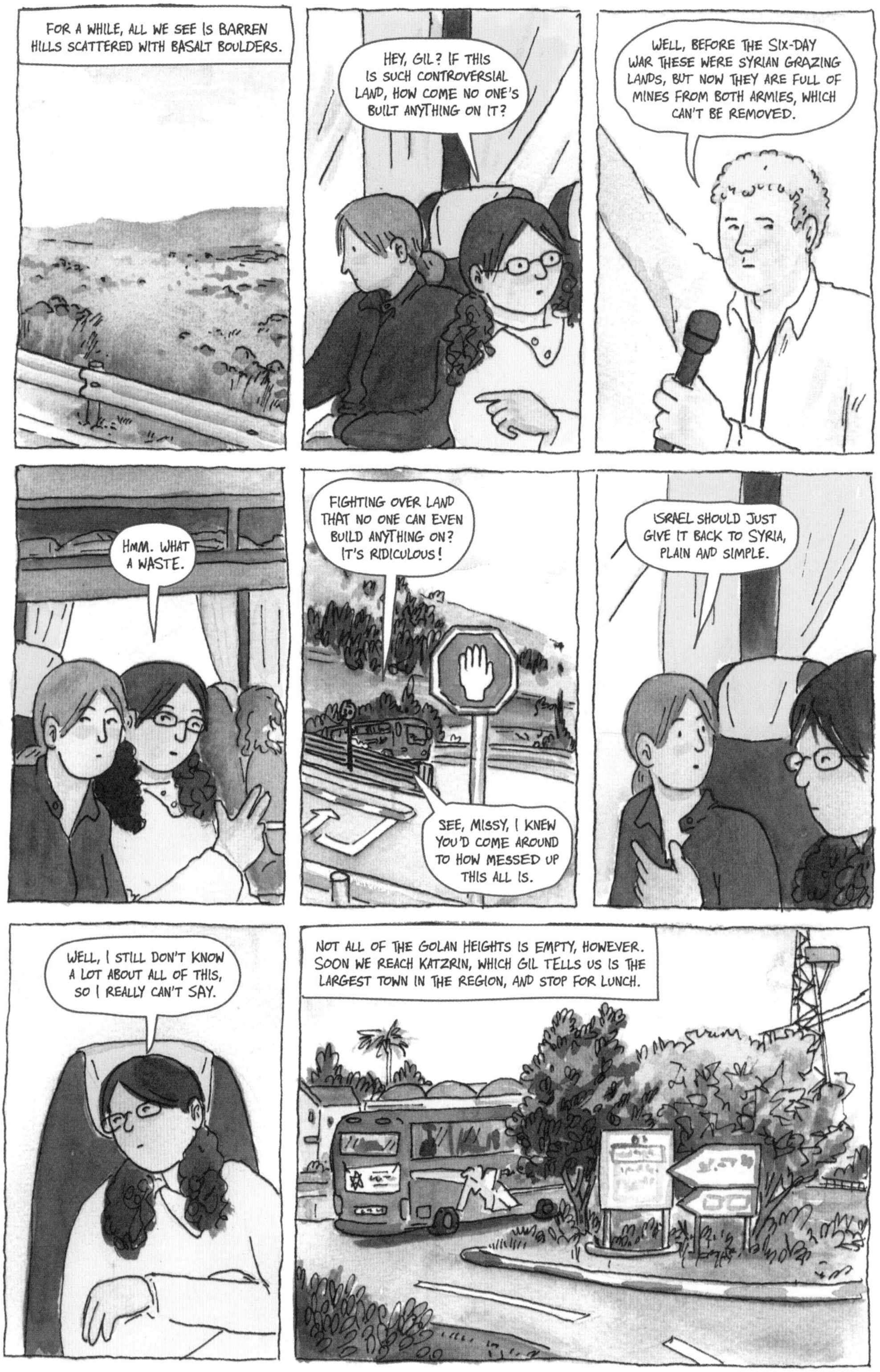
FOR A WHILE, ALL WE SEE IS BARREN HILLS SCATTERED WITH BASALT BOULDERS.
HEY, GIL? IF THIS IS SUCH CONTROVERSIAL LAND, HOW COME NO ONE'S BUILT ANYTHING ON IT?
WELL, BEFORE THE SIX-DAY WAR THESE WERE SYRIAN GRAZING LANDS, BUT NOW THEY ARE FULL OF MINES FROM BOTH ARMIES, WHICH CAN'T BE REMOVED.
HMM. WHAT A WASTE.
FIGHTING OVER LAND THAT NO ONE CAN EVEN BUILD ANYTHING ON? IT'S RIDICULOUS!
SEE, MISSY, I KNEW YOU'D COME AROUND TO HOW MESSED UP THIS ALL IS.
ISRAEL SHOULD JUST GIVE IT BACK TO SYRIA, PLAIN AND SIMPLE.
WELL, I STILL DON'T KNOW A LOT ABOUT ALL OF THIS, SO I REALLY CAN'T SAY.
NOT ALL OF THE GOLAN HEIGHTS IS EMPTY, HOWEVER. SOON WE REACH KATZRIN, WHICH GIL TELLS US IS THE LARGEST TOWN IN THE REGION, AND STOP FOR LUNCH.

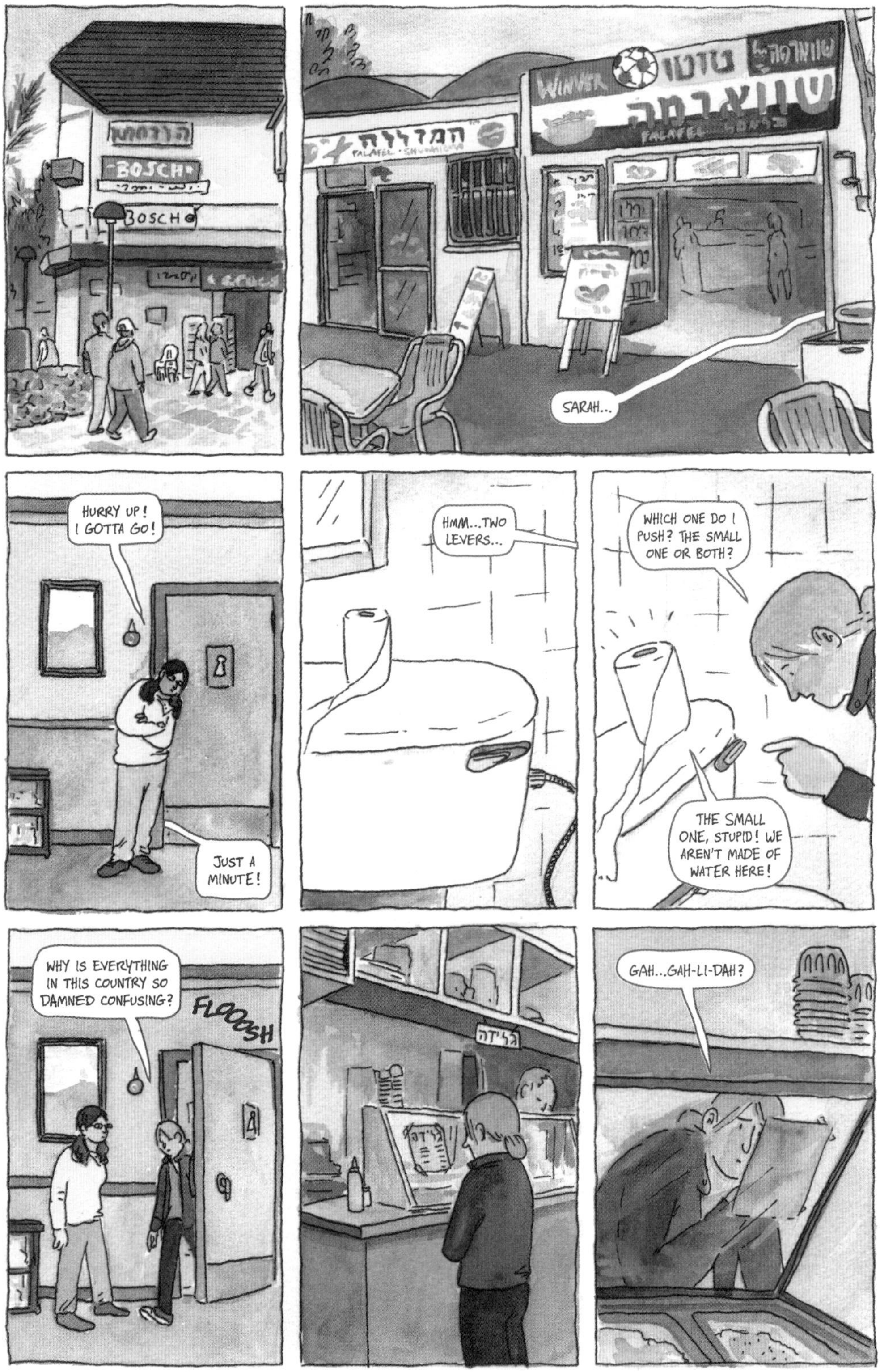
BOSCH
BOSCH
WINNER
FALAFEL
SARAH...
HURRY UP! I GOTTA GO!
JUST A MINUTE!
HMM...TWO LEVERS...
WHICH ONE DO I PUSH? THE SMALL ONE OR BOTH?
THE SMALL ONE, STUPID! WE AREN'T MADE OF WATER HERE!
WHY IS EVERYTHING IN THIS COUNTRY SO DAMNED CONFUSING?
FLOOOSH
GAH...GAH-LI-DAH?

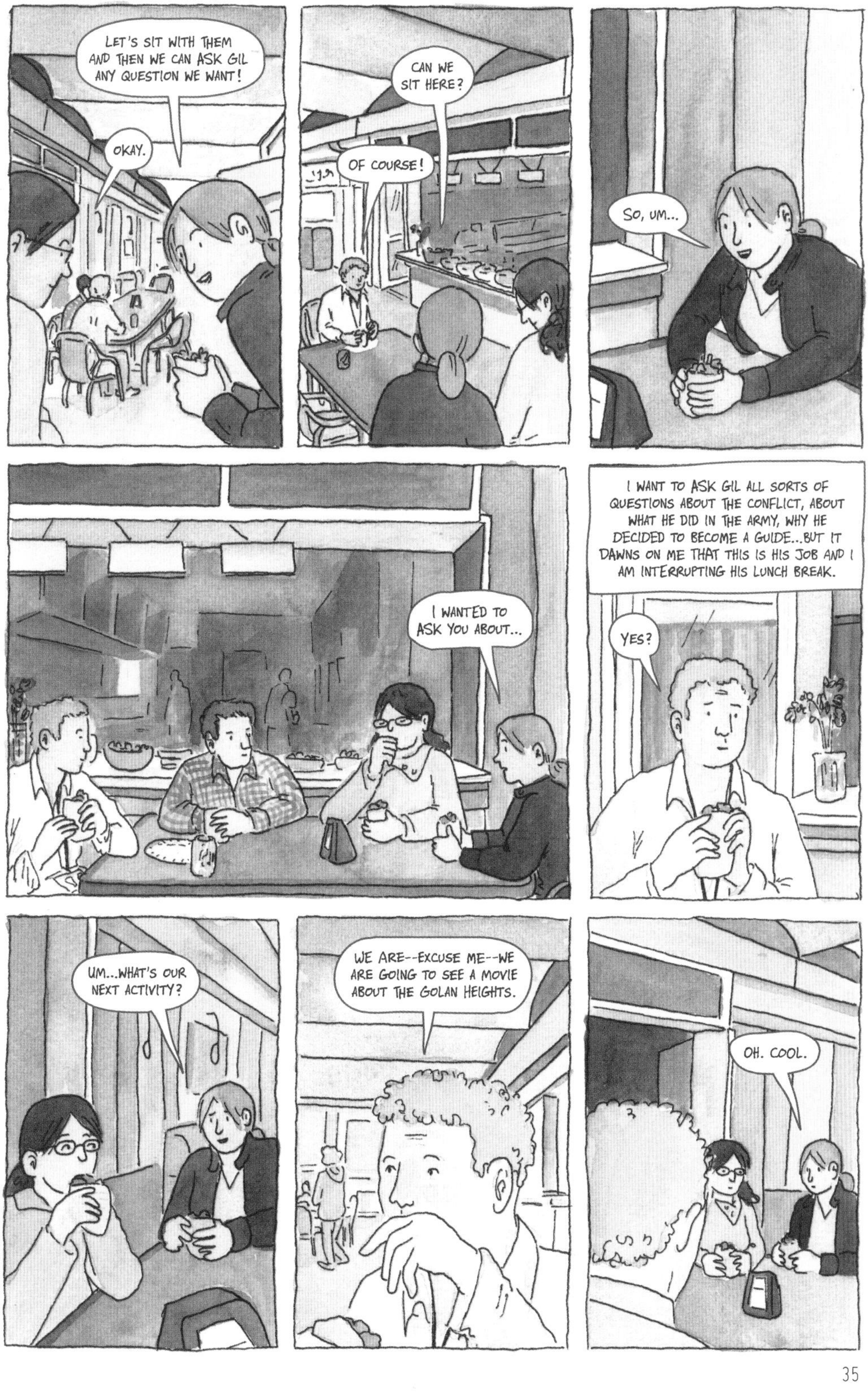
LET'S SIT WITH THEM AND THEN WE CAN ASK GIL ANY QUESTION WE WANT!
OKAY.
CAN WE SIT HERE?
OF COURSE!
SO, UM...
I WANTED TO ASK YOU ABOUT...
I WANT TO ASK GIL ALL SORTS OF QUESTIONS ABOUT THE CONFLICT, ABOUT WHAT HE DID IN THE ARMY, WHY HE DECIDED TO BECOME A GUIDE...BUT IT DAWNS ON ME THAT THIS IS HIS JOB AND I AM INTERRUPTING HIS LUNCH BREAK.
YES?
UM...WHAT'S OUR NEXT ACTIVITY?
WE ARE--EXCUSE ME--WE ARE GOING TO SEE A MOVIE ABOUT THE GOLAN HEIGHTS.
OH. COOL.

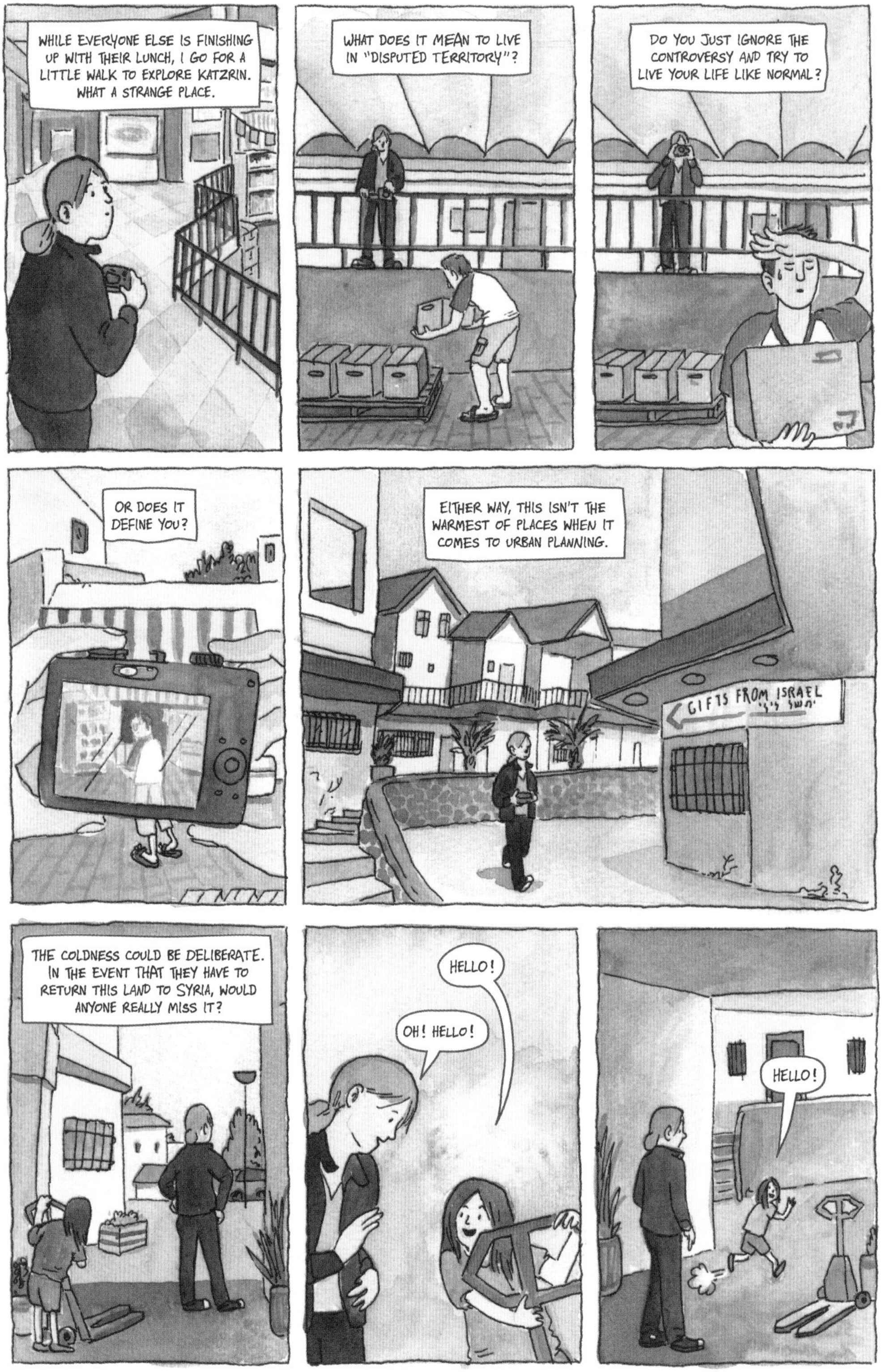
WHILE EVERYONE ELSE IS FINISHING UP WITH THEIR LUNCH, I GO FOR A LITTLE WALK TO EXPLORE KATZRIN. WHAT A STRANGE PLACE.
WHAT DOES IT MEAN TO LIVE IN "DISPUTED TERRITORY"?
DO YOU JUST IGNORE THE CONTROVERSY AND TRY TO LIVE YOUR LIFE LIKE NORMAL?
OR DOES IT DEFINE YOU?
EITHER WAY, THIS ISN'T THE WARMEST OF PLACES WHEN IT COMES TO URBAN PLANNING.
GIFTS FROM ISRAEL
THE COLDNESS COULD BE DELIBERATE. IN THE EVENT THAT THEY HAVE TO RETURN THIS LAND TO SYRIA, WOULD ANYONE REALLY MISS IT?
HELLO!
OH! HELLO!
HELLO!

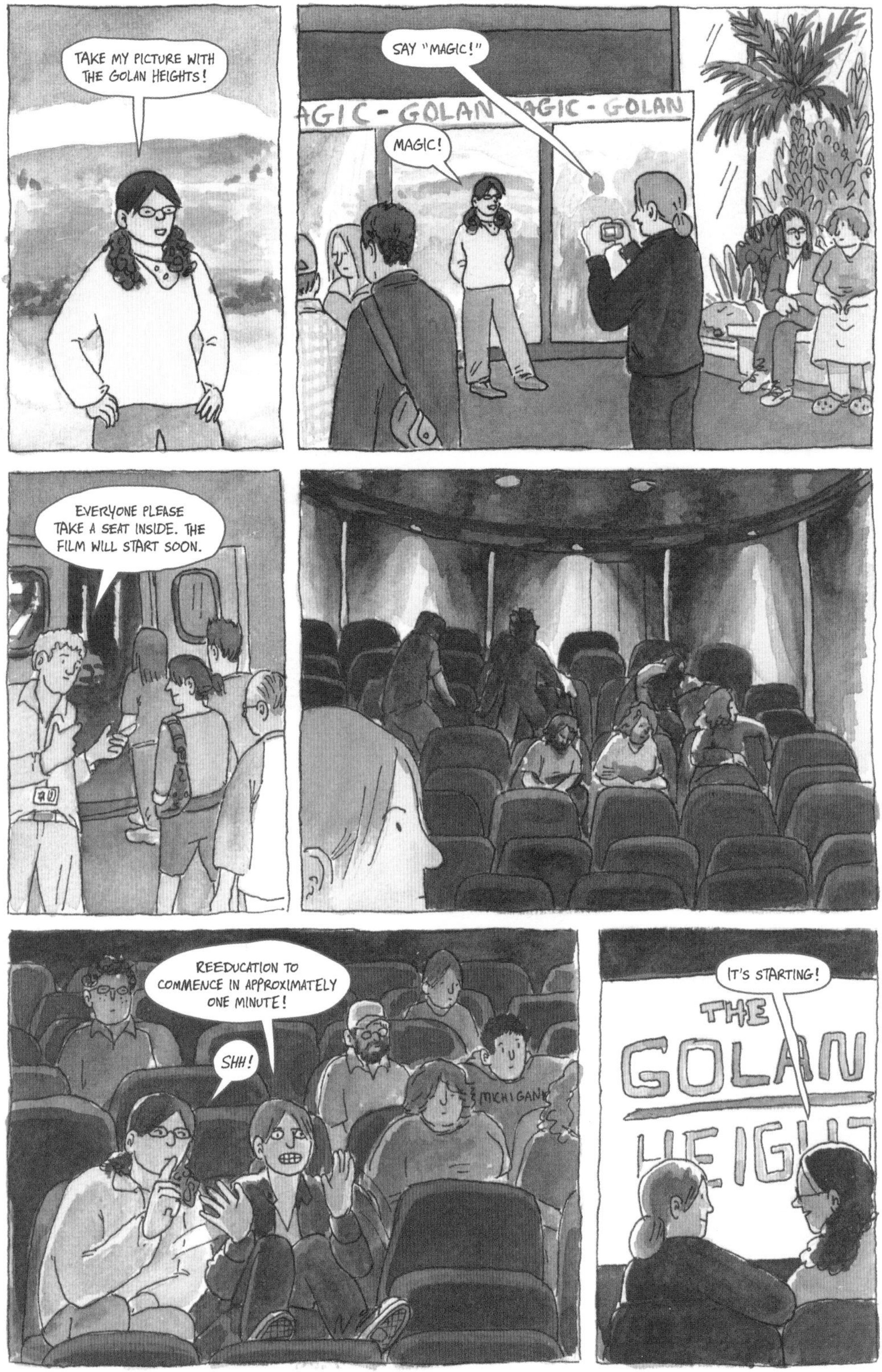
TAKE MY PICTURE WITH THE GOLAN HEIGHTS!
SAY "MAGIC!"
AGIC - GOLAN MAGIC - GOLAN
MAGIC!
EVERYONE PLEASE TAKE A SEAT INSIDE. THE FILM WILL START SOON.
REEDUCATION TO COMMENCE IN APPROXIMATELY ONE MINUTE!
SHH!
MICHIGAN
IT'S STARTING!
THE GOLAN HEIGHT

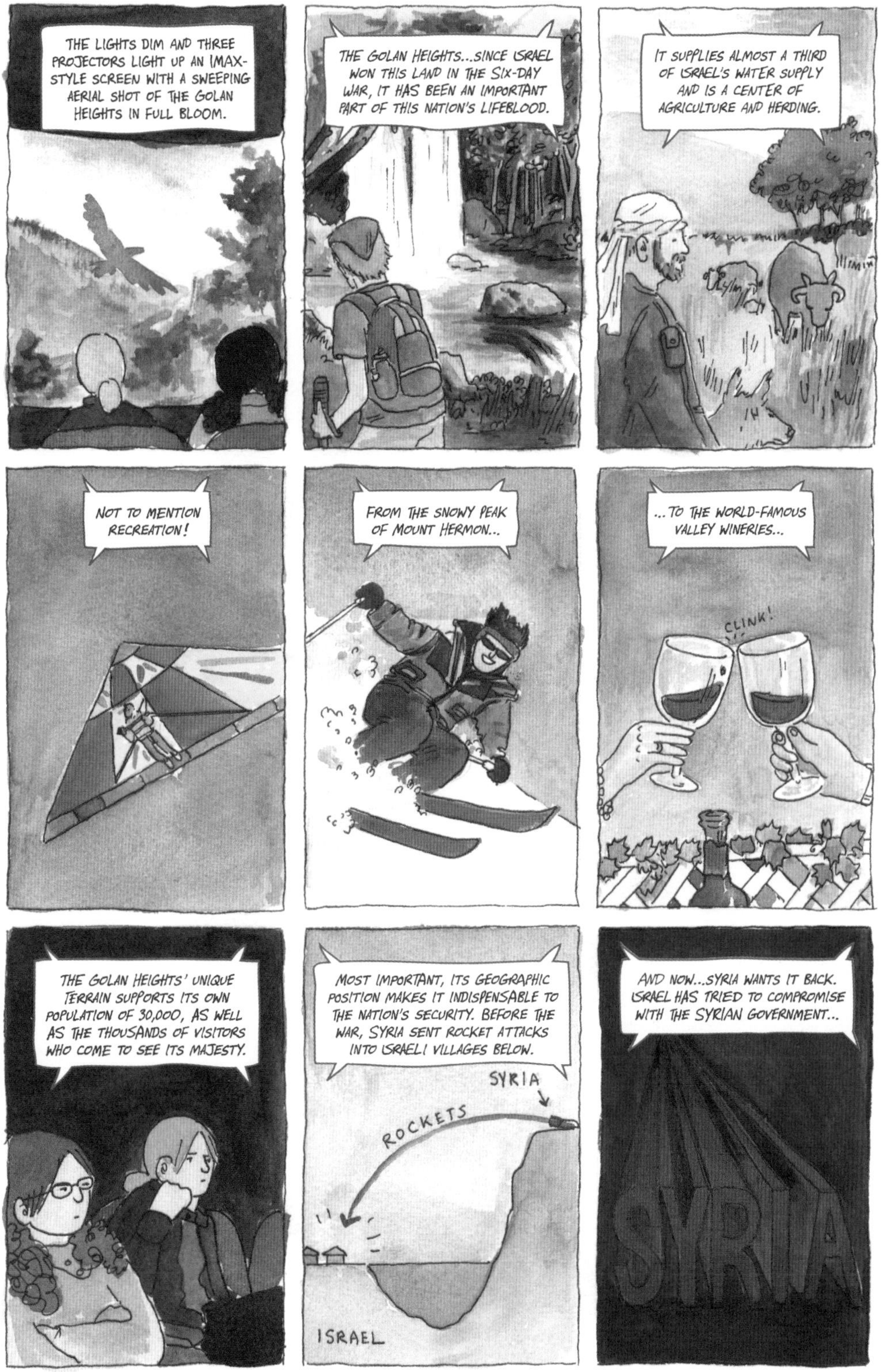
THE LIGHTS DIM AND THREE PROJECTORS LIGHT UP AN IMAX-STYLE SCREEN WITH A SWEEPING AERIAL SHOT OF THE GOLAN HEIGHTS IN FULL BLOOM.
THE GOLAN HEIGHTS...SINCE ISRAEL WON THIS LAND IN THE SIX-DAY WAR, IT HAS BEEN AN IMPORTANT PART OF THIS NATION'S LIFEBLOOD.
IT SUPPLIES ALMOST A THIRD OF ISRAEL'S WATER SUPPLY AND IS A CENTER OF AGRICULTURE AND HERDING.
NOT TO MENTION RECREATION!
FROM THE SNOWY PEAK OF MOUNT HERMON...
...TO THE WORLD-FAMOUS VALLEY WINERIES...
CLINK!
THE GOLAN HEIGHTS' UNIQUE TERRAIN SUPPORTS ITS OWN POPULATION OF 30,000, AS WELL AS THE THOUSANDS OF VISITORS WHO COME TO SEE ITS MAJESTY.
MOST IMPORTANT, ITS GEOGRAPHIC POSITION MAKES IT INDISPENSABLE TO THE NATION'S SECURITY. BEFORE THE WAR, SYRIA SENT ROCKET ATTACKS INTO ISRAELI VILLAGES BELOW.
SYRIA
ROCKETS
ISRAEL
AND NOW...SYRIA WANTS IT BACK. ISRAEL HAS TRIED TO COMPROMISE WITH THE SYRIAN GOVERNMENT...
SYRIA

41

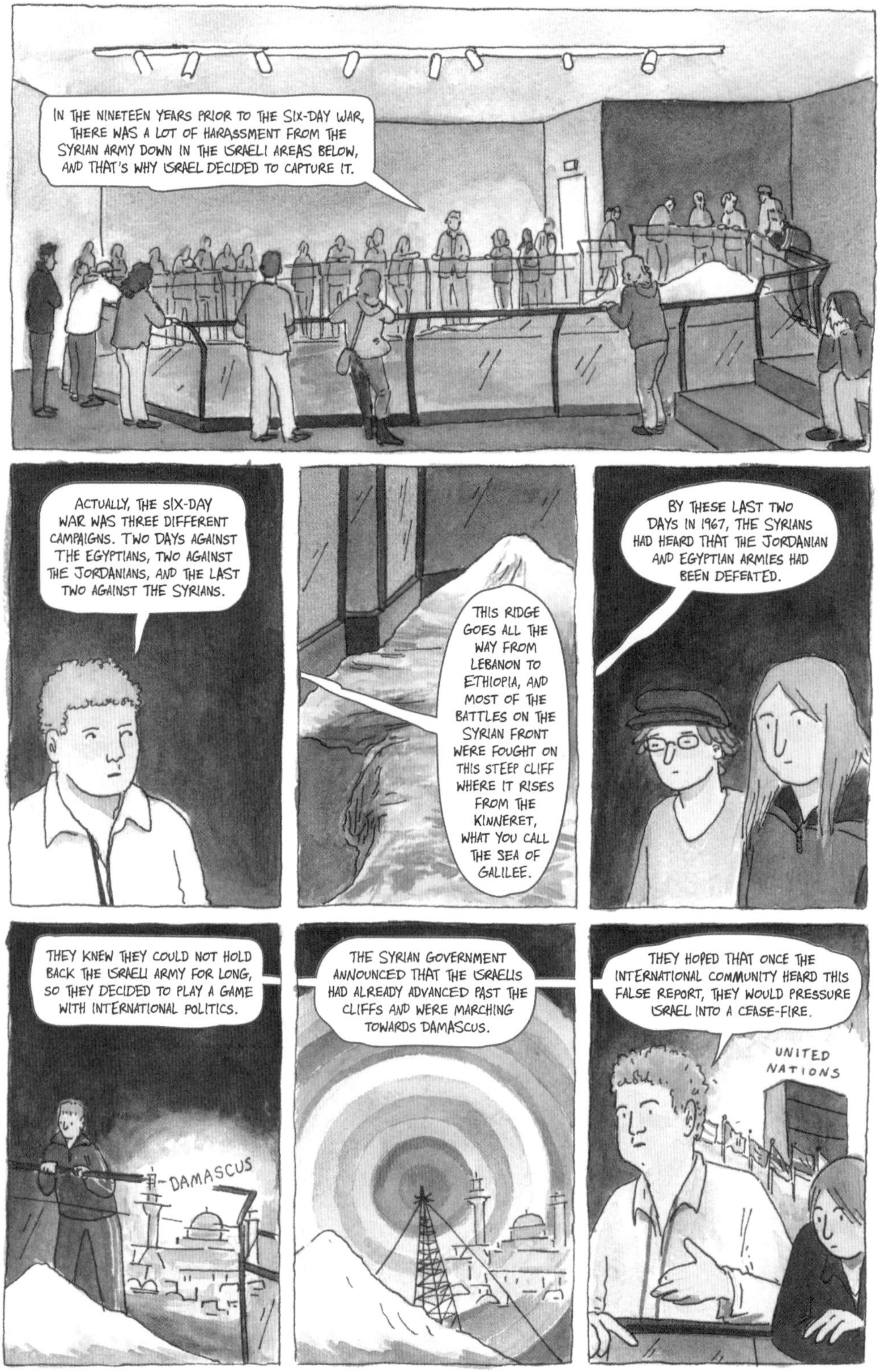
IN THE NINETEEN YEARS PRIOR TO THE SIX-DAY WAR, THERE WAS A LOT OF HARASSMENT FROM THE SYRIAN ARMY DOWN IN THE ISRAELI AREAS BELOW, AND THAT'S WHY ISRAEL DECIDED TO CAPTURE IT.
ACTUALLY, THE SIX-DAY WAR WAS THREE DIFFERENT CAMPAIGNS. TWO DAYS AGAINST THE EGYPTIANS, TWO AGAINST THE JORDANIANS, AND THE LAST TWO AGAINST THE SYRIANS.
THIS RIDGE GOES ALL THE WAY FROM LEBANON TO ETHIOPIA, AND MOST OF THE BATTLES ON THE SYRIAN FRONT WERE FOUGHT ON THIS STEEP CLIFF WHERE IT RISES FROM THE KINNERET, WHAT YOU CALL THE SEA OF GALILEE.
BY THESE LAST TWO DAYS IN 1967, THE SYRIANS HAD HEARD THAT THE JORDANIAN AND EGYPTIAN ARMIES HAD BEEN DEFEATED.
THEY KNEW THEY COULD NOT HOLD BACK THE ISRAELI ARMY FOR LONG, SO THEY DECIDED TO PLAY A GAME WITH INTERNATIONAL POLITICS.
DAMASCUS
THE SYRIAN GOVERNMENT ANNOUNCED THAT THE ISRAELIS HAD ALREADY ADVANCED PAST THE CLIFFS AND WERE MARCHING TOWARDS DAMASCUS.
THEY HOPED THAT ONCE THE INTERNATIONAL COMMUNITY HEARD THIS FALSE REPORT, THEY WOULD PRESSURE ISRAEL INTO A CEASE-FIRE.
UNITED NATIONS

47

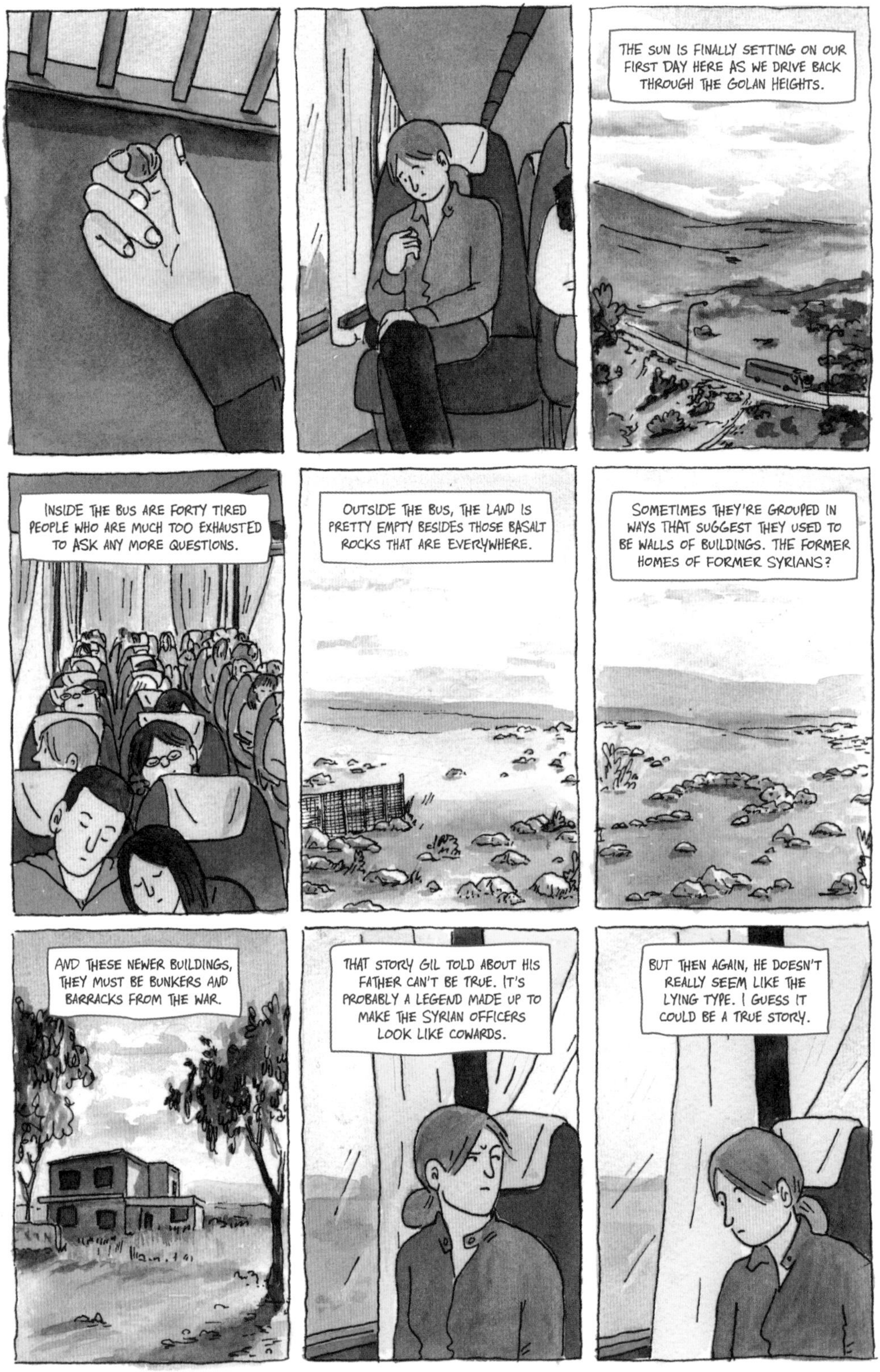
THE SUN IS FINALLY SETTING ON OUR FIRST DAY HERE AS WE DRIVE BACK THROUGH THE GOLAN HEIGHTS.
INSIDE THE BUS ARE FORTY TIRED PEOPLE WHO ARE MUCH TOO EXHAUSTED TO ASK ANY MORE QUESTIONS.
OUTSIDE THE BUS, THE LAND IS PRETTY EMPTY BESIDES THOSE BASALT ROCKS THAT ARE EVERYWHERE.
SOMETIMES THEY'RE GROUPED IN WAYS THAT SUGGEST THEY USED TO BE WALLS OF BUILDINGS. THE FORMER HOMES OF FORMER SYRIANS?
AND THESE NEWER BUILDINGS, THEY MUST BE BUNKERS AND BARRACKS FROM THE WAR.
THAT STORY GIL TOLD ABOUT HIS FATHER CAN'T BE TRUE. IT'S PROBABLY A LEGEND MADE UP TO MAKE THE SYRIAN OFFICERS LOOK LIKE COWARDS.
BUT THEN AGAIN, HE DOESN'T REALLY SEEM LIKE THE LYING TYPE. I GUESS IT COULD BE A TRUE STORY.

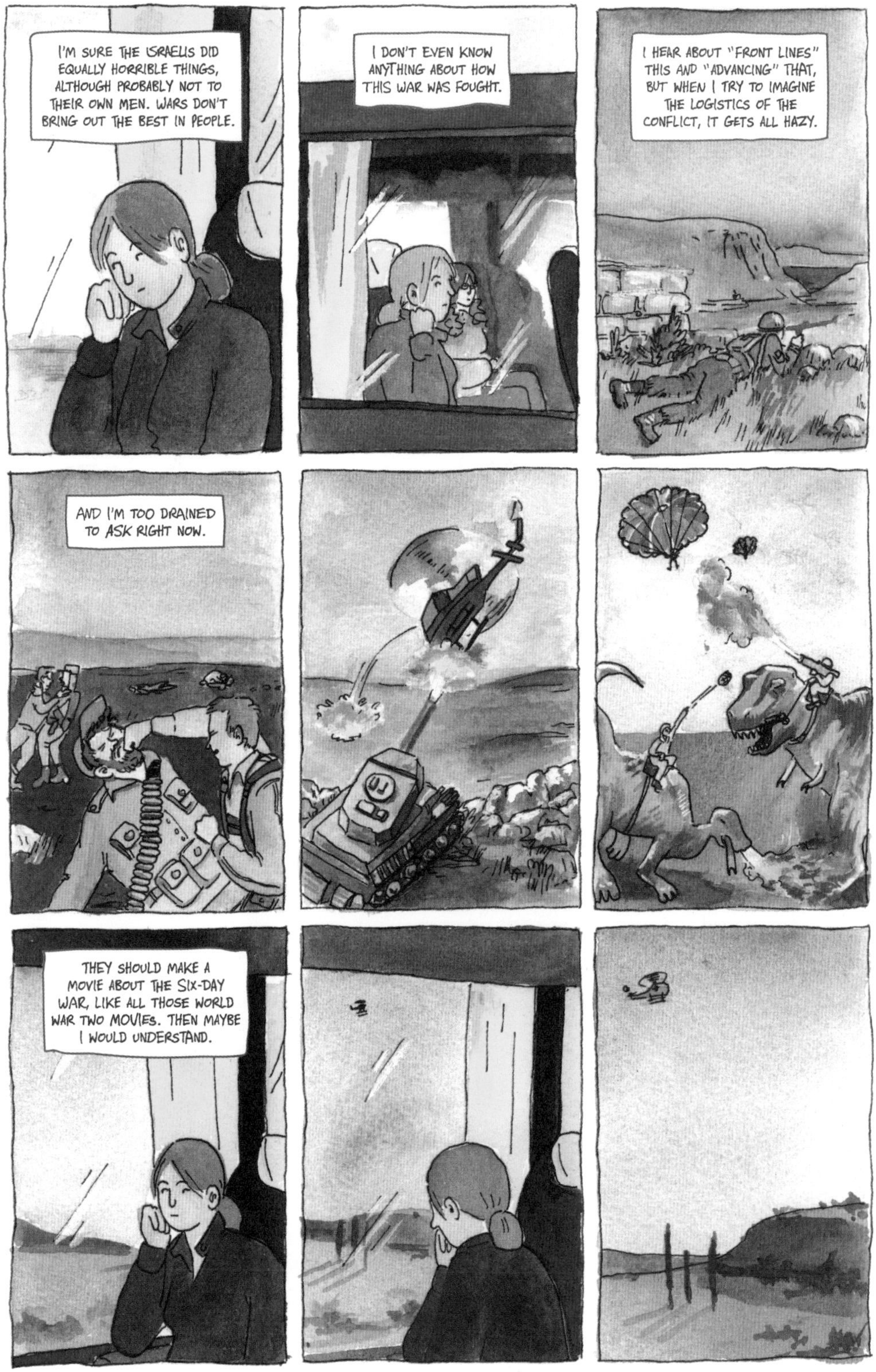
I'M SURE THE ISRAELIS DID EQUALLY HORRIBLE THINGS, ALTHOUGH PROBABLY NOT TO THEIR OWN MEN. WARS DON'T BRING OUT THE BEST IN PEOPLE.
I DON'T EVEN KNOW ANYTHING ABOUT HOW THIS WAR WAS FOUGHT.
I HEAR ABOUT "FRONT LINES" THIS AND "ADVANCING" THAT, BUT WHEN I TRY TO IMAGINE THE LOGISTICS OF THE CONFLICT, IT GETS ALL HAZY.
AND I'M TOO DRAINED TO ASK RIGHT NOW.
THEY SHOULD MAKE A MOVIE ABOUT THE SIX-DAY WAR, LIKE ALL THOSE WORLD WAR TWO MOVIES. THEN MAYBE I WOULD UNDERSTAND.

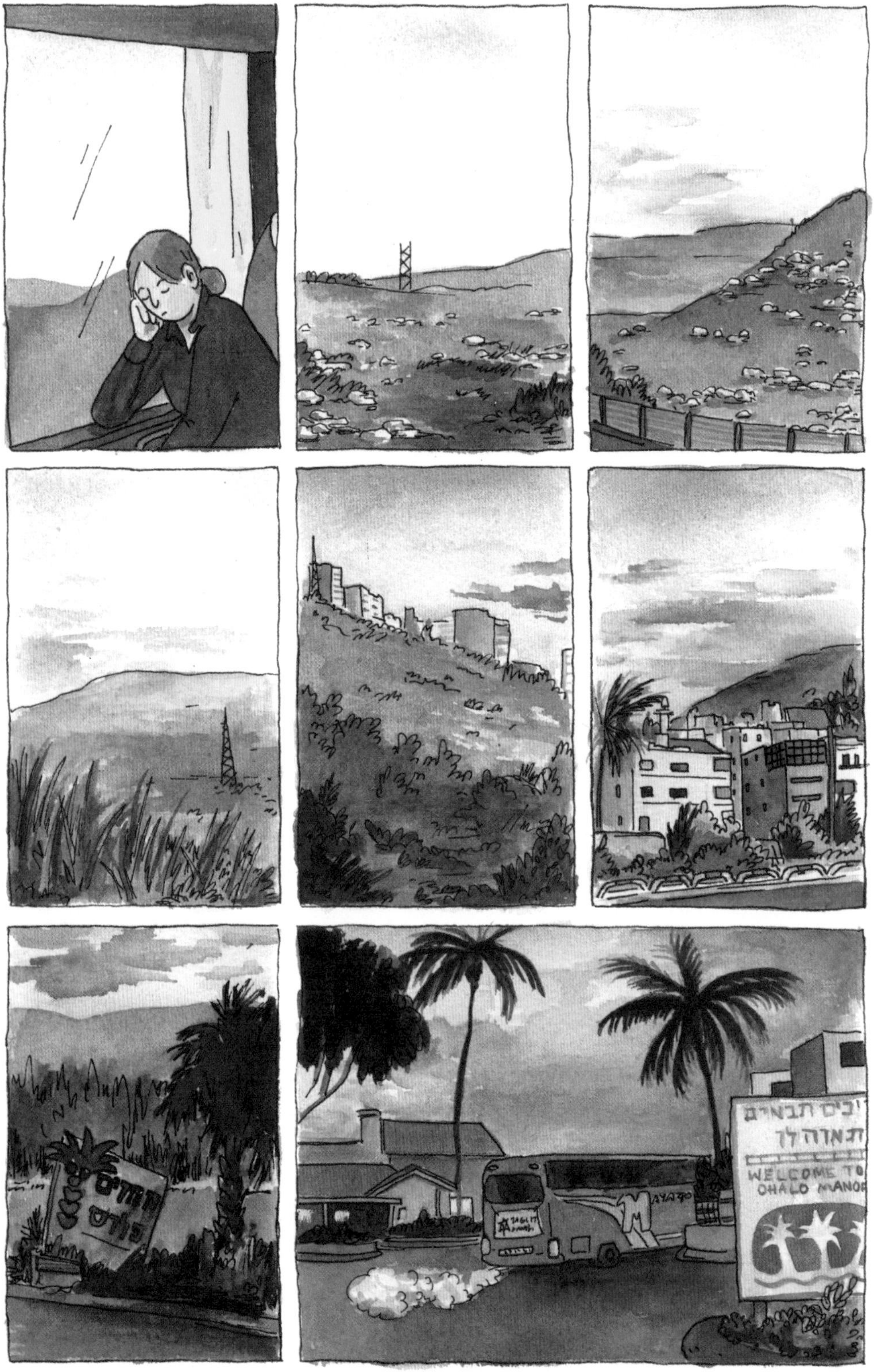
WELCOME TO
OHALO MANOR

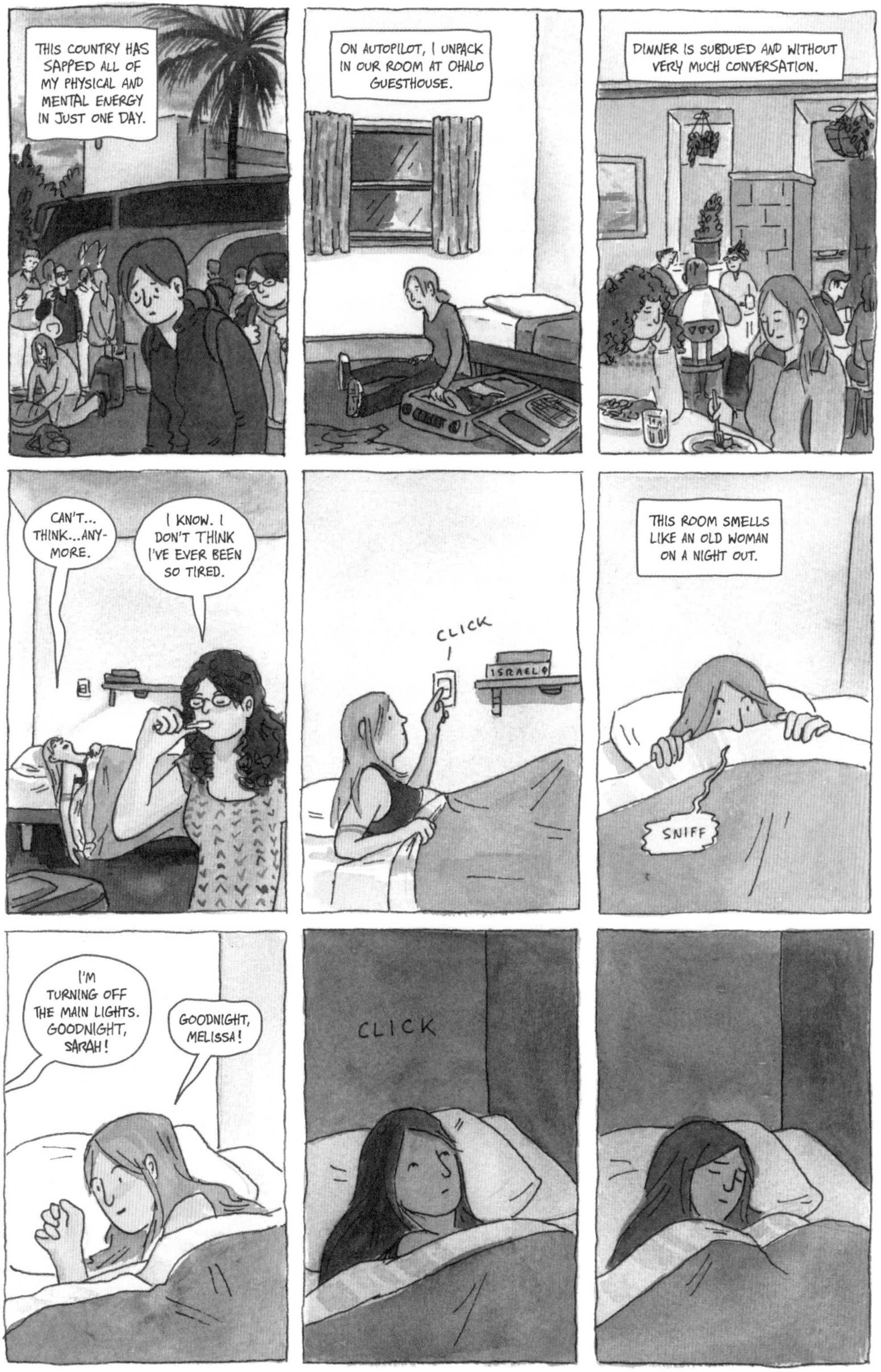
THIS COUNTRY HAS SAPPED ALL OF MY PHYSICAL AND MENTAL ENERGY IN JUST ONE DAY.
ON AUTOPILOT, I UNPACK IN OUR ROOM AT OHALO GUESTHOUSE.
DINNER IS SUBDUED AND WITHOUT VERY MUCH CONVERSATION.
CAN'T... THINK...ANY-MORE.
I KNOW. I DON'T THINK I'VE EVER BEEN SO TIRED.
CLICK
ISRAEL
THIS ROOM SMELLS LIKE AN OLD WOMAN ON A NIGHT OUT.
SNIFF
I'M TURNING OFF THE MAIN LIGHTS. GOODNIGHT, SARAH!
GOODNIGHT, MELISSA!
CLICK

52

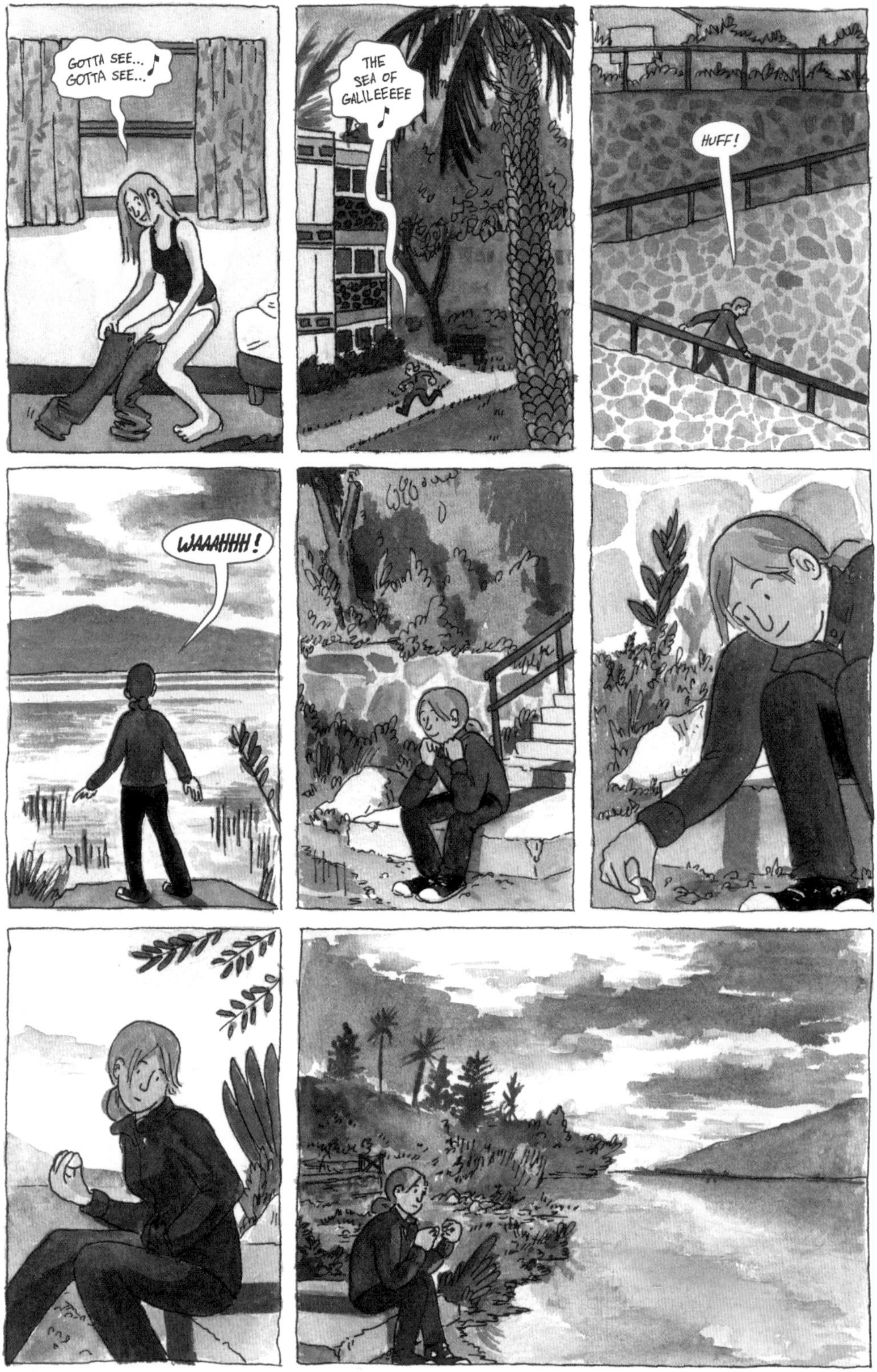
GOTTA SEE... GOTTA SEE... ♪
THE SEA OF GALILEEEEE ♪
HUFF!
WAAAHHH!

CHAPTER THREE
THE KINNERET

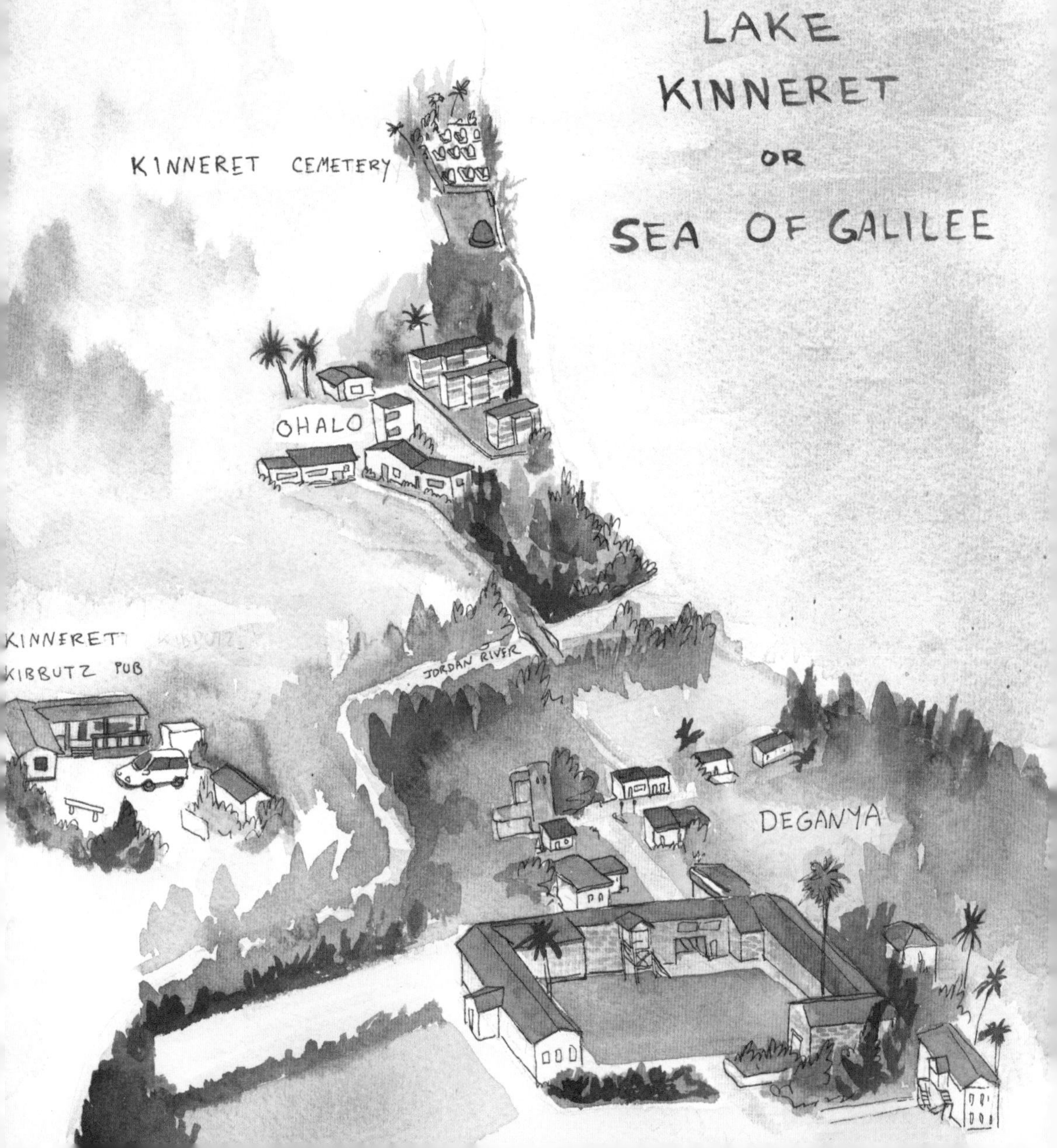
LAKE KINNERET OR SEA OF GALILEE
KINNERET CEMETERY
OHALO
KINNERET KIBBUTZ PUB
JORDAN RIVER
DEGANYA

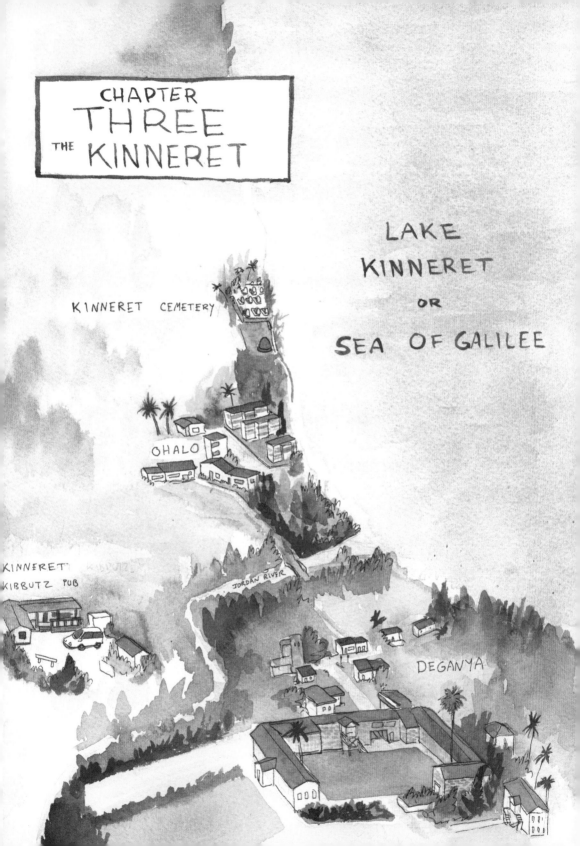

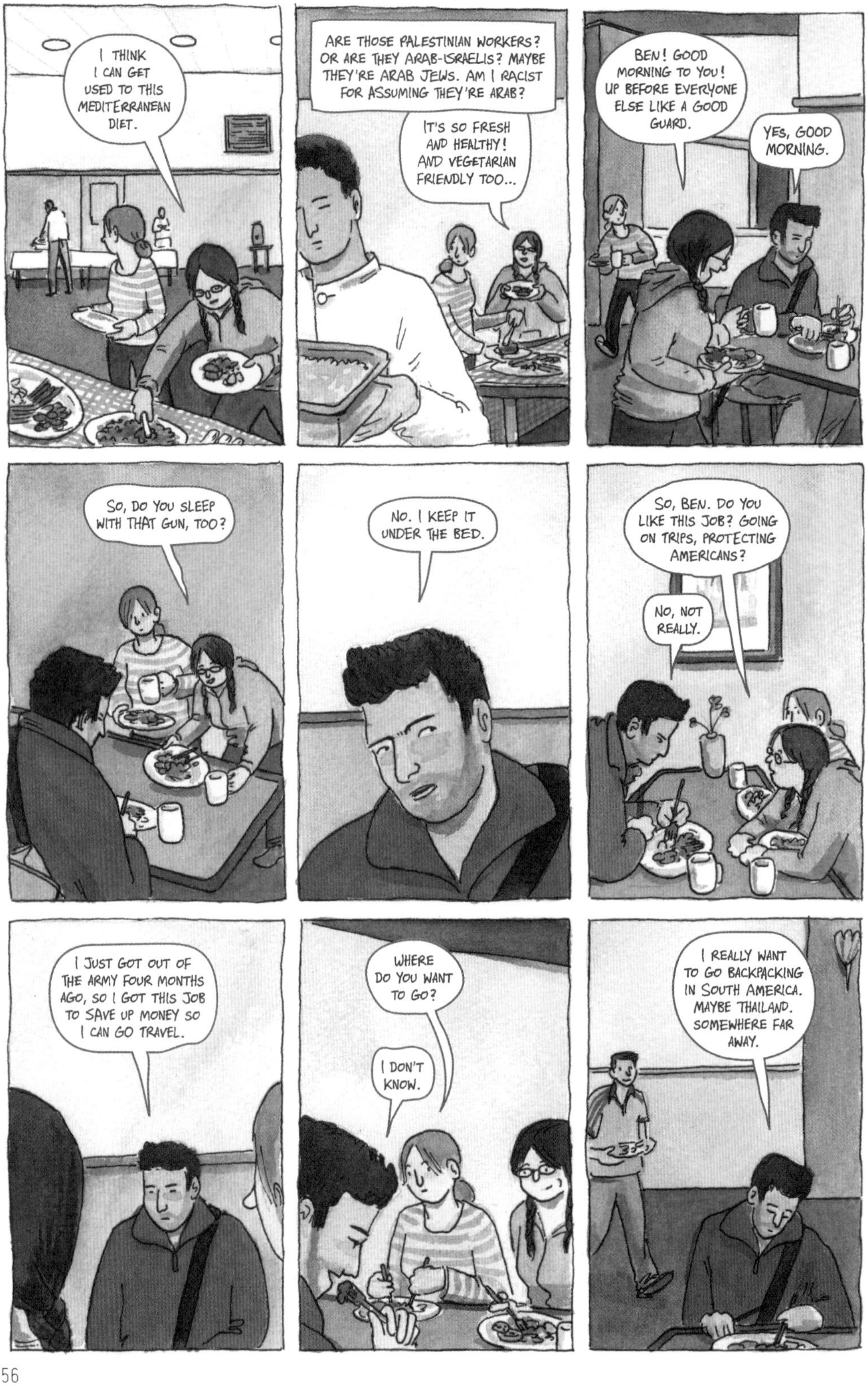
I THINK I CAN GET USED TO THIS MEDITERRANEAN DIET.
ARE THOSE PALESTINIAN WORKERS? OR ARE THEY ARAB-ISRAELIS? MAYBE THEY'RE ARAB JEWS. AM I RACIST FOR ASSUMING THEY'RE ARAB?
IT'S SO FRESH AND HEALTHY! AND VEGETARIAN FRIENDLY TOO...
BEN! GOOD MORNING TO YOU! UP BEFORE EVERYONE ELSE LIKE A GOOD GUARD.
YES, GOOD MORNING.
SO, DO YOU SLEEP WITH THAT GUN, TOO?
NO. I KEEP IT UNDER THE BED.
SO, BEN. DO YOU LIKE THIS JOB? GOING ON TRIPS, PROTECTING AMERICANS?
NO, NOT REALLY.
I JUST GOT OUT OF THE ARMY FOUR MONTHS AGO, SO I GOT THIS JOB TO SAVE UP MONEY SO I CAN GO TRAVEL.
WHERE DO YOU WANT TO GO?
I DON'T KNOW.
I REALLY WANT TO GO BACKPACKING IN SOUTH AMERICA. MAYBE THAILAND. SOMEWHERE FAR AWAY.

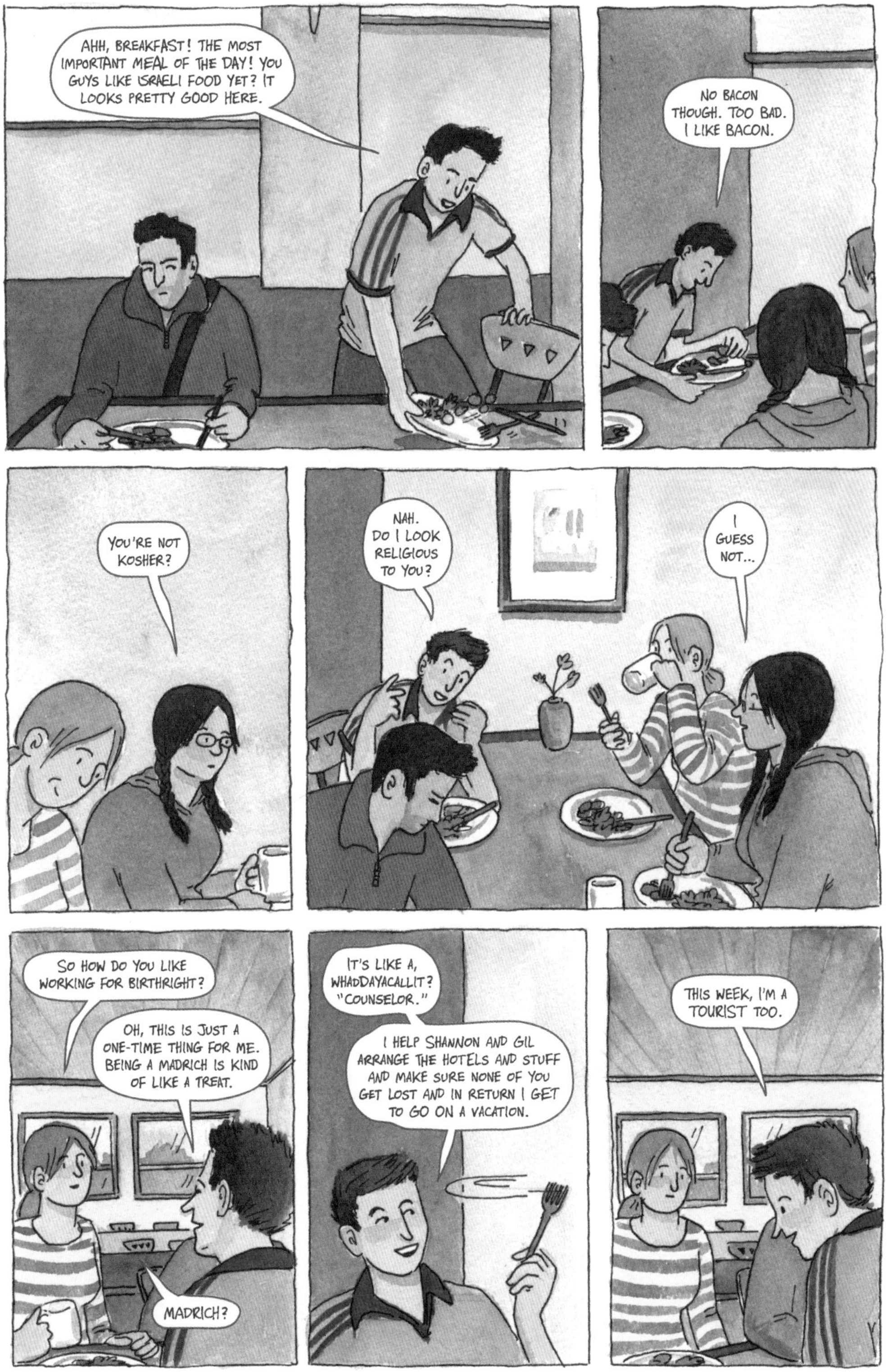
AHH, BREAKFAST! THE MOST IMPORTANT MEAL OF THE DAY! YOU GUYS LIKE ISRAELI FOOD YET? IT LOOKS PRETTY GOOD HERE.
NO BACON THOUGH. TOO BAD. I LIKE BACON.
YOU'RE NOT KOSHER?
NAH. DO I LOOK RELIGIOUS TO YOU?
I GUESS NOT...
SO HOW DO YOU LIKE WORKING FOR BIRTHRIGHT?
OH, THIS IS JUST A ONE-TIME THING FOR ME. BEING A MADRICH IS KIND OF LIKE A TREAT.
MADRICH?
IT'S LIKE A, WHADDAYACALLIT? "COUNSELOR."
I HELP SHANNON AND GIL ARRANGE THE HOTELS AND STUFF AND MAKE SURE NONE OF YOU GET LOST AND IN RETURN I GET TO GO ON A VACATION.
THIS WEEK, I'M A TOURIST TOO.

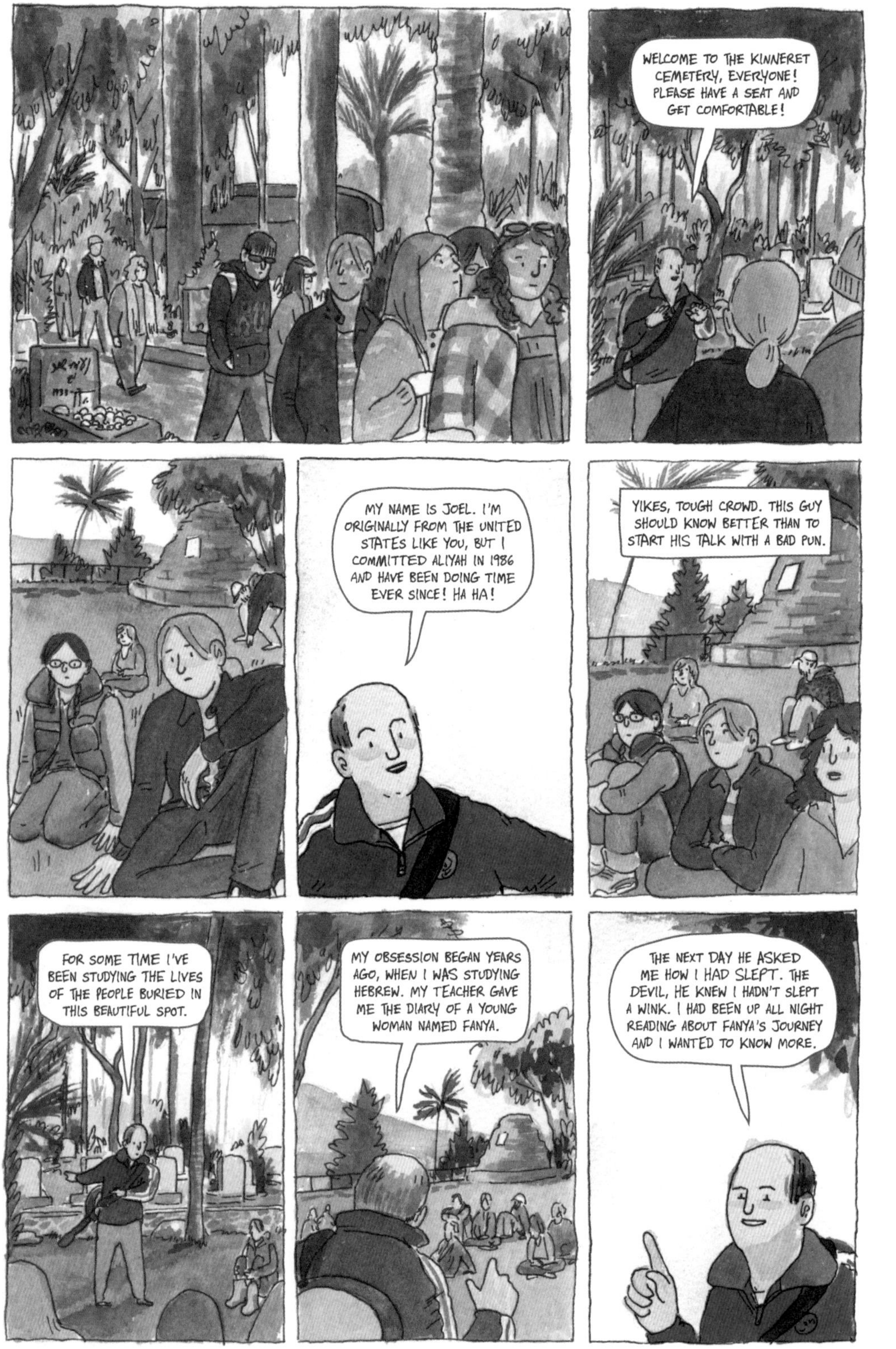
WELCOME TO THE KINNERET CEMETERY, EVERYONE! PLEASE HAVE A SEAT AND GET COMFORTABLE!
MY NAME IS JOEL. I'M ORIGINALLY FROM THE UNITED STATES LIKE YOU, BUT I COMMITTED ALIYAH IN 1986 AND HAVE BEEN DOING TIME EVER SINCE! HA HA!
YIKES, TOUGH CROWD. THIS GUY SHOULD KNOW BETTER THAN TO START HIS TALK WITH A BAD PUN.
FOR SOME TIME I'VE BEEN STUDYING THE LIVES OF THE PEOPLE BURIED IN THIS BEAUTIFUL SPOT.
MY OBSESSION BEGAN YEARS AGO, WHEN I WAS STUDYING HEBREW. MY TEACHER GAVE ME THE DIARY OF A YOUNG WOMAN NAMED FANYA.
THE NEXT DAY HE ASKED ME HOW I HAD SLEPT. THE DEVIL, HE KNEW I HADN'T SLEPT A WINK. I HAD BEEN UP ALL NIGHT READING ABOUT FANYA'S JOURNEY AND I WANTED TO KNOW MORE.

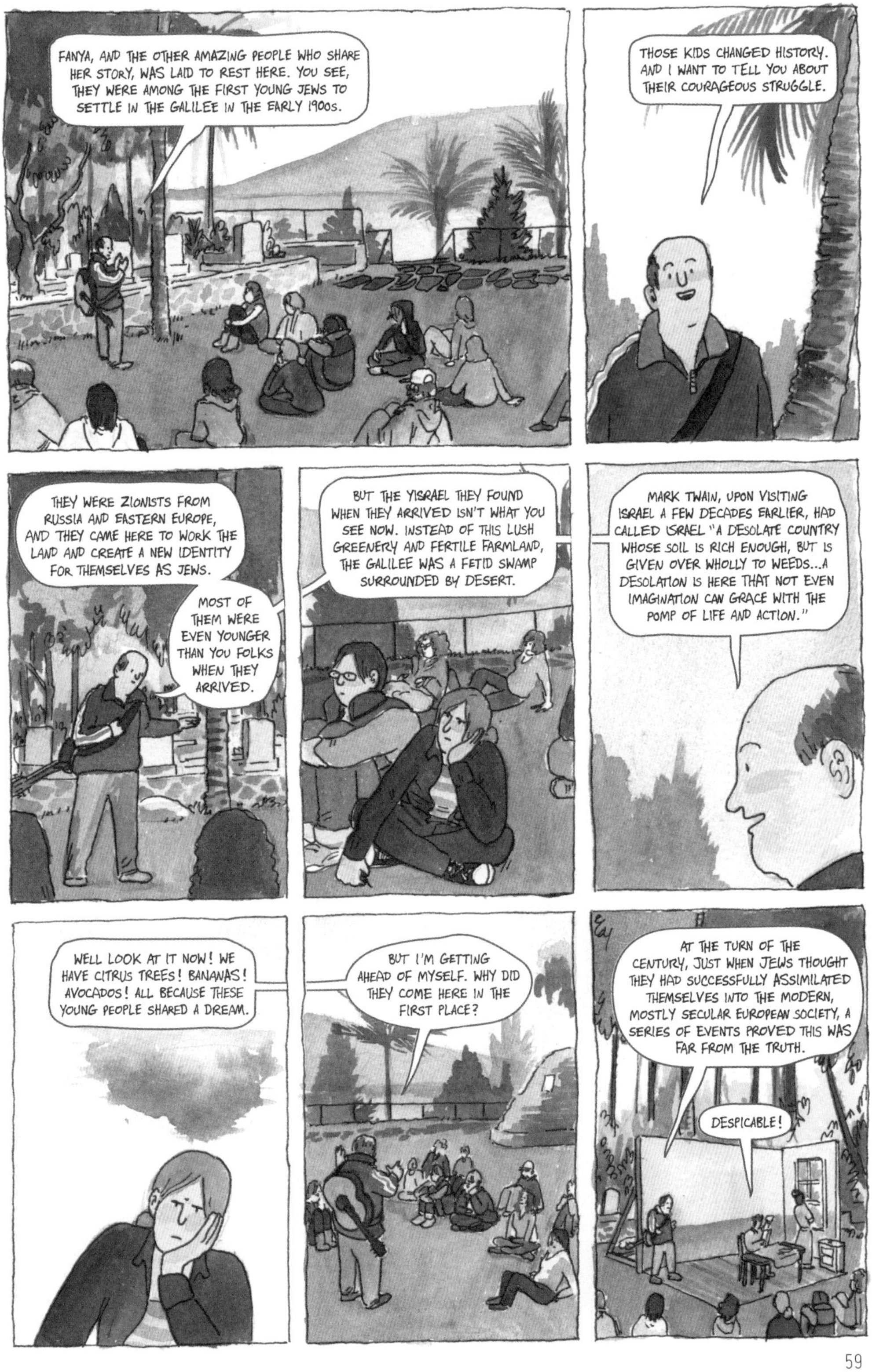
FANYA, AND THE OTHER AMAZING PEOPLE WHO SHARE HER STORY, WAS LAID TO REST HERE. YOU SEE, THEY WERE AMONG THE FIRST YOUNG JEWS TO SETTLE IN THE GALILEE IN THE EARLY 1900s.
THOSE KIDS CHANGED HISTORY. AND I WANT TO TELL YOU ABOUT THEIR COURAGEOUS STRUGGLE.
THEY WERE ZIONISTS FROM RUSSIA AND EASTERN EUROPE, AND THEY CAME HERE TO WORK THE LAND AND CREATE A NEW IDENTITY FOR THEMSELVES AS JEWS.
MOST OF THEM WERE EVEN YOUNGER THAN YOU FOLKS WHEN THEY ARRIVED.
BUT THE YISRAEL THEY FOUND WHEN THEY ARRIVED ISN'T WHAT YOU SEE NOW. INSTEAD OF THIS LUSH GREENERY AND FERTILE FARMLAND, THE GALILEE WAS A FETID SWAMP SURROUNDED BY DESERT.
MARK TWAIN, UPON VISITING ISRAEL A FEW DECADES EARLIER, HAD CALLED ISRAEL "A DESOLATE COUNTRY WHOSE SOIL IS RICH ENOUGH, BUT IS GIVEN OVER WHOLLY TO WEEDS...A DESOLATION IS HERE THAT NOT EVEN IMAGINATION CAN GRACE WITH THE POMP OF LIFE AND ACTION."
WELL LOOK AT IT NOW! WE HAVE CITRUS TREES! BANANAS! AVOCADOS! ALL BECAUSE THESE YOUNG PEOPLE SHARED A DREAM.
BUT I'M GETTING AHEAD OF MYSELF. WHY DID THEY COME HERE IN THE FIRST PLACE?
AT THE TURN OF THE CENTURY, JUST WHEN JEWS THOUGHT THEY HAD SUCCESSFULLY ASSIMILATED THEMSELVES INTO THE MODERN, MOSTLY SECULAR EUROPEAN SOCIETY, A SERIES OF EVENTS PROVED THIS WAS FAR FROM THE TRUTH.
DESPICABLE!

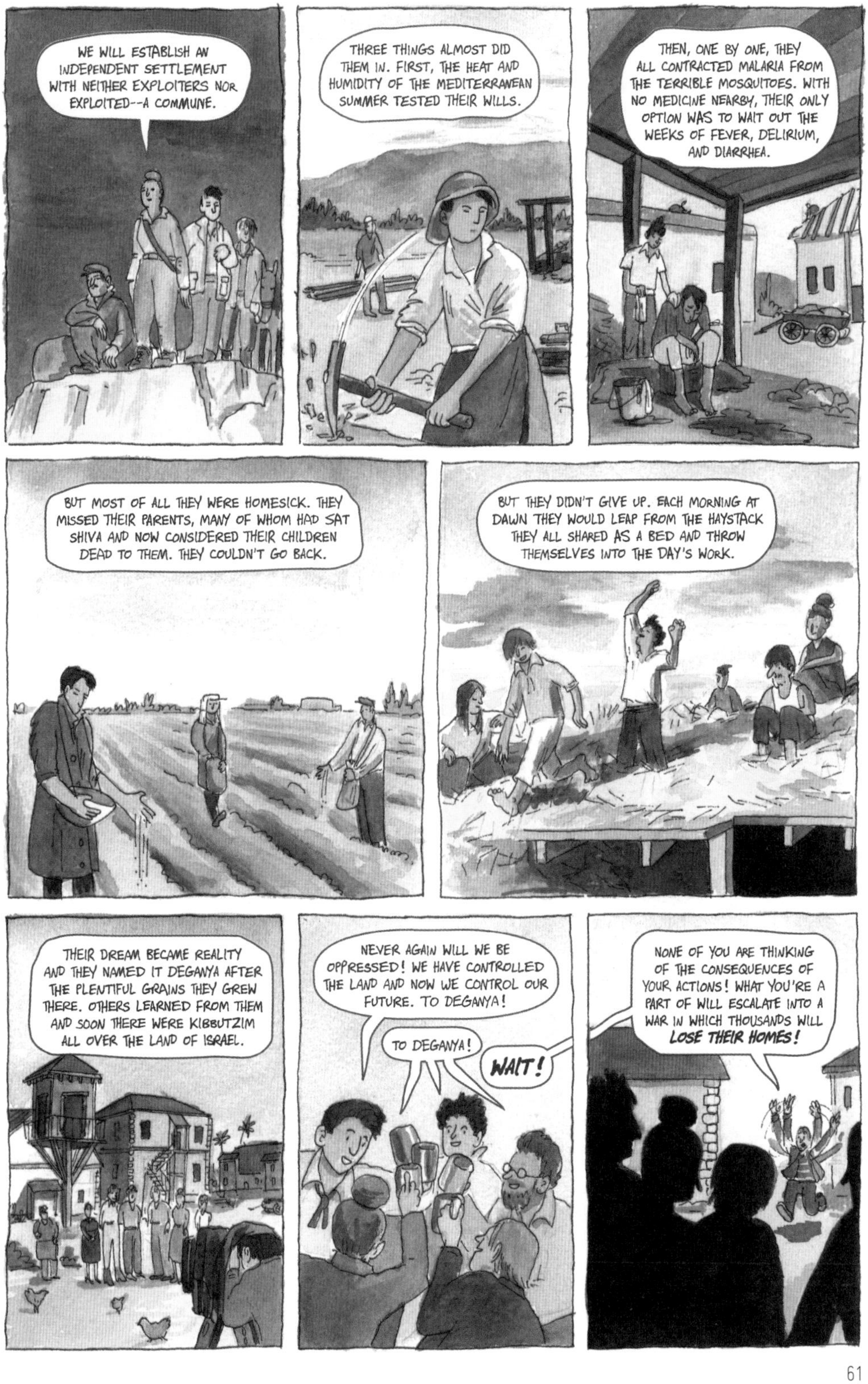
WE WILL ESTABLISH AN INDEPENDENT SETTLEMENT WITH NEITHER EXPLOITERS NOR EXPLOITED--A COMMUNE.
THREE THINGS ALMOST DID THEM IN. FIRST, THE HEAT AND HUMIDITY OF THE MEDITERRANEAN SUMMER TESTED THEIR WILLS.
THEN, ONE BY ONE, THEY ALL CONTRACTED MALARIA FROM THE TERRIBLE MOSQUITOES. WITH NO MEDICINE NEARBY, THEIR ONLY OPTION WAS TO WAIT OUT THE WEEKS OF FEVER, DELIRIUM, AND DIARRHEA.
BUT MOST OF ALL THEY WERE HOMESICK. THEY MISSED THEIR PARENTS, MANY OF WHOM HAD SAT SHIVA AND NOW CONSIDERED THEIR CHILDREN DEAD TO THEM. THEY COULDN'T GO BACK.
BUT THEY DIDN'T GIVE UP. EACH MORNING AT DAWN THEY WOULD LEAP FROM THE HAYSTACK THEY ALL SHARED AS A BED AND THROW THEMSELVES INTO THE DAY'S WORK.
THEIR DREAM BECAME REALITY AND THEY NAMED IT DEGANYA AFTER THE PLENTIFUL GRAINS THEY GREW THERE. OTHERS LEARNED FROM THEM AND SOON THERE WERE KIBBUTZIM ALL OVER THE LAND OF ISRAEL.
NEVER AGAIN WILL WE BE OPPRESSED! WE HAVE CONTROLLED THE LAND AND NOW WE CONTROL OUR FUTURE. TO DEGANYA!
TO DEGANYA!
WAIT!
NONE OF YOU ARE THINKING OF THE CONSEQUENCES OF YOUR ACTIONS! WHAT YOU'RE A PART OF WILL ESCALATE INTO A WAR IN WHICH THOUSANDS WILL **LOSE THEIR HOMES!**

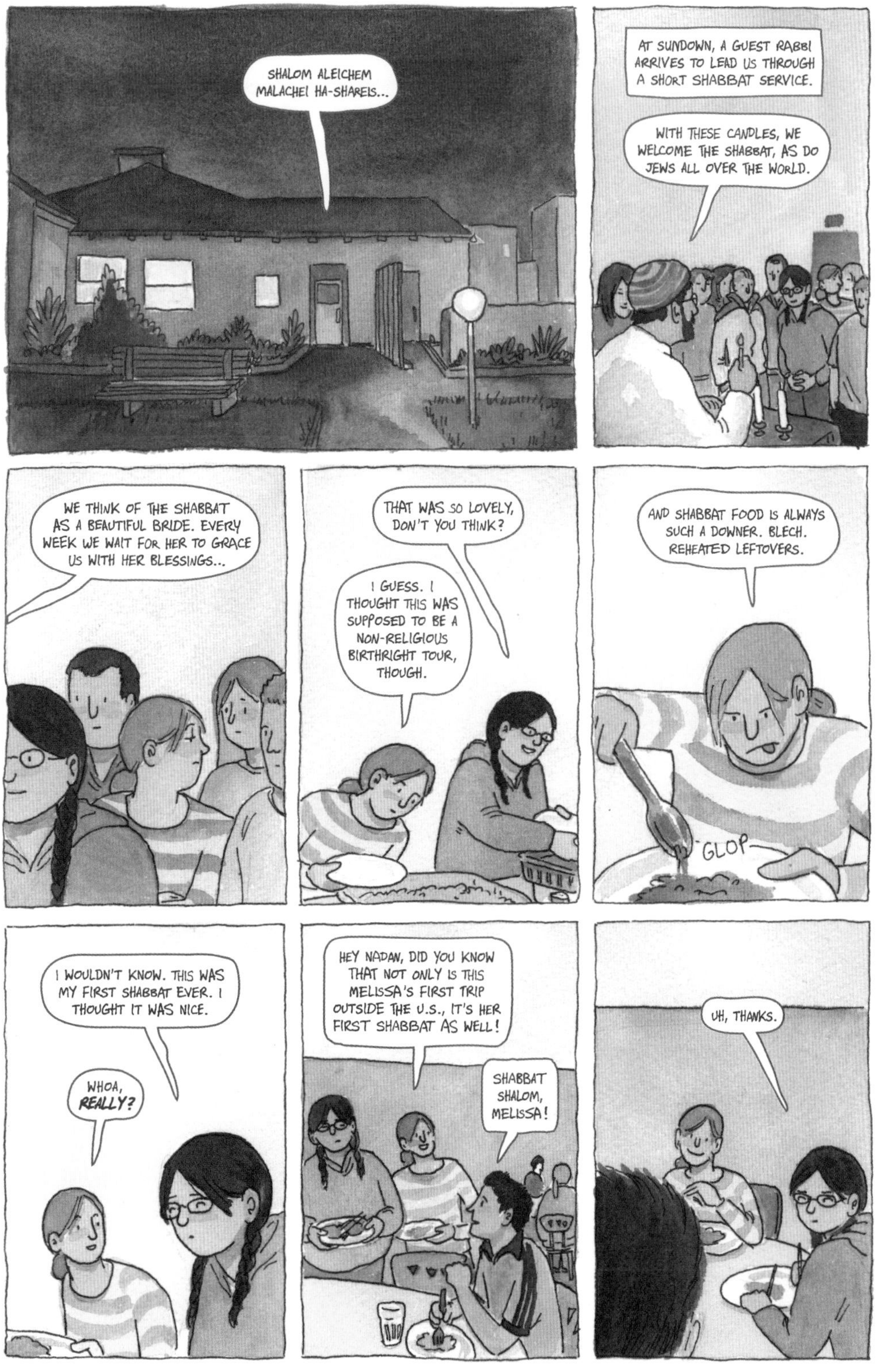
SHALOM ALEICHEM MALACHEI HA-SHAREIS...
AT SUNDOWN, A GUEST RABBI ARRIVES TO LEAD US THROUGH A SHORT SHABBAT SERVICE.
WITH THESE CANDLES, WE WELCOME THE SHABBAT, AS DO JEWS ALL OVER THE WORLD.
WE THINK OF THE SHABBAT AS A BEAUTIFUL BRIDE. EVERY WEEK WE WAIT FOR HER TO GRACE US WITH HER BLESSINGS...
THAT WAS SO LOVELY, DON'T YOU THINK?
I GUESS. I THOUGHT THIS WAS SUPPOSED TO BE A NON-RELIGIOUS BIRTHRIGHT TOUR, THOUGH.
AND SHABBAT FOOD IS ALWAYS SUCH A DOWNER. BLECH. REHEATED LEFTOVERS.
GLOP
I WOULDN'T KNOW. THIS WAS MY FIRST SHABBAT EVER. I THOUGHT IT WAS NICE.
WHOA, **REALLY?**
HEY NADAN, DID YOU KNOW THAT NOT ONLY IS THIS MELISSA'S FIRST TRIP OUTSIDE THE U.S., IT'S HER FIRST SHABBAT AS WELL!
SHABBAT SHALOM, MELISSA!
UH, THANKS.

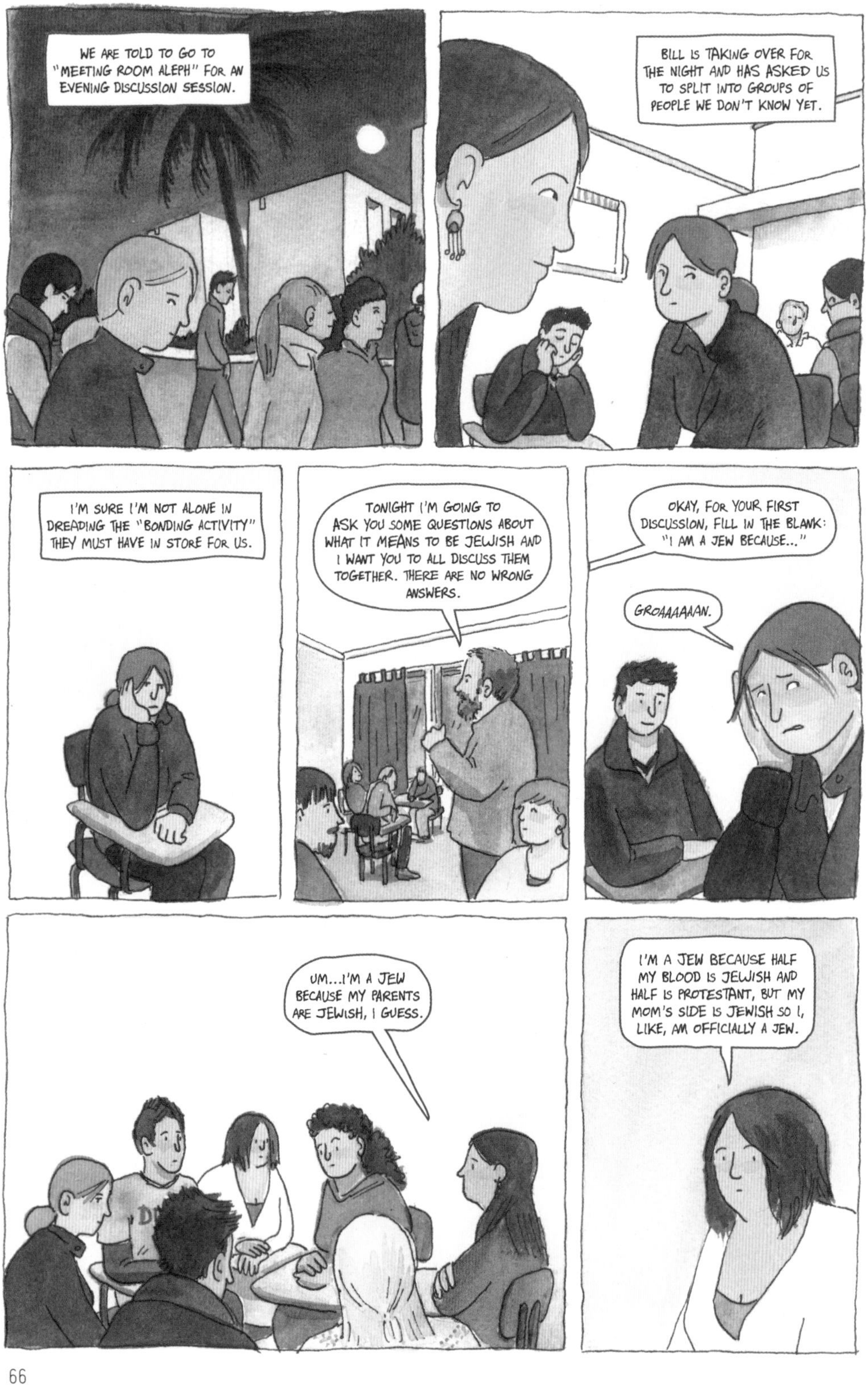

WE ARE TOLD TO GO TO "MEETING ROOM ALEPH" FOR AN EVENING DISCUSSION SESSION.
BILL IS TAKING OVER FOR THE NIGHT AND HAS ASKED US TO SPLIT INTO GROUPS OF PEOPLE WE DON'T KNOW YET.
I'M SURE I'M NOT ALONE IN DREADING THE "BONDING ACTIVITY" THEY MUST HAVE IN STORE FOR US.
TONIGHT I'M GOING TO ASK YOU SOME QUESTIONS ABOUT WHAT IT MEANS TO BE JEWISH AND I WANT YOU TO ALL DISCUSS THEM TOGETHER. THERE ARE NO WRONG ANSWERS.
OKAY, FOR YOUR FIRST DISCUSSION, FILL IN THE BLANK: "I AM A JEW BECAUSE..."
GROAAAAAAN.
UM...I'M A JEW BECAUSE MY PARENTS ARE JEWISH, I GUESS.
I'M A JEW BECAUSE HALF MY BLOOD IS JEWISH AND HALF IS PROTESTANT, BUT MY MOM'S SIDE IS JEWISH SO I, LIKE, AM OFFICIALLY A JEW.

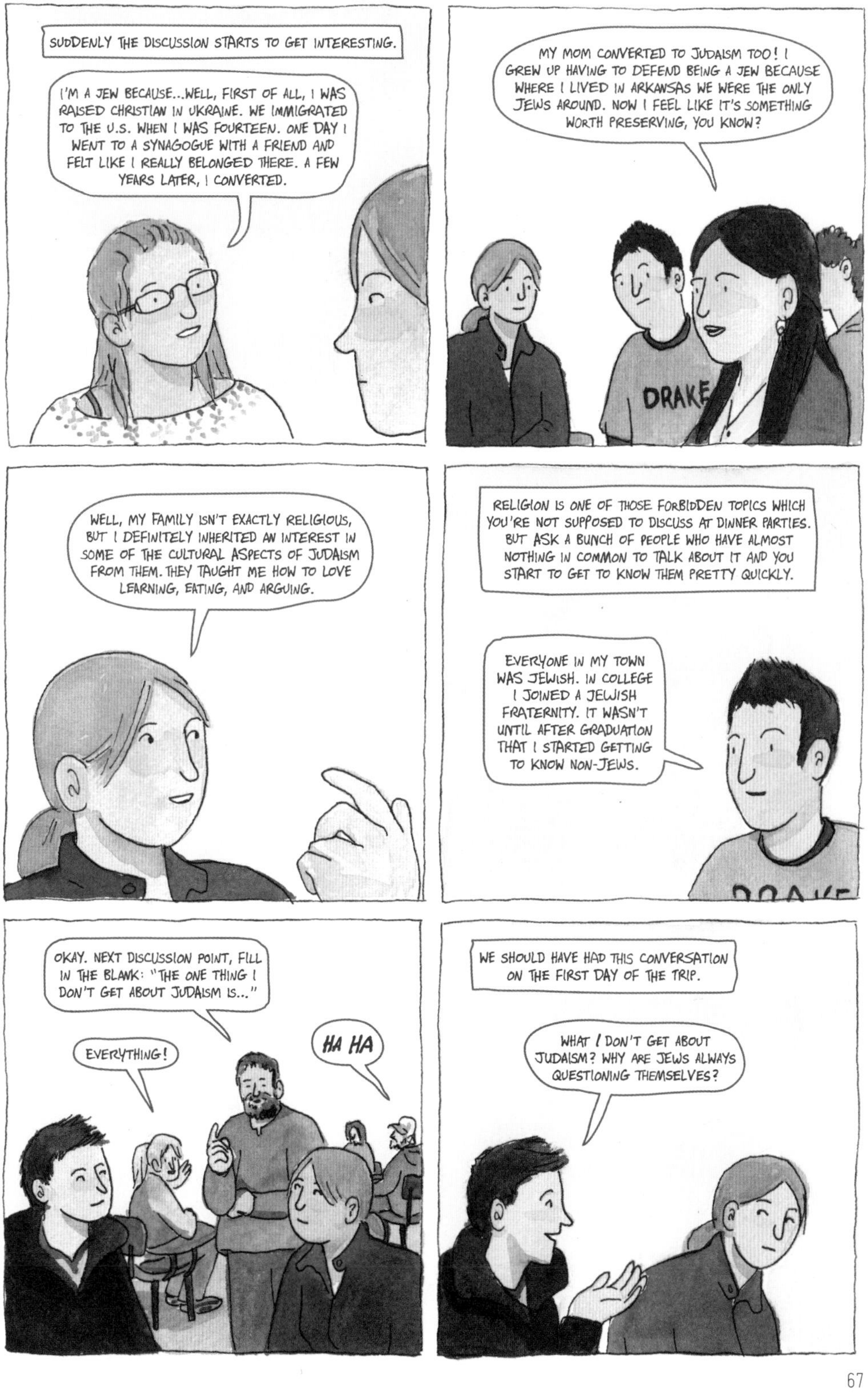
SUDDENLY THE DISCUSSION STARTS TO GET INTERESTING.
I'M A JEW BECAUSE...WELL, FIRST OF ALL, I WAS RAISED CHRISTIAN IN UKRAINE. WE IMMIGRATED TO THE U.S. WHEN I WAS FOURTEEN. ONE DAY I WENT TO A SYNAGOGUE WITH A FRIEND AND FELT LIKE I REALLY BELONGED THERE. A FEW YEARS LATER, I CONVERTED.
MY MOM CONVERTED TO JUDAISM TOO! I GREW UP HAVING TO DEFEND BEING A JEW BECAUSE WHERE I LIVED IN ARKANSAS WE WERE THE ONLY JEWS AROUND. NOW I FEEL LIKE IT'S SOMETHING WORTH PRESERVING, YOU KNOW?
DRAKE
WELL, MY FAMILY ISN'T EXACTLY RELIGIOUS, BUT I DEFINITELY INHERITED AN INTEREST IN SOME OF THE CULTURAL ASPECTS OF JUDAISM FROM THEM. THEY TAUGHT ME HOW TO LOVE LEARNING, EATING, AND ARGUING.
RELIGION IS ONE OF THOSE FORBIDDEN TOPICS WHICH YOU'RE NOT SUPPOSED TO DISCUSS AT DINNER PARTIES. BUT ASK A BUNCH OF PEOPLE WHO HAVE ALMOST NOTHING IN COMMON TO TALK ABOUT IT AND YOU START TO GET TO KNOW THEM PRETTY QUICKLY.
EVERYONE IN MY TOWN WAS JEWISH. IN COLLEGE I JOINED A JEWISH FRATERNITY. IT WASN'T UNTIL AFTER GRADUATION THAT I STARTED GETTING TO KNOW NON-JEWS.
OKAY. NEXT DISCUSSION POINT, FILL IN THE BLANK: "THE ONE THING I DON'T GET ABOUT JUDAISM IS..."
EVERYTHING!
HA HA
WE SHOULD HAVE HAD THIS CONVERSATION ON THE FIRST DAY OF THE TRIP.
WHAT I DON'T GET ABOUT JUDAISM? WHY ARE JEWS ALWAYS QUESTIONING THEMSELVES?

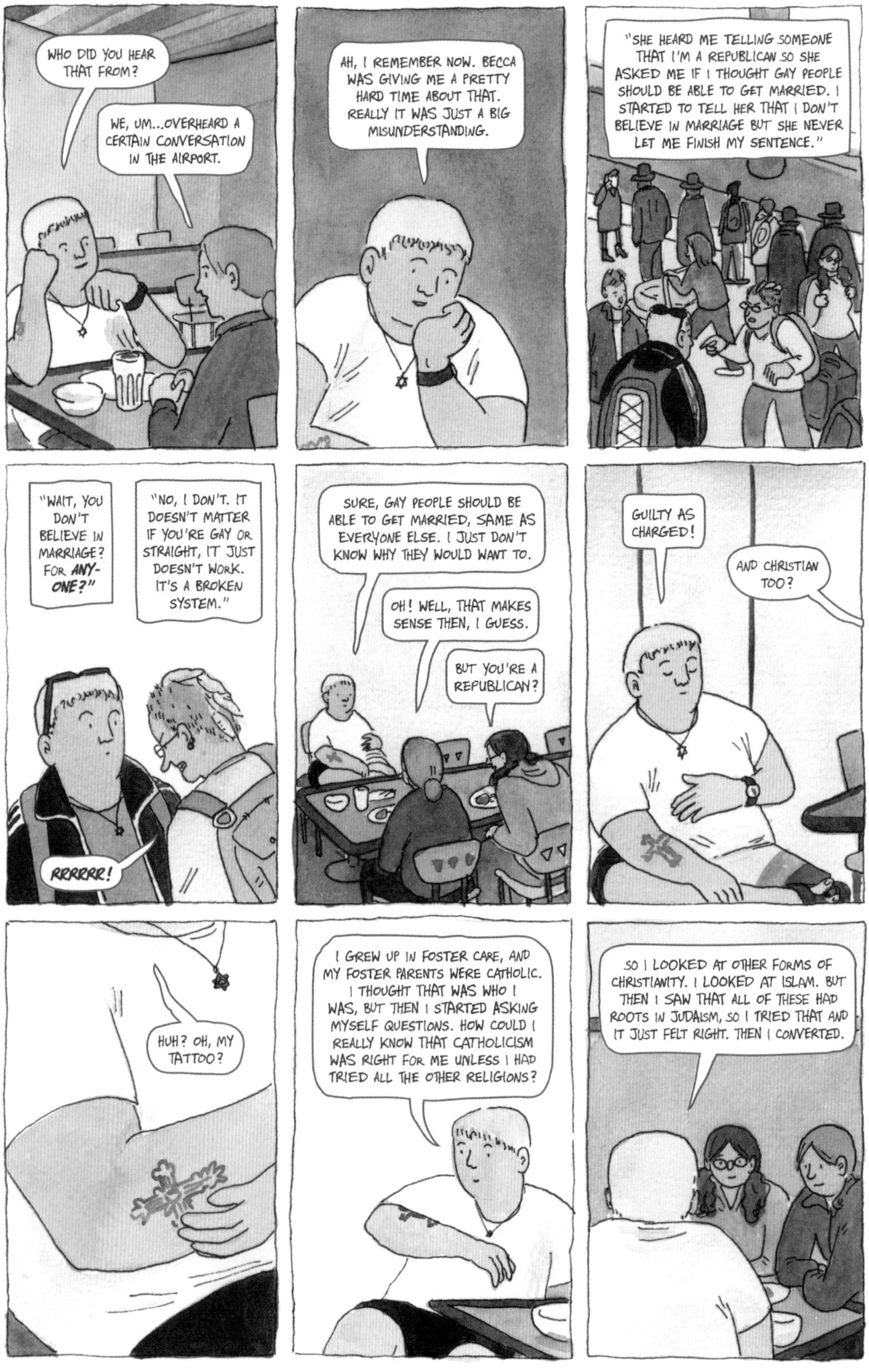
WHO DID YOU HEAR THAT FROM?
WE, UM...OVERHEARD A CERTAIN CONVERSATION IN THE AIRPORT.
AH, I REMEMBER NOW. BECCA WAS GIVING ME A PRETTY HARD TIME ABOUT THAT. REALLY IT WAS JUST A BIG MISUNDERSTANDING.
"SHE HEARD ME TELLING SOMEONE THAT I'M A REPUBLICAN SO SHE ASKED ME IF I THOUGHT GAY PEOPLE SHOULD BE ABLE TO GET MARRIED. I STARTED TO TELL HER THAT I DON'T BELIEVE IN MARRIAGE BUT SHE NEVER LET ME FINISH MY SENTENCE."
"WAIT, YOU DON'T BELIEVE IN MARRIAGE? FOR ANY-ONE?"
"NO, I DON'T. IT DOESN'T MATTER IF YOU'RE GAY OR STRAIGHT, IT JUST DOESN'T WORK. IT'S A BROKEN SYSTEM."
RRRRRR!
SURE, GAY PEOPLE SHOULD BE ABLE TO GET MARRIED, SAME AS EVERYONE ELSE. I JUST DON'T KNOW WHY THEY WOULD WANT TO.
OH! WELL, THAT MAKES SENSE THEN, I GUESS.
BUT YOU'RE A REPUBLICAN?
GUILTY AS CHARGED!
AND CHRISTIAN TOO?
HUH? OH, MY TATTOO?
I GREW UP IN FOSTER CARE, AND MY FOSTER PARENTS WERE CATHOLIC. I THOUGHT THAT WAS WHO I WAS, BUT THEN I STARTED ASKING MYSELF QUESTIONS. HOW COULD I REALLY KNOW THAT CATHOLICISM WAS RIGHT FOR ME UNLESS I HAD TRIED ALL THE OTHER RELIGIONS?
SO I LOOKED AT OTHER FORMS OF CHRISTIANITY. I LOOKED AT ISLAM. BUT THEN I SAW THAT ALL OF THESE HAD ROOTS IN JUDAISM, SO I TRIED THAT AND IT JUST FELT RIGHT. THEN I CONVERTED.

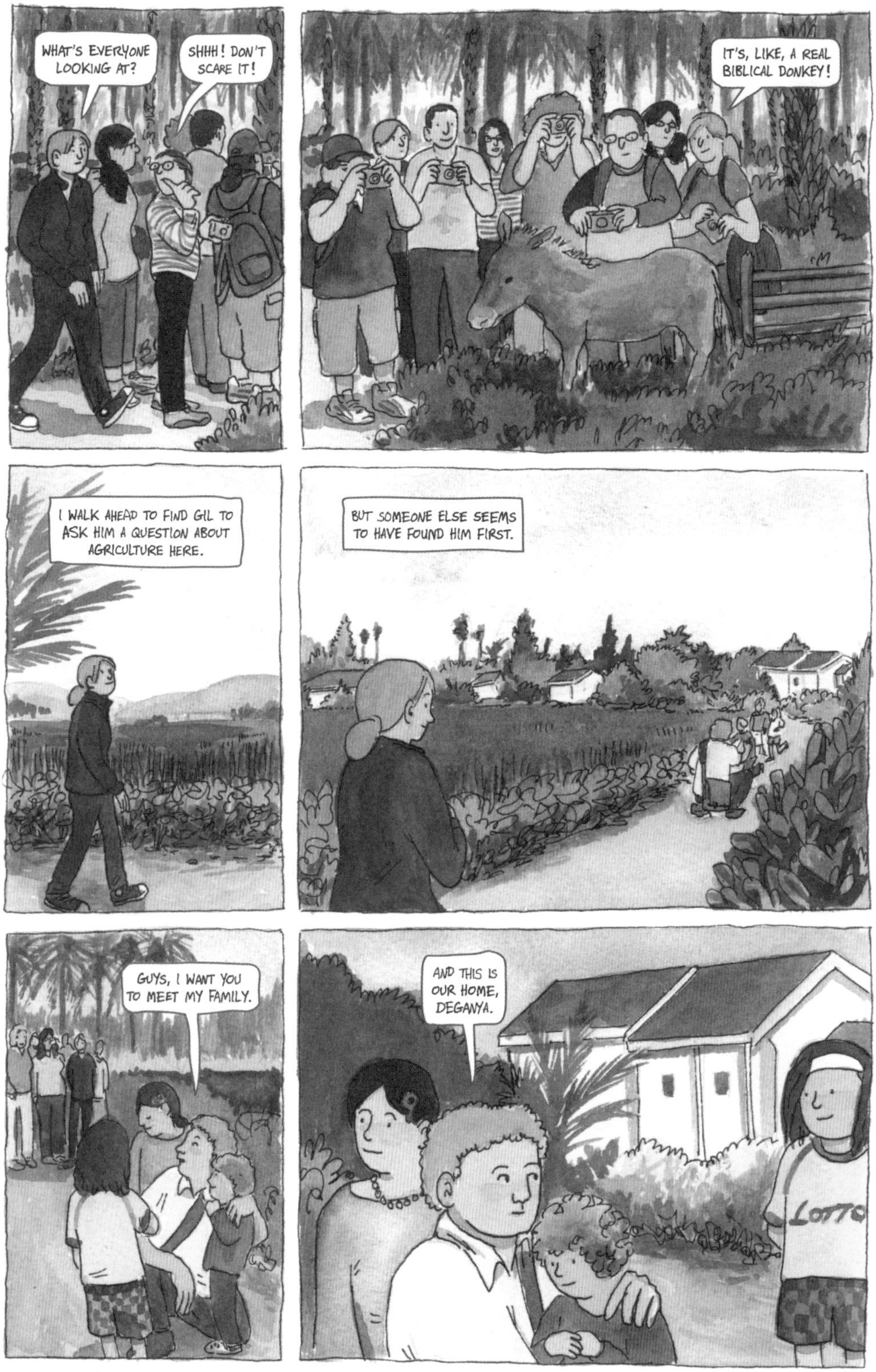
WHAT'S EVERYONE LOOKING AT?
SHHH! DON'T SCARE IT!
IT'S, LIKE, A REAL BIBLICAL DONKEY!
I WALK AHEAD TO FIND GIL TO ASK HIM A QUESTION ABOUT AGRICULTURE HERE.
BUT SOMEONE ELSE SEEMS TO HAVE FOUND HIM FIRST.
GUYS, I WANT YOU TO MEET MY FAMILY.
AND THIS IS OUR HOME, DEGANYA.
LOTTO

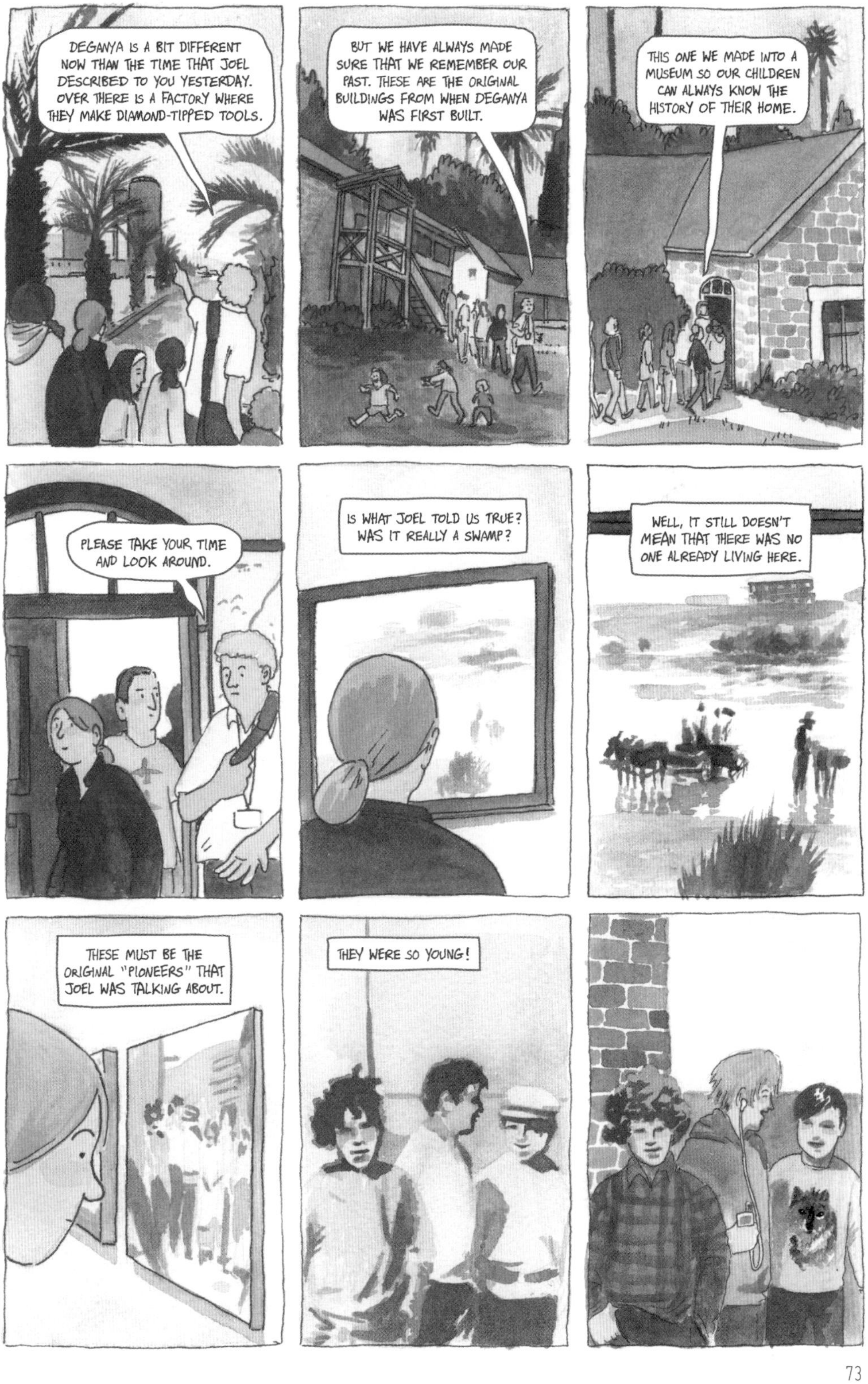
DEGANYA IS A BIT DIFFERENT NOW THAN THE TIME THAT JOEL DESCRIBED TO YOU YESTERDAY. OVER THERE IS A FACTORY WHERE THEY MAKE DIAMOND-TIPPED TOOLS.
BUT WE HAVE ALWAYS MADE SURE THAT WE REMEMBER OUR PAST. THESE ARE THE ORIGINAL BUILDINGS FROM WHEN DEGANYA WAS FIRST BUILT.
THIS ONE WE MADE INTO A MUSEUM SO OUR CHILDREN CAN ALWAYS KNOW THE HISTORY OF THEIR HOME.
PLEASE TAKE YOUR TIME AND LOOK AROUND.
IS WHAT JOEL TOLD US TRUE? WAS IT REALLY A SWAMP?
WELL, IT STILL DOESN'T MEAN THAT THERE WAS NO ONE ALREADY LIVING HERE.
THESE MUST BE THE ORIGINAL "PIONEERS" THAT JOEL WAS TALKING ABOUT.
THEY WERE SO YOUNG!

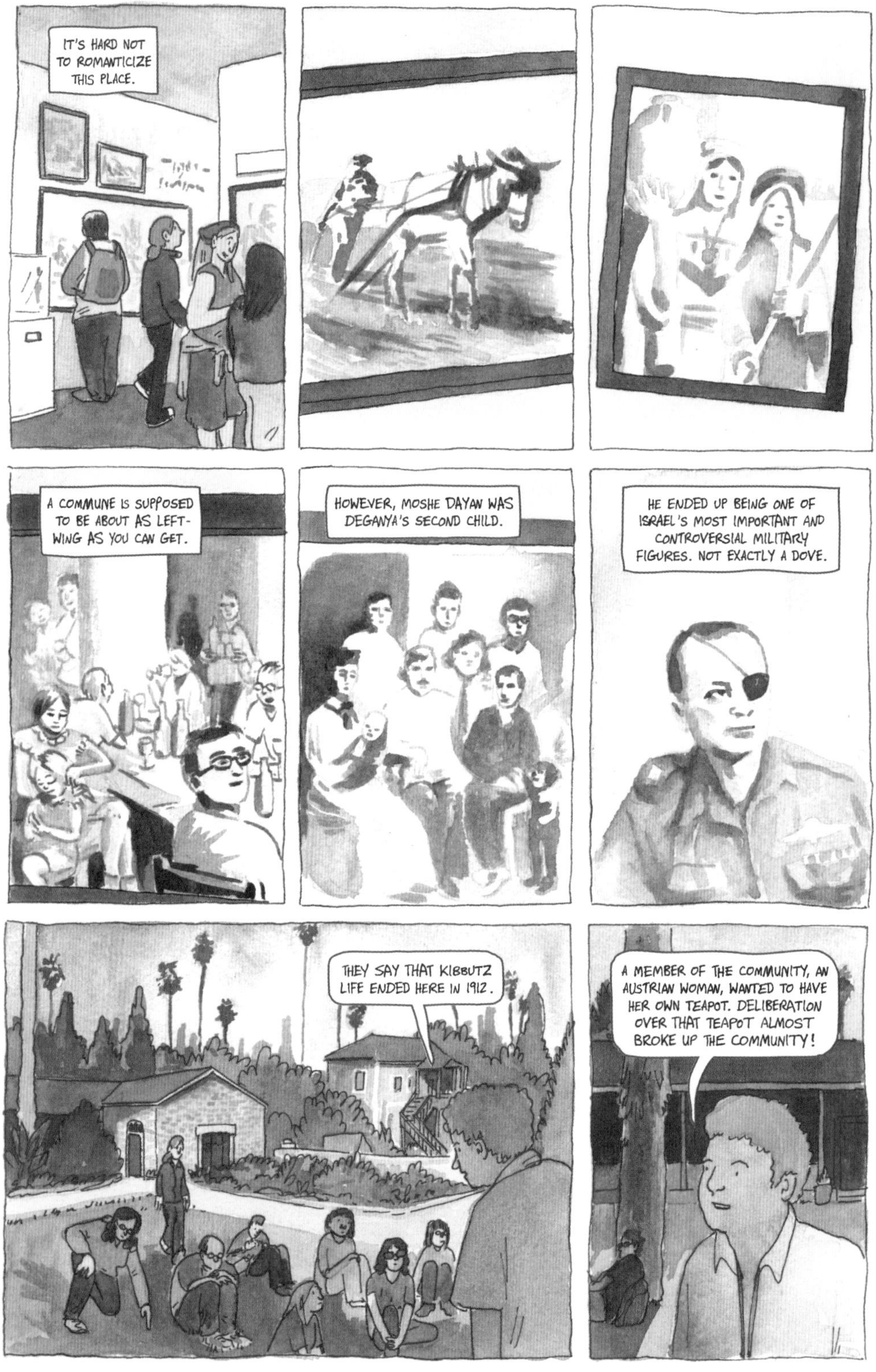
IT'S HARD NOT TO ROMANTICIZE THIS PLACE.
A COMMUNE IS SUPPOSED TO BE ABOUT AS LEFT-WING AS YOU CAN GET.
HOWEVER, MOSHE DAYAN WAS DEGANYA'S SECOND CHILD.
HE ENDED UP BEING ONE OF ISRAEL'S MOST IMPORTANT AND CONTROVERSIAL MILITARY FIGURES. NOT EXACTLY A DOVE.
THEY SAY THAT KIBBUTZ LIFE ENDED HERE IN 1912.
A MEMBER OF THE COMMUNITY, AN AUSTRIAN WOMAN, WANTED TO HAVE HER OWN TEAPOT. DELIBERATION OVER THAT TEAPOT ALMOST BROKE UP THE COMMUNITY!

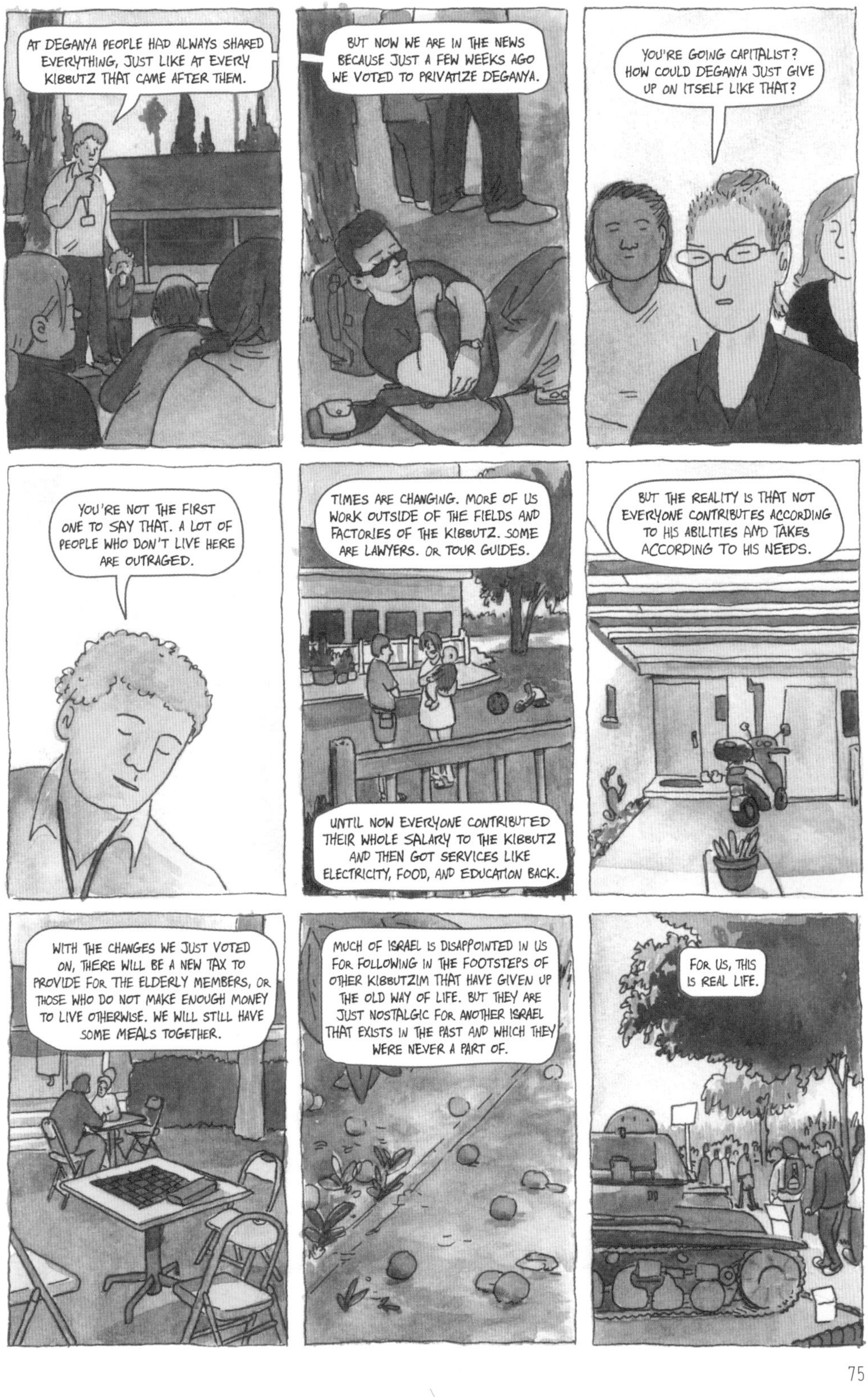
AT DEGANYA PEOPLE HAD ALWAYS SHARED EVERYTHING, JUST LIKE AT EVERY KIBBUTZ THAT CAME AFTER THEM.
BUT NOW WE ARE IN THE NEWS BECAUSE JUST A FEW WEEKS AGO WE VOTED TO PRIVATIZE DEGANYA.
YOU'RE GOING CAPITALIST? HOW COULD DEGANYA JUST GIVE UP ON ITSELF LIKE THAT?
YOU'RE NOT THE FIRST ONE TO SAY THAT. A LOT OF PEOPLE WHO DON'T LIVE HERE ARE OUTRAGED.
TIMES ARE CHANGING. MORE OF US WORK OUTSIDE OF THE FIELDS AND FACTORIES OF THE KIBBUTZ. SOME ARE LAWYERS. OR TOUR GUIDES.
UNTIL NOW EVERYONE CONTRIBUTED THEIR WHOLE SALARY TO THE KIBBUTZ AND THEN GOT SERVICES LIKE ELECTRICITY, FOOD, AND EDUCATION BACK.
BUT THE REALITY IS THAT NOT EVERYONE CONTRIBUTES ACCORDING TO HIS ABILITIES AND TAKES ACCORDING TO HIS NEEDS.
WITH THE CHANGES WE JUST VOTED ON, THERE WILL BE A NEW TAX TO PROVIDE FOR THE ELDERLY MEMBERS, OR THOSE WHO DO NOT MAKE ENOUGH MONEY TO LIVE OTHERWISE. WE WILL STILL HAVE SOME MEALS TOGETHER.
MUCH OF ISRAEL IS DISAPPOINTED IN US FOR FOLLOWING IN THE FOOTSTEPS OF OTHER KIBBUTZIM THAT HAVE GIVEN UP THE OLD WAY OF LIFE. BUT THEY ARE JUST NOSTALGIC FOR ANOTHER ISRAEL THAT EXISTS IN THE PAST AND WHICH THEY WERE NEVER A PART OF.
FOR US, THIS IS REAL LIFE.

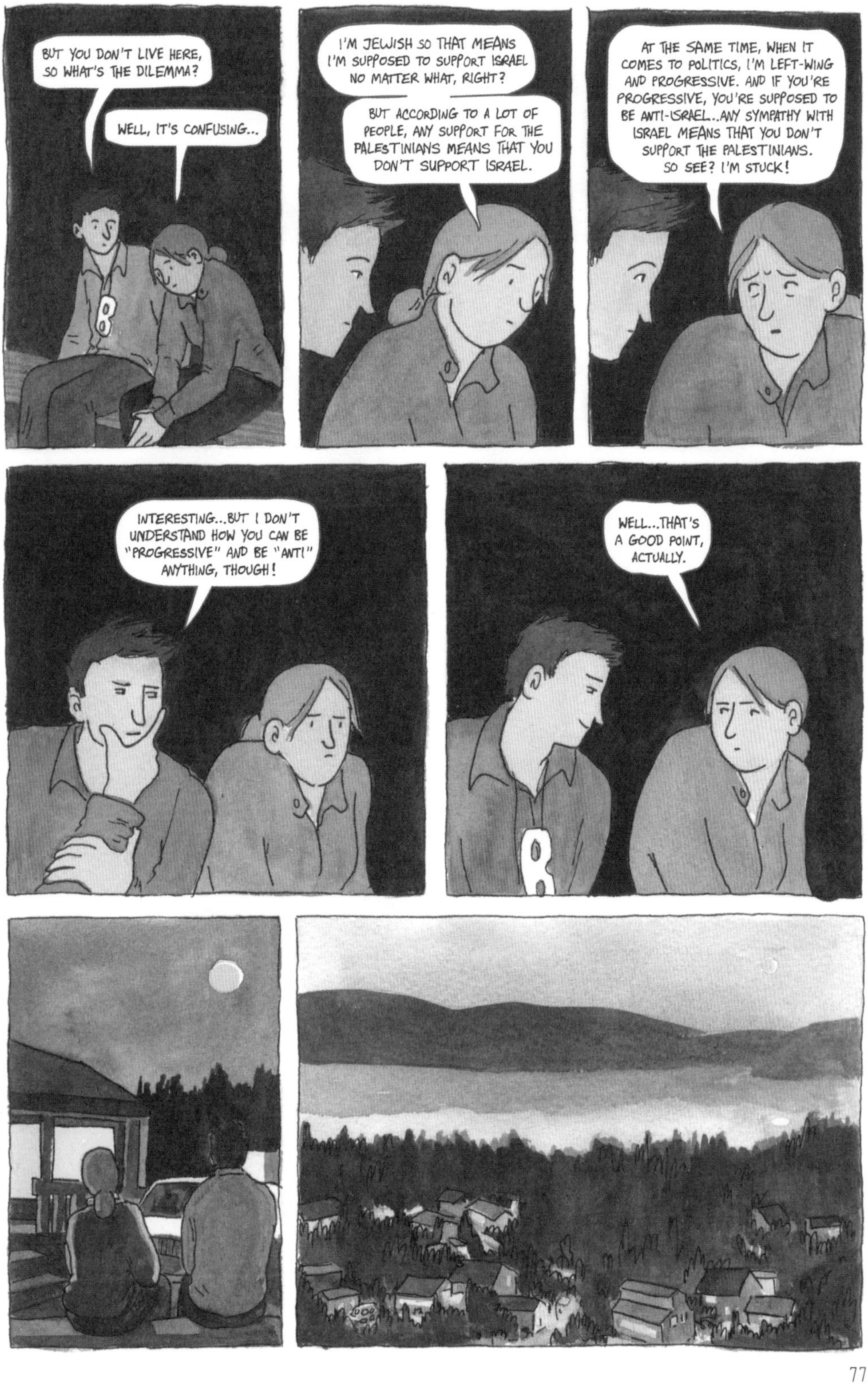

BUT YOU DON'T LIVE HERE, SO WHAT'S THE DILEMMA?
WELL, IT'S CONFUSING...
I'M JEWISH SO THAT MEANS I'M SUPPOSED TO SUPPORT ISRAEL NO MATTER WHAT, RIGHT?
BUT ACCORDING TO A LOT OF PEOPLE, ANY SUPPORT FOR THE PALESTINIANS MEANS THAT YOU DON'T SUPPORT ISRAEL.
AT THE SAME TIME, WHEN IT COMES TO POLITICS, I'M LEFT-WING AND PROGRESSIVE. AND IF YOU'RE PROGRESSIVE, YOU'RE SUPPOSED TO BE ANTI-ISRAEL...ANY SYMPATHY WITH ISRAEL MEANS THAT YOU DON'T SUPPORT THE PALESTINIANS. SO SEE? I'M STUCK!
INTERESTING...BUT I DON'T UNDERSTAND HOW YOU CAN BE "PROGRESSIVE" AND BE "ANTI" ANYTHING, THOUGH!
WELL...THAT'S A GOOD POINT, ACTUALLY.

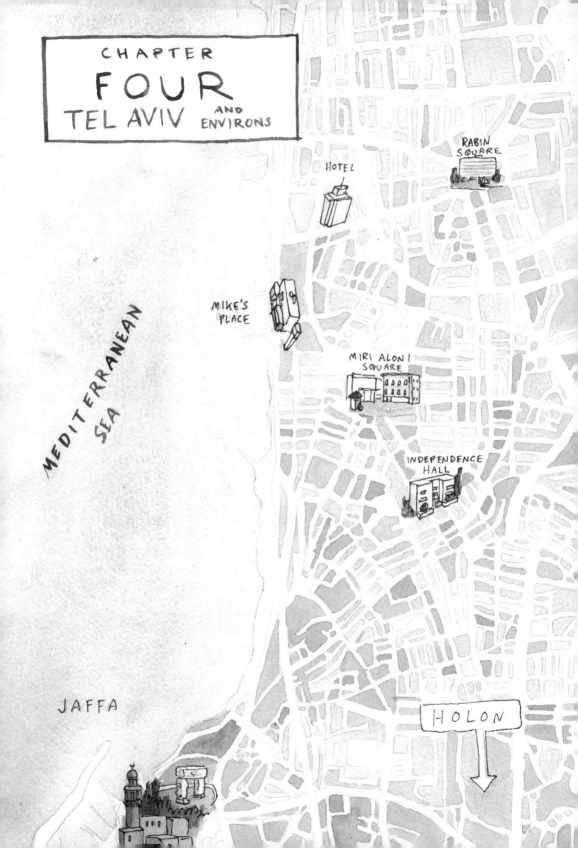

CHAPTER
FOUR
TEL AVIV AND ENVIRONS

RABIN SQUARE

HOTEL

MIKE'S PLACE

MIRI ALONI SQUARE

INDEPENDENCE HALL

MEDITERRANEAN SEA

JAFFA

HOLON

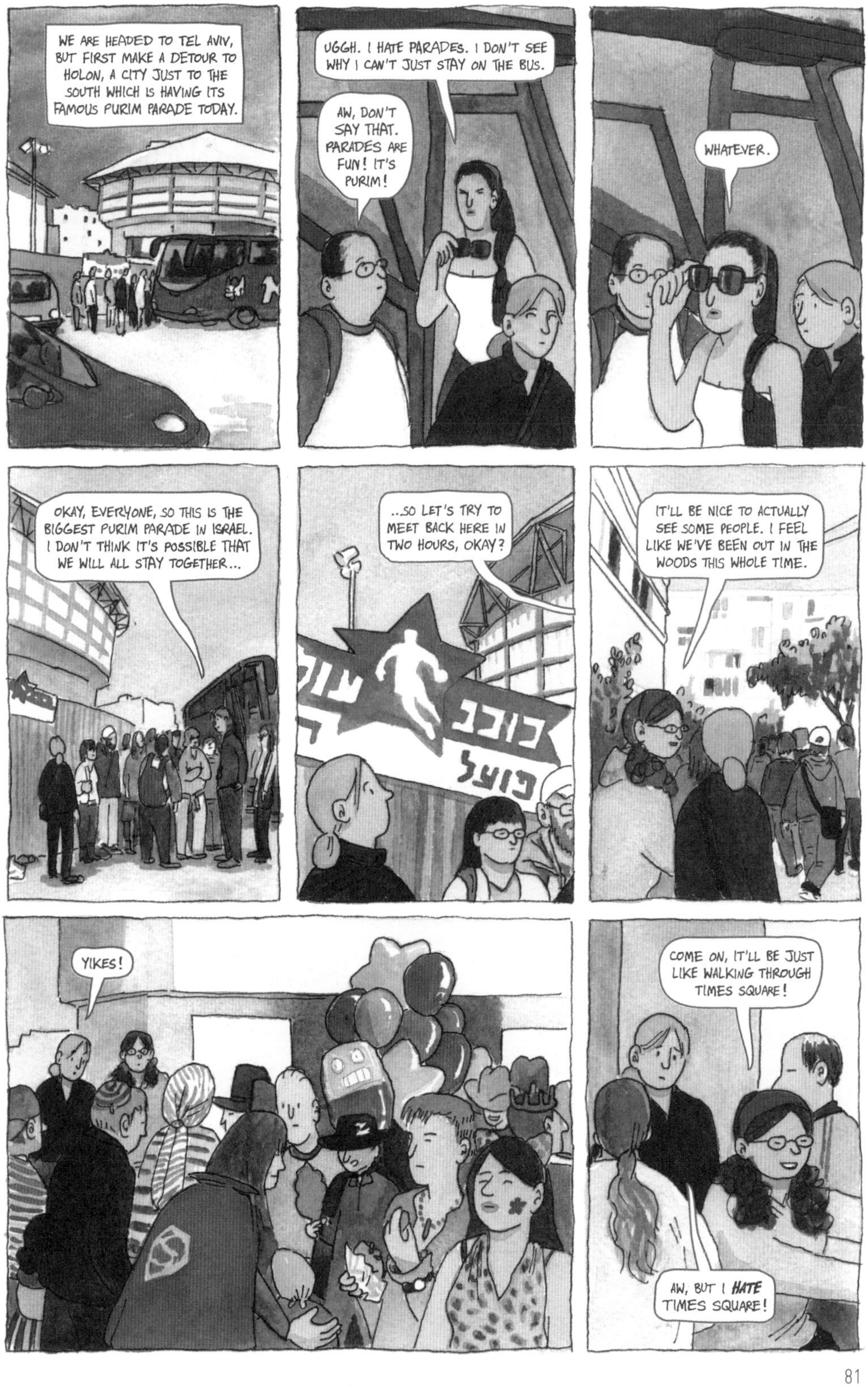
WE ARE HEADED TO TEL AVIV, BUT FIRST MAKE A DETOUR TO HOLON, A CITY JUST TO THE SOUTH WHICH IS HAVING ITS FAMOUS PURIM PARADE TODAY.
UGGH. I HATE PARADES. I DON'T SEE WHY I CAN'T JUST STAY ON THE BUS.
AW, DON'T SAY THAT. PARADES ARE FUN! IT'S PURIM!
WHATEVER.
OKAY, EVERYONE, SO THIS IS THE BIGGEST PURIM PARADE IN ISRAEL. I DON'T THINK IT'S POSSIBLE THAT WE WILL ALL STAY TOGETHER...
...SO LET'S TRY TO MEET BACK HERE IN TWO HOURS, OKAY?
IT'LL BE NICE TO ACTUALLY SEE SOME PEOPLE. I FEEL LIKE WE'VE BEEN OUT IN THE WOODS THIS WHOLE TIME.
YIKES!
COME ON, IT'LL BE JUST LIKE WALKING THROUGH TIMES SQUARE!
AW, BUT I **HATE** TIMES SQUARE!

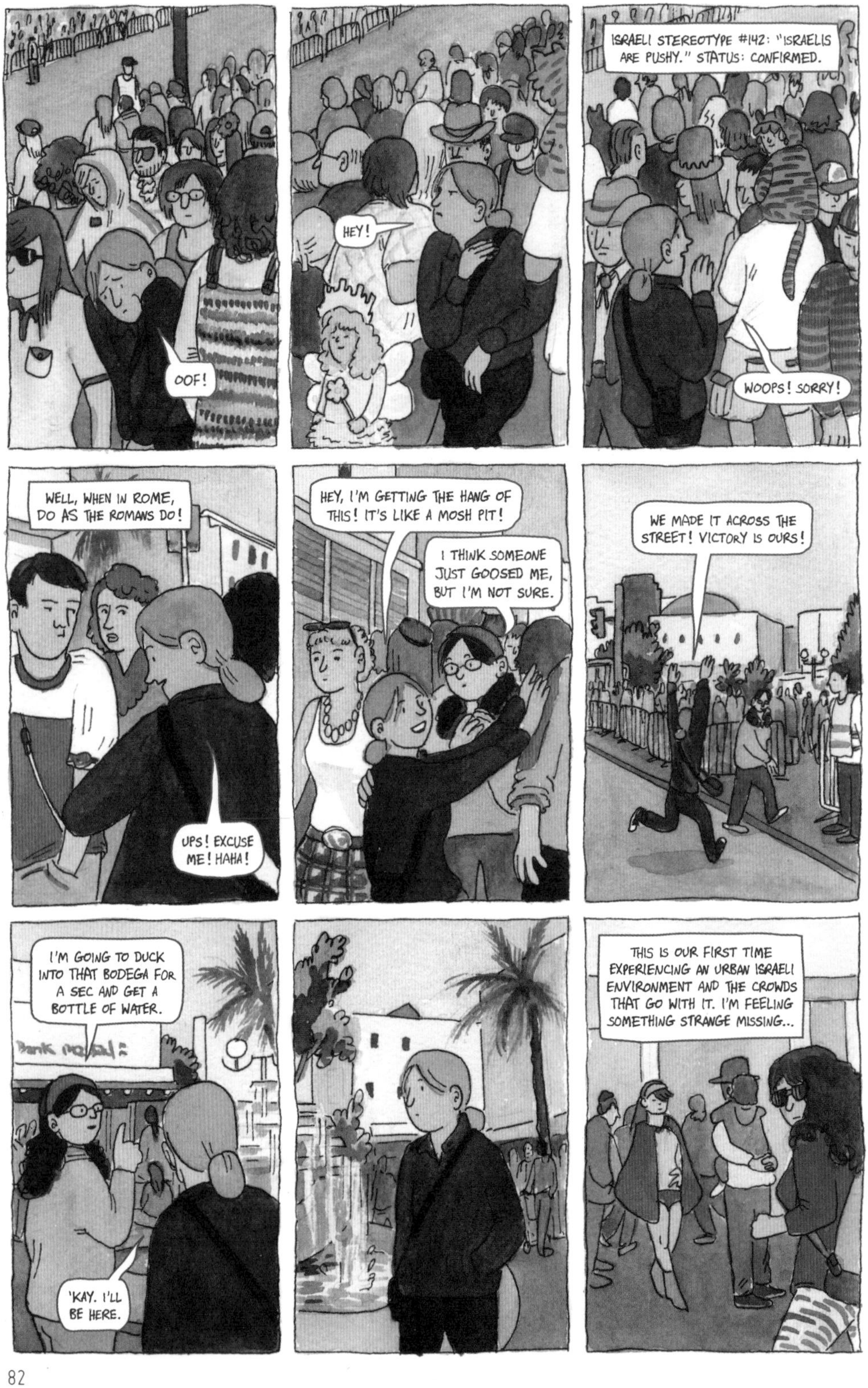
OOF!
HEY!
ISRAELI STEREOTYPE #142: "ISRAELIS ARE PUSHY." STATUS: CONFIRMED.
WOOPS! SORRY!
WELL, WHEN IN ROME, DO AS THE ROMANS DO!
UPS! EXCUSE ME! HAHA!
HEY, I'M GETTING THE HANG OF THIS! IT'S LIKE A MOSH PIT!
I THINK SOMEONE JUST GOOSED ME, BUT I'M NOT SURE.
WE MADE IT ACROSS THE STREET! VICTORY IS OURS!
I'M GOING TO DUCK INTO THAT BODEGA FOR A SEC AND GET A BOTTLE OF WATER.
'KAY. I'LL BE HERE.
THIS IS OUR FIRST TIME EXPERIENCING AN URBAN ISRAELI ENVIRONMENT AND THE CROWDS THAT GO WITH IT. I'M FEELING SOMETHING STRANGE MISSING...

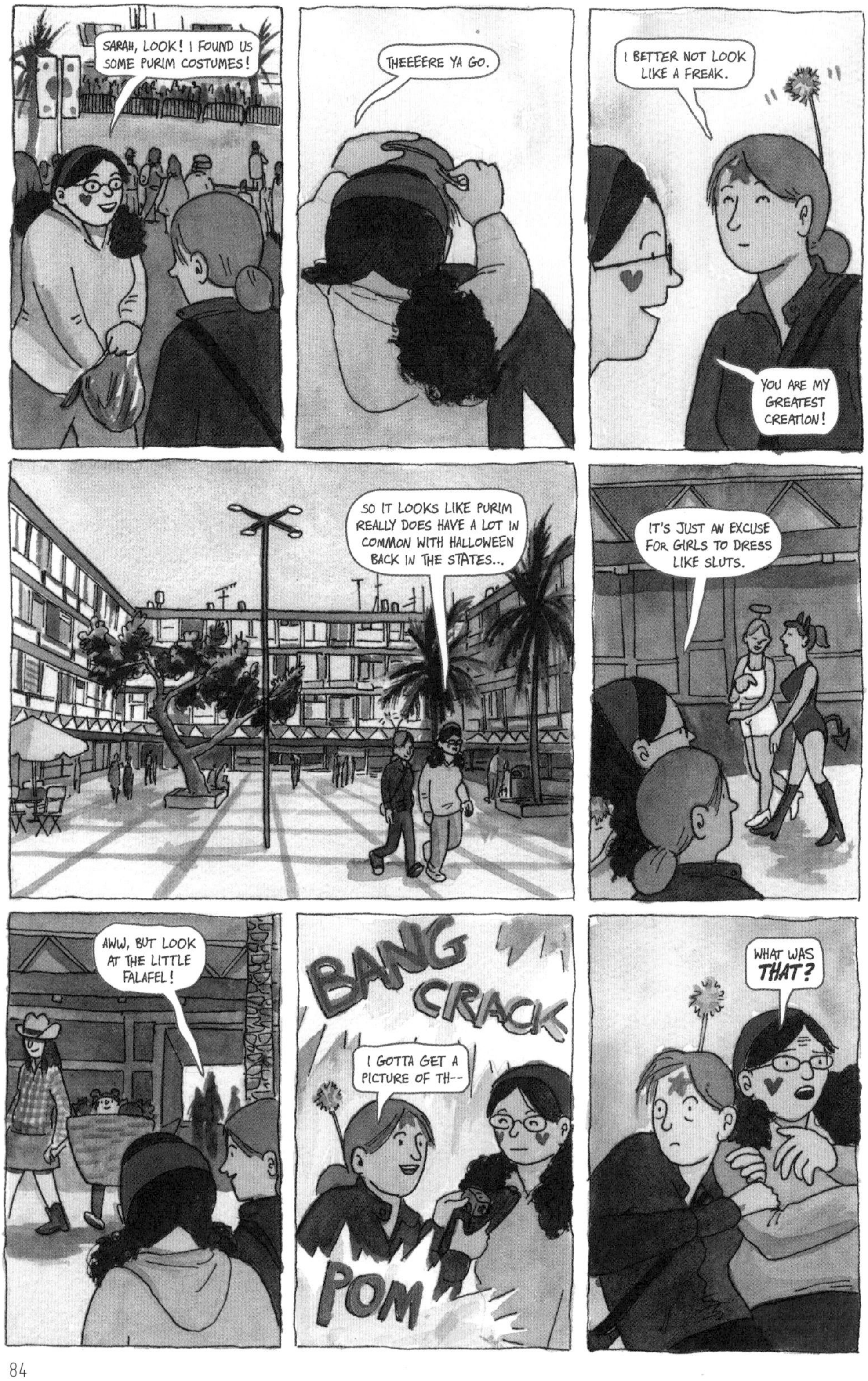
SARAH, LOOK! I FOUND US SOME PURIM COSTUMES!
THEEEERE YA GO.
I BETTER NOT LOOK LIKE A FREAK.
YOU ARE MY GREATEST CREATION!
SO IT LOOKS LIKE PURIM REALLY DOES HAVE A LOT IN COMMON WITH HALLOWEEN BACK IN THE STATES...
IT'S JUST AN EXCUSE FOR GIRLS TO DRESS LIKE SLUTS.
AWW, BUT LOOK AT THE LITTLE FALAFEL!
BANG
CRACK
I GOTTA GET A PICTURE OF TH--
POM
WHAT WAS THAT?

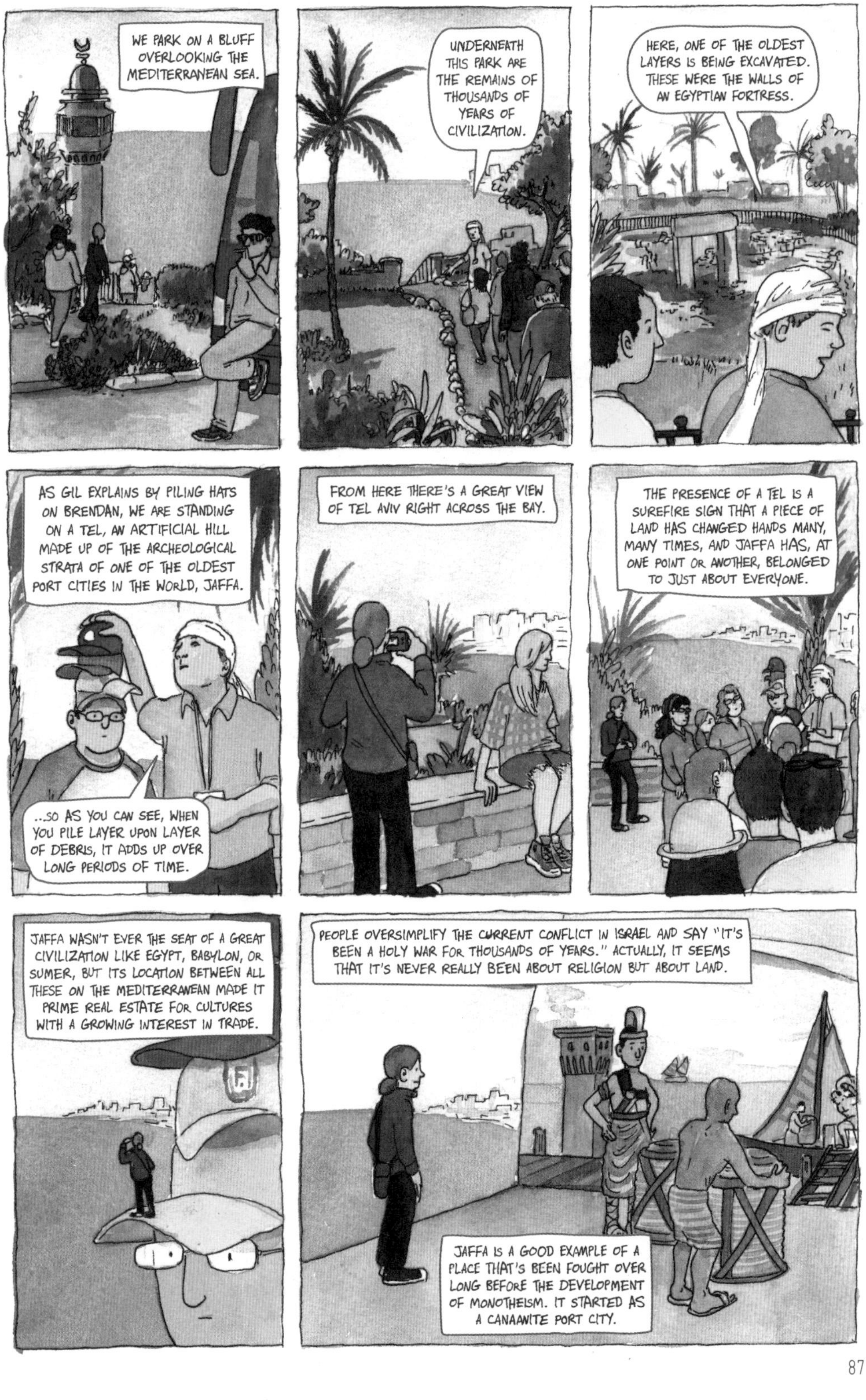
WE PARK ON A BLUFF OVERLOOKING THE MEDITERRANEAN SEA.
UNDERNEATH THIS PARK ARE THE REMAINS OF THOUSANDS OF YEARS OF CIVILIZATION.
HERE, ONE OF THE OLDEST LAYERS IS BEING EXCAVATED. THESE WERE THE WALLS OF AN EGYPTIAN FORTRESS.
AS GIL EXPLAINS BY PILING HATS ON BRENDAN, WE ARE STANDING ON A TEL, AN ARTIFICIAL HILL MADE UP OF THE ARCHEOLOGICAL STRATA OF ONE OF THE OLDEST PORT CITIES IN THE WORLD, JAFFA.
...SO AS YOU CAN SEE, WHEN YOU PILE LAYER UPON LAYER OF DEBRIS, IT ADDS UP OVER LONG PERIODS OF TIME.
FROM HERE THERE'S A GREAT VIEW OF TEL AVIV RIGHT ACROSS THE BAY.
THE PRESENCE OF A TEL IS A SUREFIRE SIGN THAT A PIECE OF LAND HAS CHANGED HANDS MANY, MANY TIMES, AND JAFFA HAS, AT ONE POINT OR ANOTHER, BELONGED TO JUST ABOUT EVERYONE.
JAFFA WASN'T EVER THE SEAT OF A GREAT CIVILIZATION LIKE EGYPT, BABYLON, OR SUMER, BUT ITS LOCATION BETWEEN ALL THESE ON THE MEDITERRANEAN MADE IT PRIME REAL ESTATE FOR CULTURES WITH A GROWING INTEREST IN TRADE.
PEOPLE OVERSIMPLIFY THE CURRENT CONFLICT IN ISRAEL AND SAY "IT'S BEEN A HOLY WAR FOR THOUSANDS OF YEARS." ACTUALLY, IT SEEMS THAT IT'S NEVER REALLY BEEN ABOUT RELIGION BUT ABOUT LAND.
JAFFA IS A GOOD EXAMPLE OF A PLACE THAT'S BEEN FOUGHT OVER LONG BEFORE THE DEVELOPMENT OF MONOTHEISM. IT STARTED AS A CANAANITE PORT CITY.

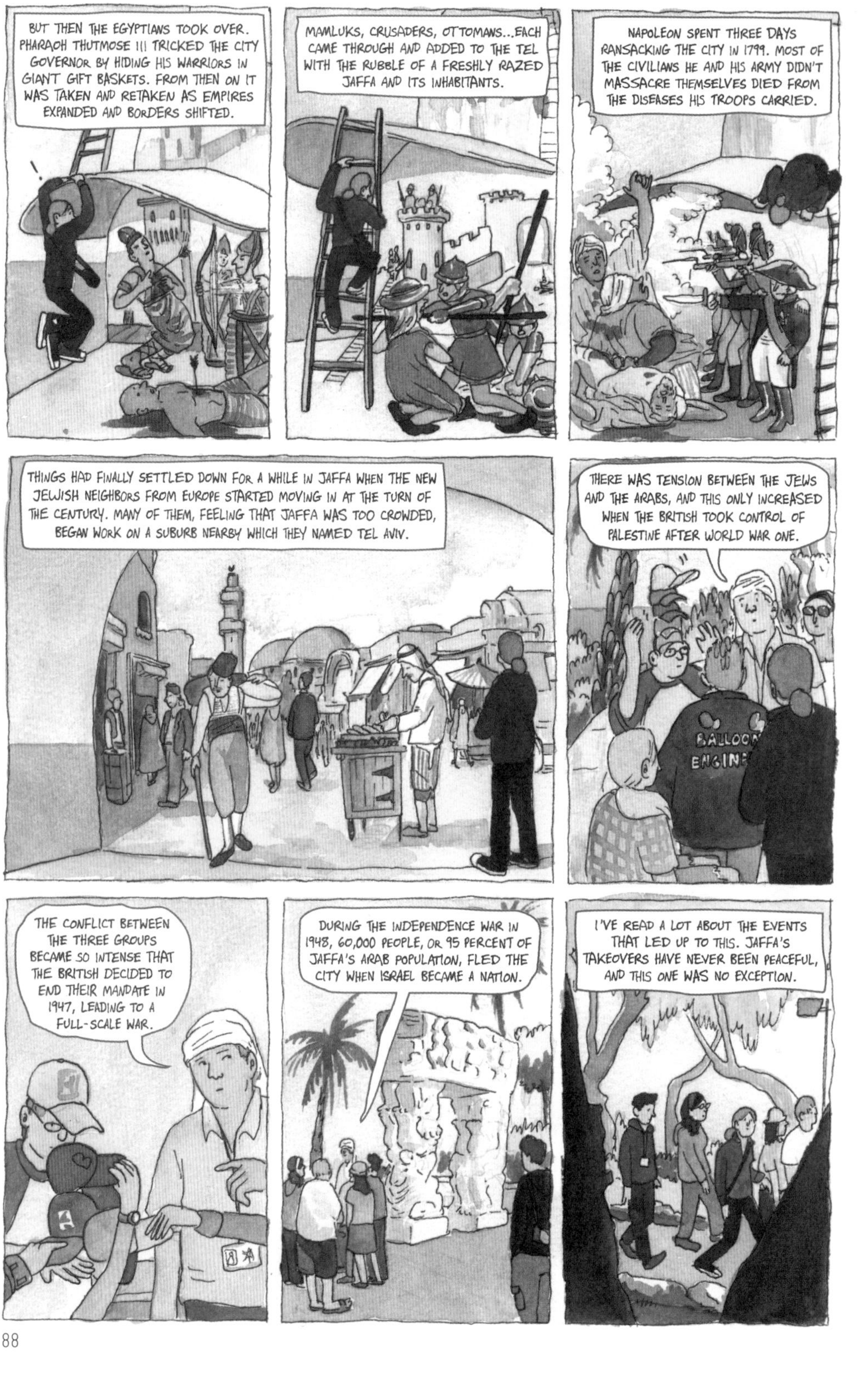
BUT THEN THE EGYPTIANS TOOK OVER. PHARAOH THUTMOSE III TRICKED THE CITY GOVERNOR BY HIDING HIS WARRIORS IN GIANT GIFT BASKETS. FROM THEN ON IT WAS TAKEN AND RETAKEN AS EMPIRES EXPANDED AND BORDERS SHIFTED.
!
MAMLUKS, CRUSADERS, OTTOMANS...EACH CAME THROUGH AND ADDED TO THE TEL WITH THE RUBBLE OF A FRESHLY RAZED JAFFA AND ITS INHABITANTS.
NAPOLEON SPENT THREE DAYS RANSACKING THE CITY IN 1799. MOST OF THE CIVILIANS HE AND HIS ARMY DIDN'T MASSACRE THEMSELVES DIED FROM THE DISEASES HIS TROOPS CARRIED.
THINGS HAD FINALLY SETTLED DOWN FOR A WHILE IN JAFFA WHEN THE NEW JEWISH NEIGHBORS FROM EUROPE STARTED MOVING IN AT THE TURN OF THE CENTURY. MANY OF THEM, FEELING THAT JAFFA WAS TOO CROWDED, BEGAN WORK ON A SUBURB NEARBY WHICH THEY NAMED TEL AVIV.
THERE WAS TENSION BETWEEN THE JEWS AND THE ARABS, AND THIS ONLY INCREASED WHEN THE BRITISH TOOK CONTROL OF PALESTINE AFTER WORLD WAR ONE.
BALLOON
ENGINE
THE CONFLICT BETWEEN THE THREE GROUPS BECAME SO INTENSE THAT THE BRITISH DECIDED TO END THEIR MANDATE IN 1947, LEADING TO A FULL-SCALE WAR.
DURING THE INDEPENDENCE WAR IN 1948, 60,000 PEOPLE, OR 95 PERCENT OF JAFFA'S ARAB POPULATION, FLED THE CITY WHEN ISRAEL BECAME A NATION.
I'VE READ A LOT ABOUT THE EVENTS THAT LED UP TO THIS. JAFFA'S TAKEOVERS HAVE NEVER BEEN PEACEFUL, AND THIS ONE WAS NO EXCEPTION.

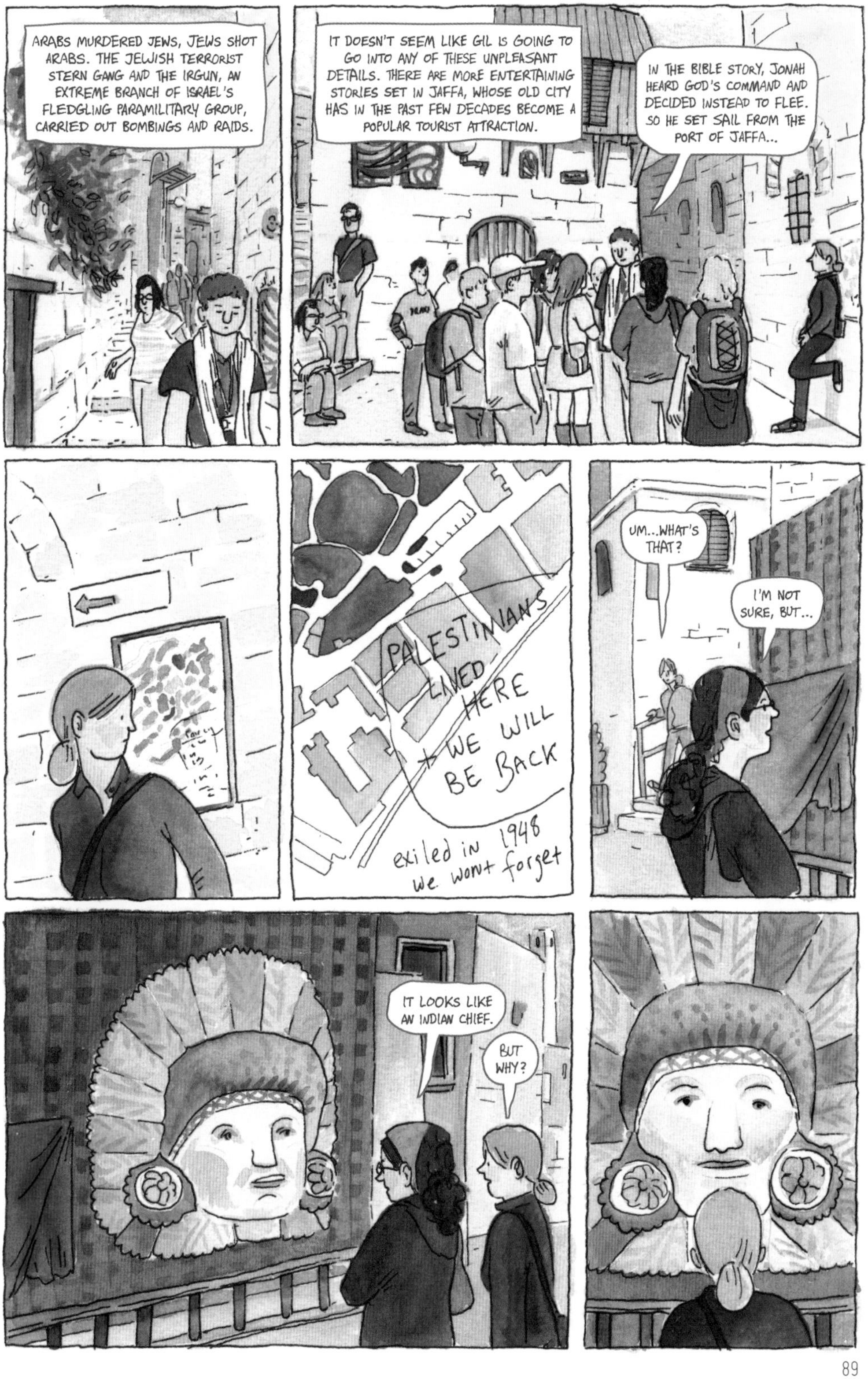
ARABS MURDERED JEWS, JEWS SHOT ARABS. THE JEWISH TERRORIST STERN GANG AND THE IRGUN, AN EXTREME BRANCH OF ISRAEL'S FLEDGLING PARAMILITARY GROUP, CARRIED OUT BOMBINGS AND RAIDS.
IT DOESN'T SEEM LIKE GIL IS GOING TO GO INTO ANY OF THESE UNPLEASANT DETAILS. THERE ARE MORE ENTERTAINING STORIES SET IN JAFFA, WHOSE OLD CITY HAS IN THE PAST FEW DECADES BECOME A POPULAR TOURIST ATTRACTION.
IN THE BIBLE STORY, JONAH HEARD GOD'S COMMAND AND DECIDED INSTEAD TO FLEE. SO HE SET SAIL FROM THE PORT OF JAFFA...
PALESTINIANS LIVED HERE + WE WILL BE BACK
exiled in 1948 we wont forget
UM...WHAT'S THAT?
I'M NOT SURE, BUT...
IT LOOKS LIKE AN INDIAN CHIEF.
BUT WHY?

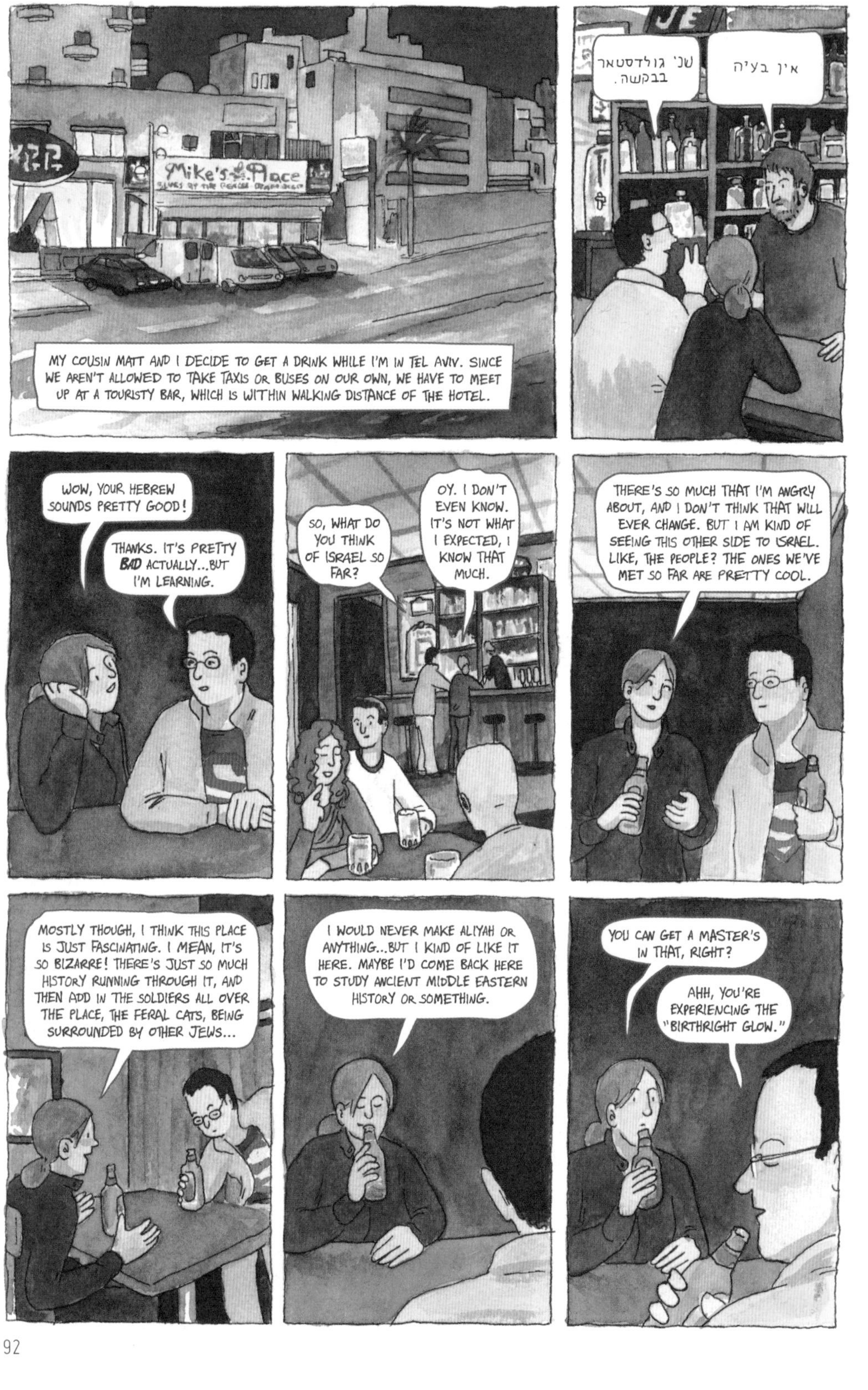
Mike's Place
MY COUSIN MATT AND I DECIDE TO GET A DRINK WHILE I'M IN TEL AVIV. SINCE WE AREN'T ALLOWED TO TAKE TAXIS OR BUSES ON OUR OWN, WE HAVE TO MEET UP AT A TOURISTY BAR, WHICH IS WITHIN WALKING DISTANCE OF THE HOTEL.
שני גולדסטאר בבקשה.
אין בעיה
WOW, YOUR HEBREW SOUNDS PRETTY GOOD!
THANKS. IT'S PRETTY **BAD** ACTUALLY...BUT I'M LEARNING.
SO, WHAT DO YOU THINK OF ISRAEL SO FAR?
OY. I DON'T EVEN KNOW. IT'S NOT WHAT I EXPECTED, I KNOW THAT MUCH.
THERE'S SO MUCH THAT I'M ANGRY ABOUT, AND I DON'T THINK THAT WILL EVER CHANGE. BUT I AM KIND OF SEEING THIS OTHER SIDE TO ISRAEL. LIKE, THE PEOPLE? THE ONES WE'VE MET SO FAR ARE PRETTY COOL.
MOSTLY THOUGH, I THINK THIS PLACE IS JUST FASCINATING. I MEAN, IT'S SO BIZARRE! THERE'S JUST SO MUCH HISTORY RUNNING THROUGH IT, AND THEN ADD IN THE SOLDIERS ALL OVER THE PLACE, THE FERAL CATS, BEING SURROUNDED BY OTHER JEWS...
I WOULD NEVER MAKE ALIYAH OR ANYTHING...BUT I KIND OF LIKE IT HERE. MAYBE I'D COME BACK HERE TO STUDY ANCIENT MIDDLE EASTERN HISTORY OR SOMETHING.
YOU CAN GET A MASTER'S IN THAT, RIGHT?
AHH, YOU'RE EXPERIENCING THE "BIRTHRIGHT GLOW."

94

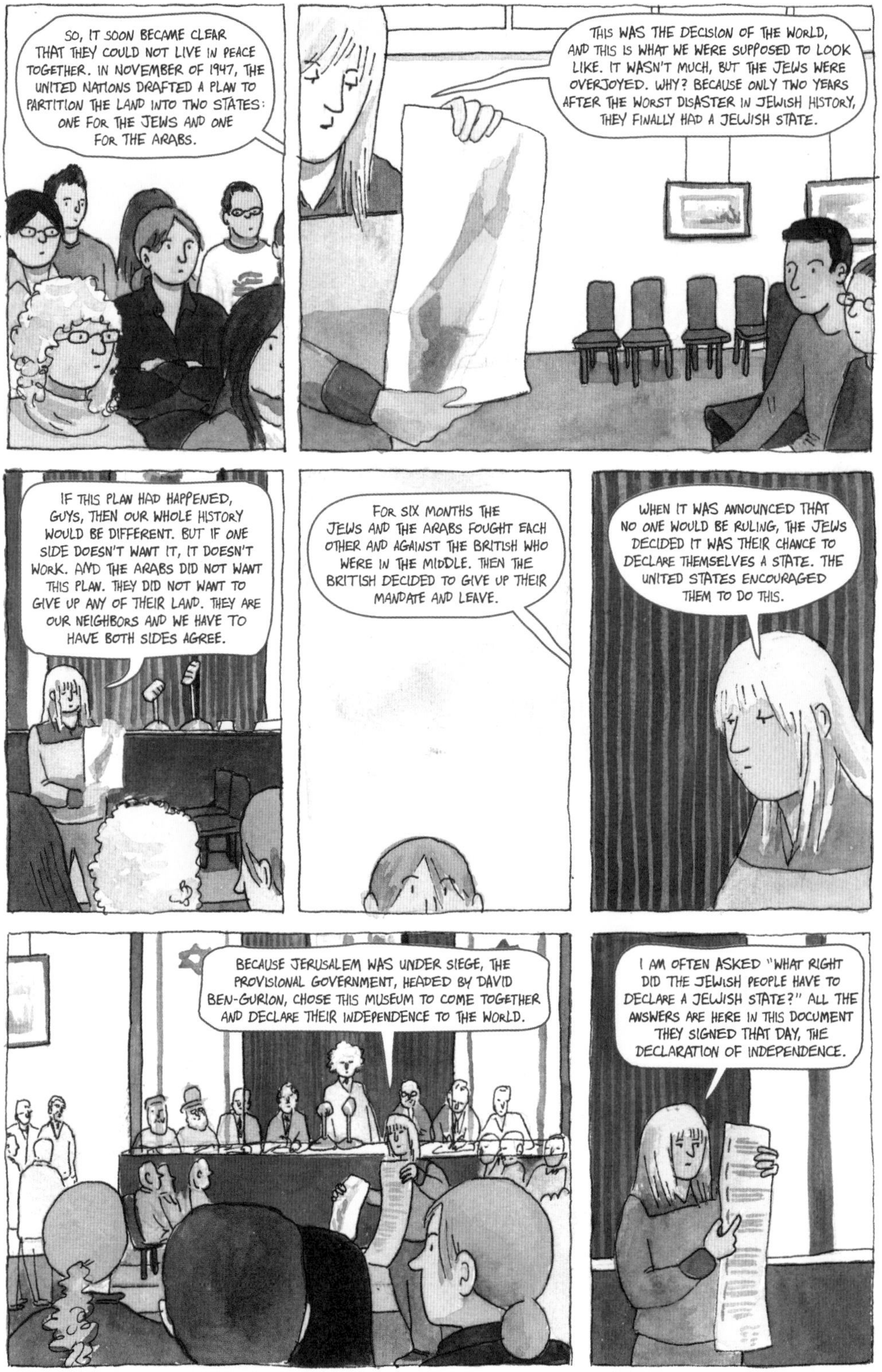

SO, IT SOON BECAME CLEAR THAT THEY COULD NOT LIVE IN PEACE TOGETHER. IN NOVEMBER OF 1947, THE UNITED NATIONS DRAFTED A PLAN TO PARTITION THE LAND INTO TWO STATES: ONE FOR THE JEWS AND ONE FOR THE ARABS.
THIS WAS THE DECISION OF THE WORLD, AND THIS IS WHAT WE WERE SUPPOSED TO LOOK LIKE. IT WASN'T MUCH, BUT THE JEWS WERE OVERJOYED. WHY? BECAUSE ONLY TWO YEARS AFTER THE WORST DISASTER IN JEWISH HISTORY, THEY FINALLY HAD A JEWISH STATE.
IF THIS PLAN HAD HAPPENED, GUYS, THEN OUR WHOLE HISTORY WOULD BE DIFFERENT. BUT IF ONE SIDE DOESN'T WANT IT, IT DOESN'T WORK. AND THE ARABS DID NOT WANT THIS PLAN. THEY DID NOT WANT TO GIVE UP ANY OF THEIR LAND. THEY ARE OUR NEIGHBORS AND WE HAVE TO HAVE BOTH SIDES AGREE.
FOR SIX MONTHS THE JEWS AND THE ARABS FOUGHT EACH OTHER AND AGAINST THE BRITISH WHO WERE IN THE MIDDLE. THEN THE BRITISH DECIDED TO GIVE UP THEIR MANDATE AND LEAVE.
WHEN IT WAS ANNOUNCED THAT NO ONE WOULD BE RULING, THE JEWS DECIDED IT WAS THEIR CHANCE TO DECLARE THEMSELVES A STATE. THE UNITED STATES ENCOURAGED THEM TO DO THIS.
BECAUSE JERUSALEM WAS UNDER SIEGE, THE PROVISIONAL GOVERNMENT, HEADED BY DAVID BEN-GURION, CHOSE THIS MUSEUM TO COME TOGETHER AND DECLARE THEIR INDEPENDENCE TO THE WORLD.
I AM OFTEN ASKED "WHAT RIGHT DID THE JEWISH PEOPLE HAVE TO DECLARE A JEWISH STATE?" ALL THE ANSWERS ARE HERE IN THIS DOCUMENT THEY SIGNED THAT DAY, THE DECLARATION OF INDEPENDENCE.

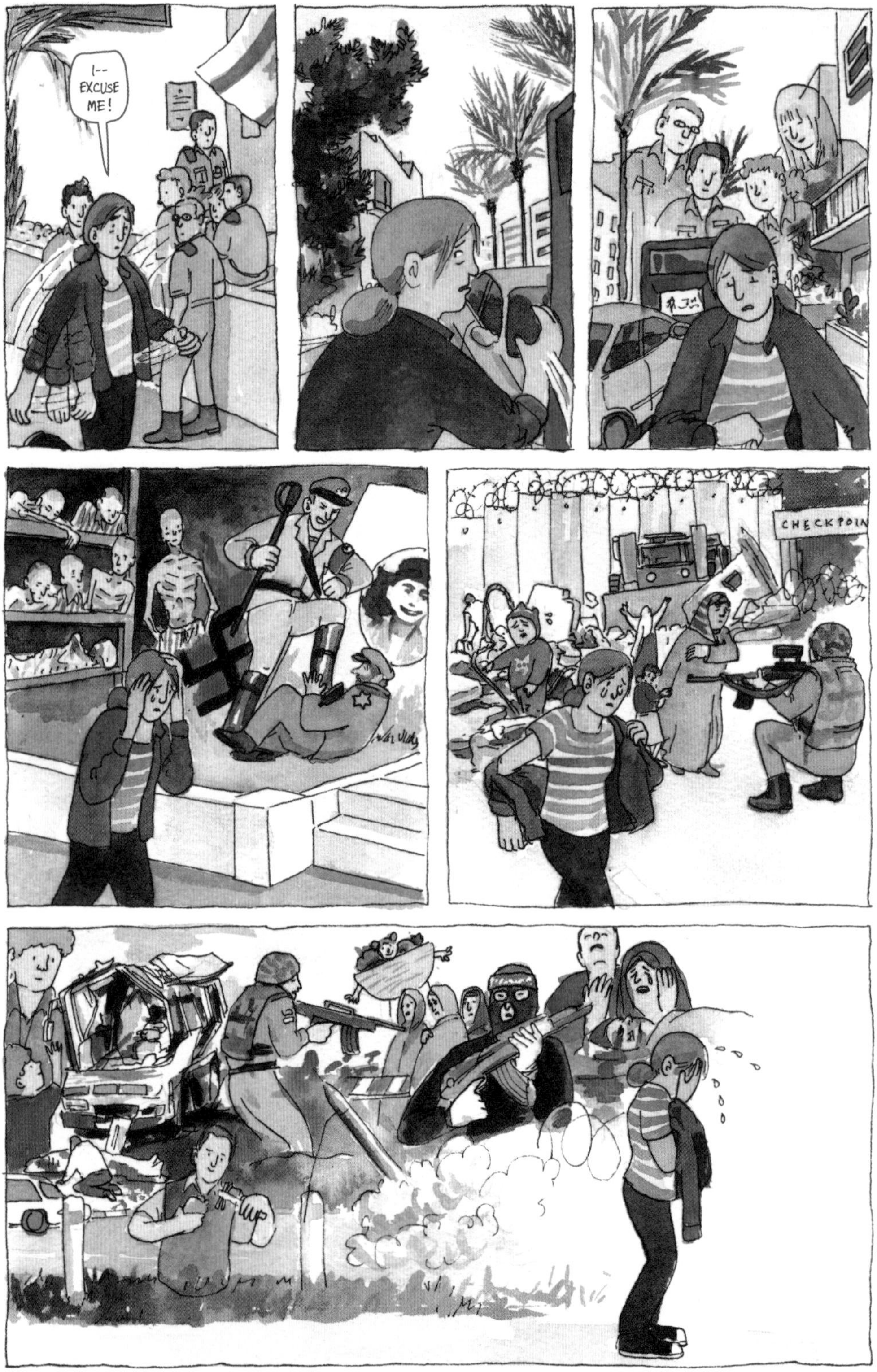
I-- EXCUSE ME!
CHECKPOIN

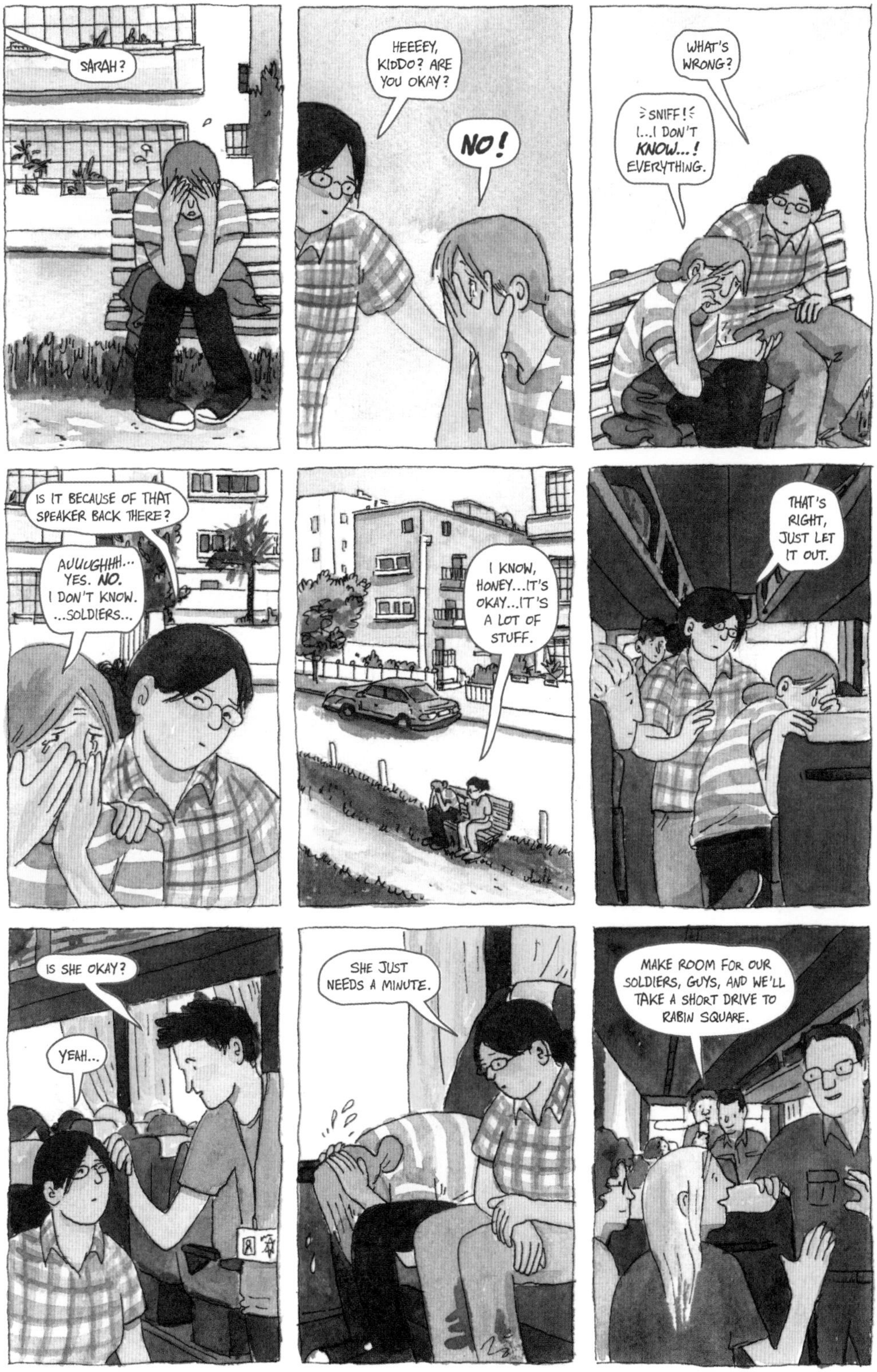
SARAH?
HEEEEY, KIDDO? ARE YOU OKAY?
NO!
WHAT'S WRONG?
SNIFF! I...I DON'T **KNOW...!** EVERYTHING.
IS IT BECAUSE OF THAT SPEAKER BACK THERE?
AUUUGHHH... YES. **NO.** I DON'T KNOW. ...SOLDIERS...
I KNOW, HONEY...IT'S OKAY...IT'S A LOT OF STUFF.
THAT'S RIGHT, JUST LET IT OUT.
IS SHE OKAY?
YEAH...
SHE JUST NEEDS A MINUTE.
MAKE ROOM FOR OUR SOLDIERS, GUYS, AND WE'LL TAKE A SHORT DRIVE TO RABIN SQUARE.

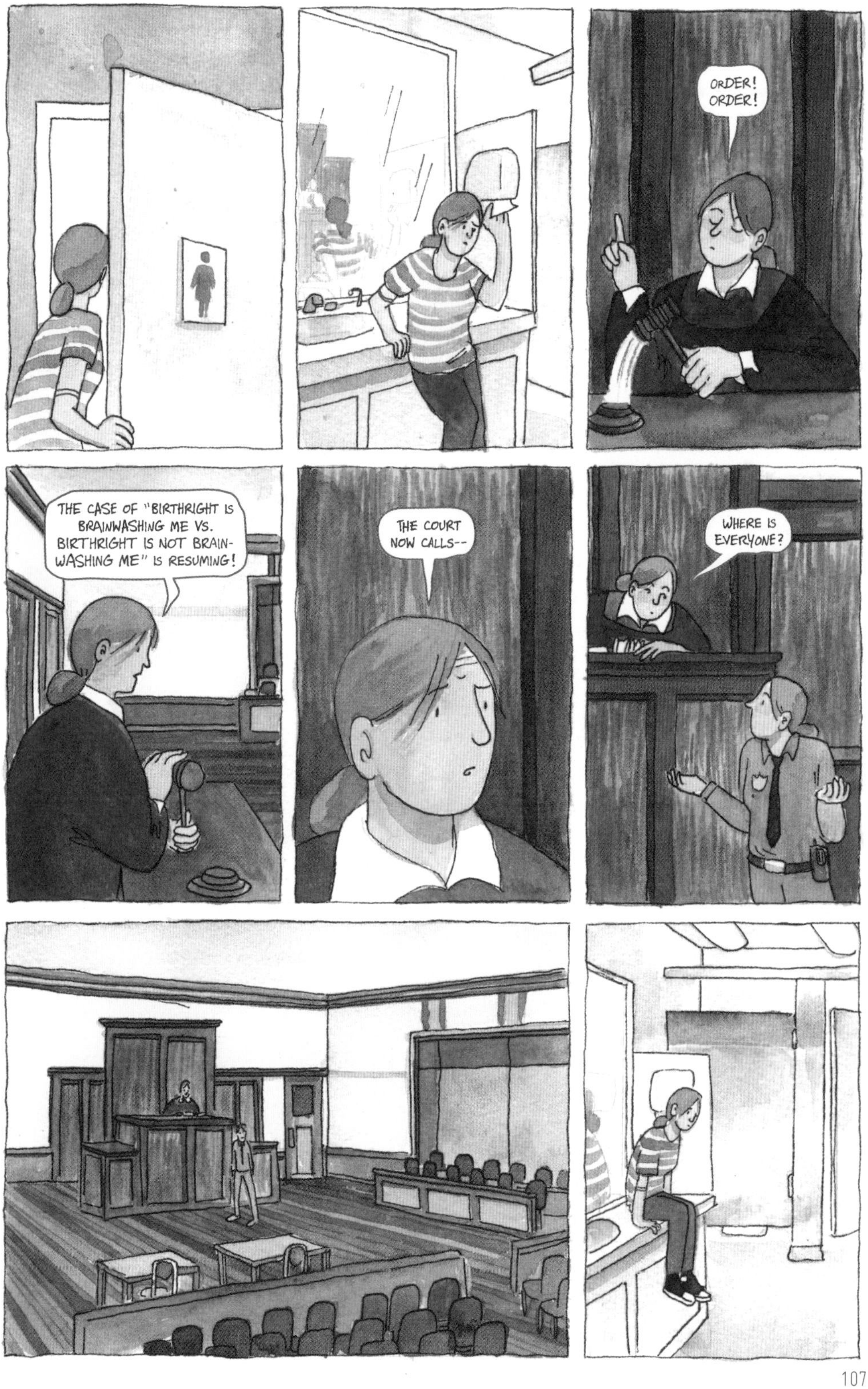
ORDER! ORDER!
THE CASE OF "BIRTHRIGHT IS BRAINWASHING ME VS. BIRTHRIGHT IS NOT BRAIN-WASHING ME" IS RESUMING!
THE COURT NOW CALLS--
WHERE IS EVERYONE?

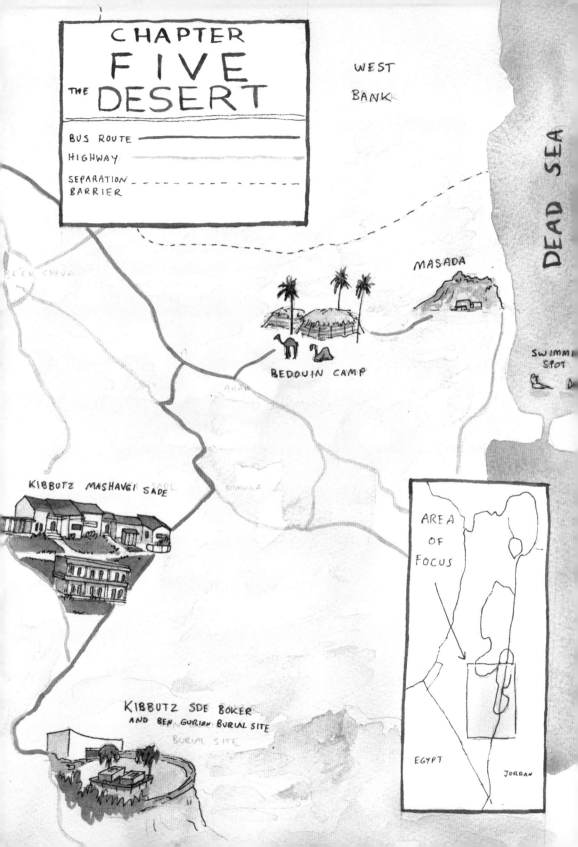

CHAPTER FIVE
THE DESERT

BUS ROUTE	————
HIGHWAY	
SEPARATION BARRIER	- - - - -

WEST BANK

DEAD SEA

BEER SHEVA

MASADA

SWIMMING SPOT

BEDOUIN CAMP

KIBBUTZ MASHAVEI SADE

DIMONA

AREA OF FOCUS

KIBBUTZ SDE BOKER
AND BEN GURION BURIAL SITE
BURIAL SITE

EGYPT

JORDAN

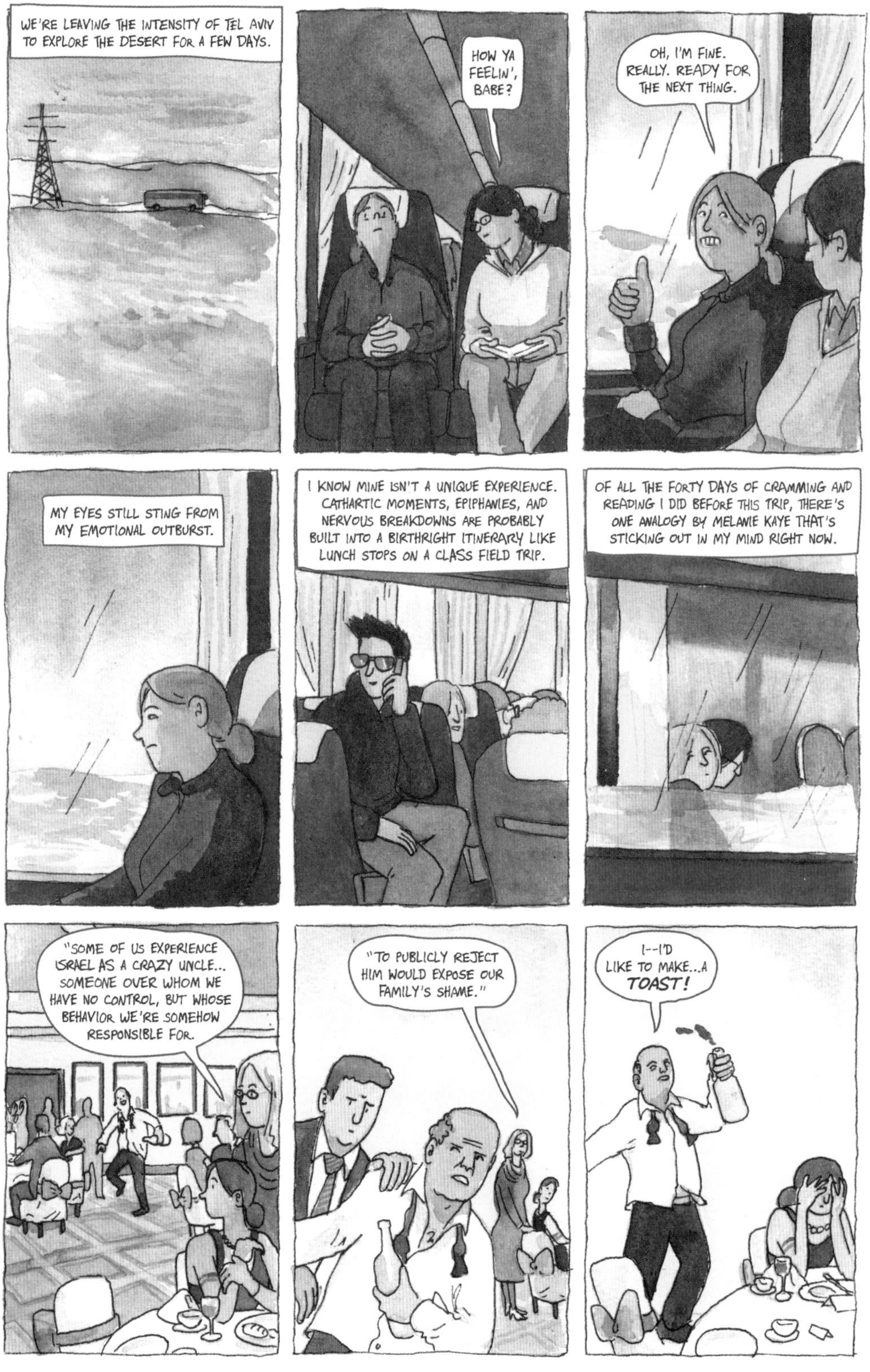
WE'RE LEAVING THE INTENSITY OF TEL AVIV TO EXPLORE THE DESERT FOR A FEW DAYS.
HOW YA FEELIN', BABE?
OH, I'M FINE. REALLY. READY FOR THE NEXT THING.
MY EYES STILL STING FROM MY EMOTIONAL OUTBURST.
I KNOW MINE ISN'T A UNIQUE EXPERIENCE. CATHARTIC MOMENTS, EPIPHANIES, AND NERVOUS BREAKDOWNS ARE PROBABLY BUILT INTO A BIRTHRIGHT ITINERARY LIKE LUNCH STOPS ON A CLASS FIELD TRIP.
OF ALL THE FORTY DAYS OF CRAMMING AND READING I DID BEFORE THIS TRIP, THERE'S ONE ANALOGY BY MELANIE KAYE THAT'S STICKING OUT IN MY MIND RIGHT NOW.
"SOME OF US EXPERIENCE ISRAEL AS A CRAZY UNCLE... SOMEONE OVER WHOM WE HAVE NO CONTROL, BUT WHOSE BEHAVIOR WE'RE SOMEHOW RESPONSIBLE FOR.
"TO PUBLICLY REJECT HIM WOULD EXPOSE OUR FAMILY'S SHAME."
I--I'D LIKE TO MAKE...A TOAST!

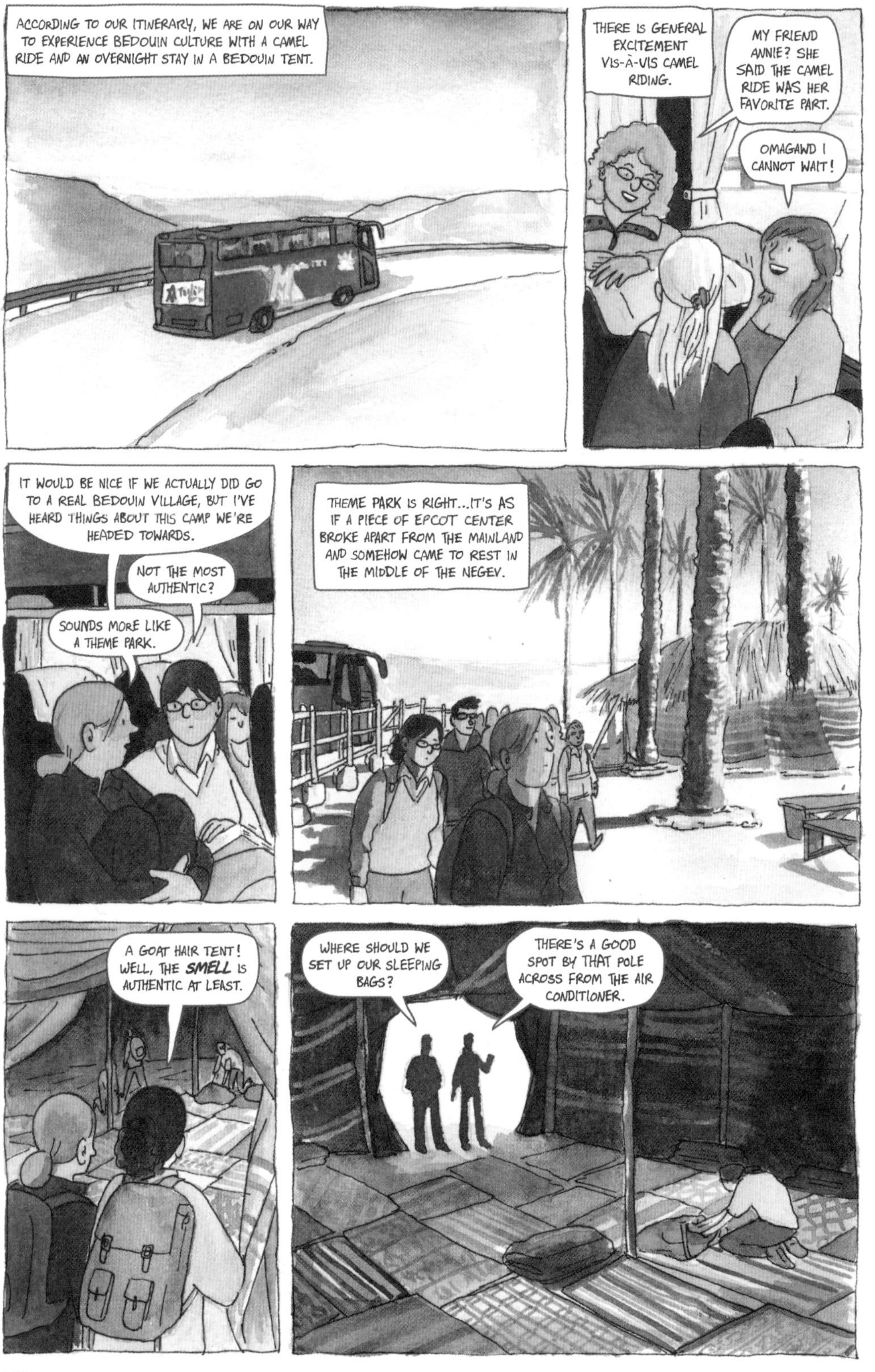
ACCORDING TO OUR ITINERARY, WE ARE ON OUR WAY TO EXPERIENCE BEDOUIN CULTURE WITH A CAMEL RIDE AND AN OVERNIGHT STAY IN A BEDOUIN TENT.
THERE IS GENERAL EXCITEMENT VIS-À-VIS CAMEL RIDING.
MY FRIEND ANNIE? SHE SAID THE CAMEL RIDE WAS HER FAVORITE PART.
OMAGAWD I CANNOT WAIT!
IT WOULD BE NICE IF WE ACTUALLY DID GO TO A REAL BEDOUIN VILLAGE, BUT I'VE HEARD THINGS ABOUT THIS CAMP WE'RE HEADED TOWARDS.
NOT THE MOST AUTHENTIC?
SOUNDS MORE LIKE A THEME PARK.
THEME PARK IS RIGHT...IT'S AS IF A PIECE OF EPCOT CENTER BROKE APART FROM THE MAINLAND AND SOMEHOW CAME TO REST IN THE MIDDLE OF THE NEGEV.
A GOAT HAIR TENT! WELL, THE SMELL IS AUTHENTIC AT LEAST.
WHERE SHOULD WE SET UP OUR SLEEPING BAGS?
THERE'S A GOOD SPOT BY THAT POLE ACROSS FROM THE AIR CONDITIONER.

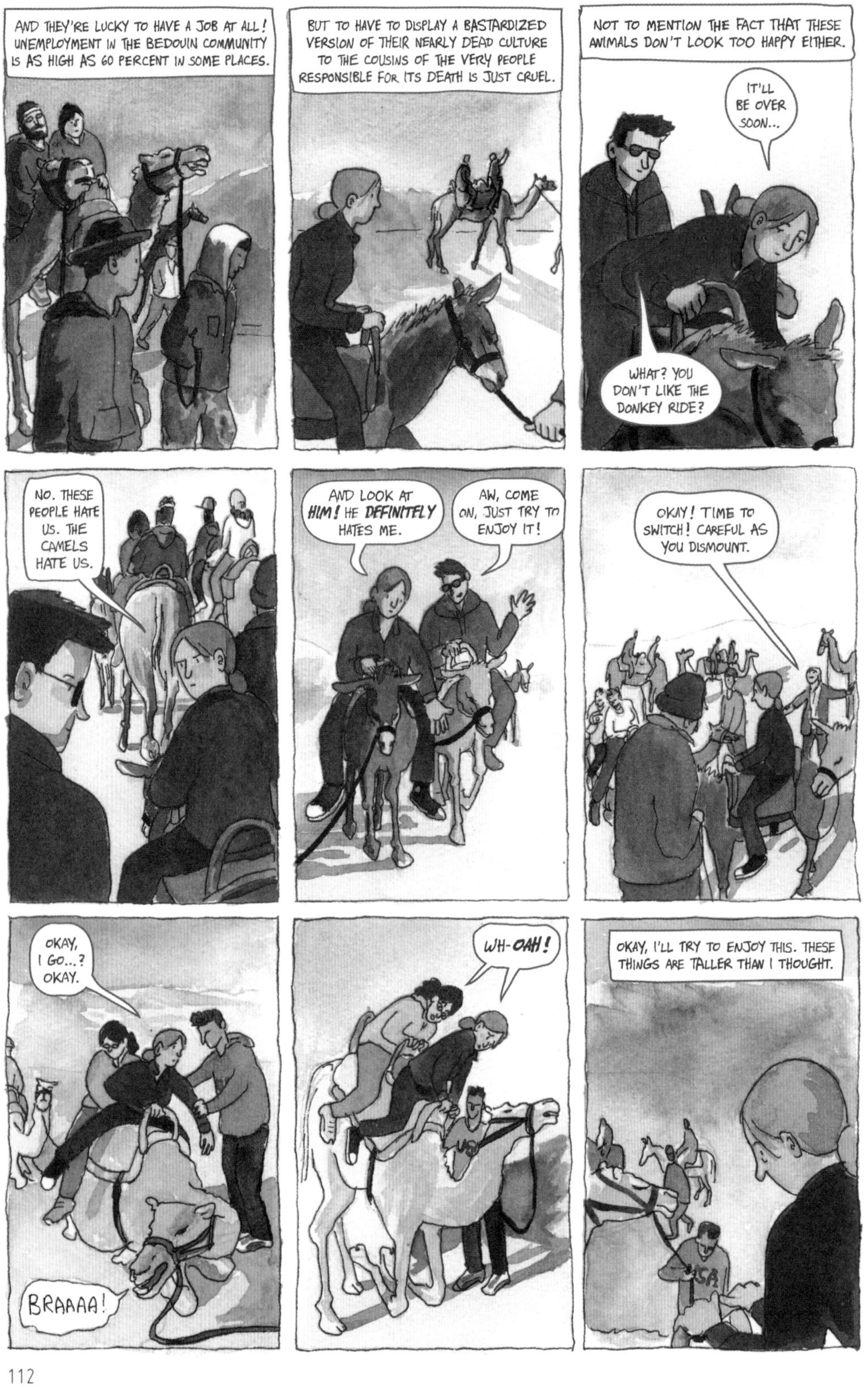
AND THEY'RE LUCKY TO HAVE A JOB AT ALL! UNEMPLOYMENT IN THE BEDOUIN COMMUNITY IS AS HIGH AS 60 PERCENT IN SOME PLACES.
BUT TO HAVE TO DISPLAY A BASTARDIZED VERSION OF THEIR NEARLY DEAD CULTURE TO THE COUSINS OF THE VERY PEOPLE RESPONSIBLE FOR ITS DEATH IS JUST CRUEL.
NOT TO MENTION THE FACT THAT THESE ANIMALS DON'T LOOK TOO HAPPY EITHER.
IT'LL BE OVER SOON...
WHAT? YOU DON'T LIKE THE DONKEY RIDE?
NO. THESE PEOPLE HATE US. THE CAMELS HATE US.
AND LOOK AT **HIM!** HE **DEFINITELY** HATES ME.
AW, COME ON, JUST TRY TO ENJOY IT!
OKAY! TIME TO SWITCH! CAREFUL AS YOU DISMOUNT.
OKAY, I GO...? OKAY.
BRAAAA!
WH-**OAH!**
OKAY, I'LL TRY TO ENJOY THIS. THESE THINGS ARE TALLER THAN I THOUGHT.

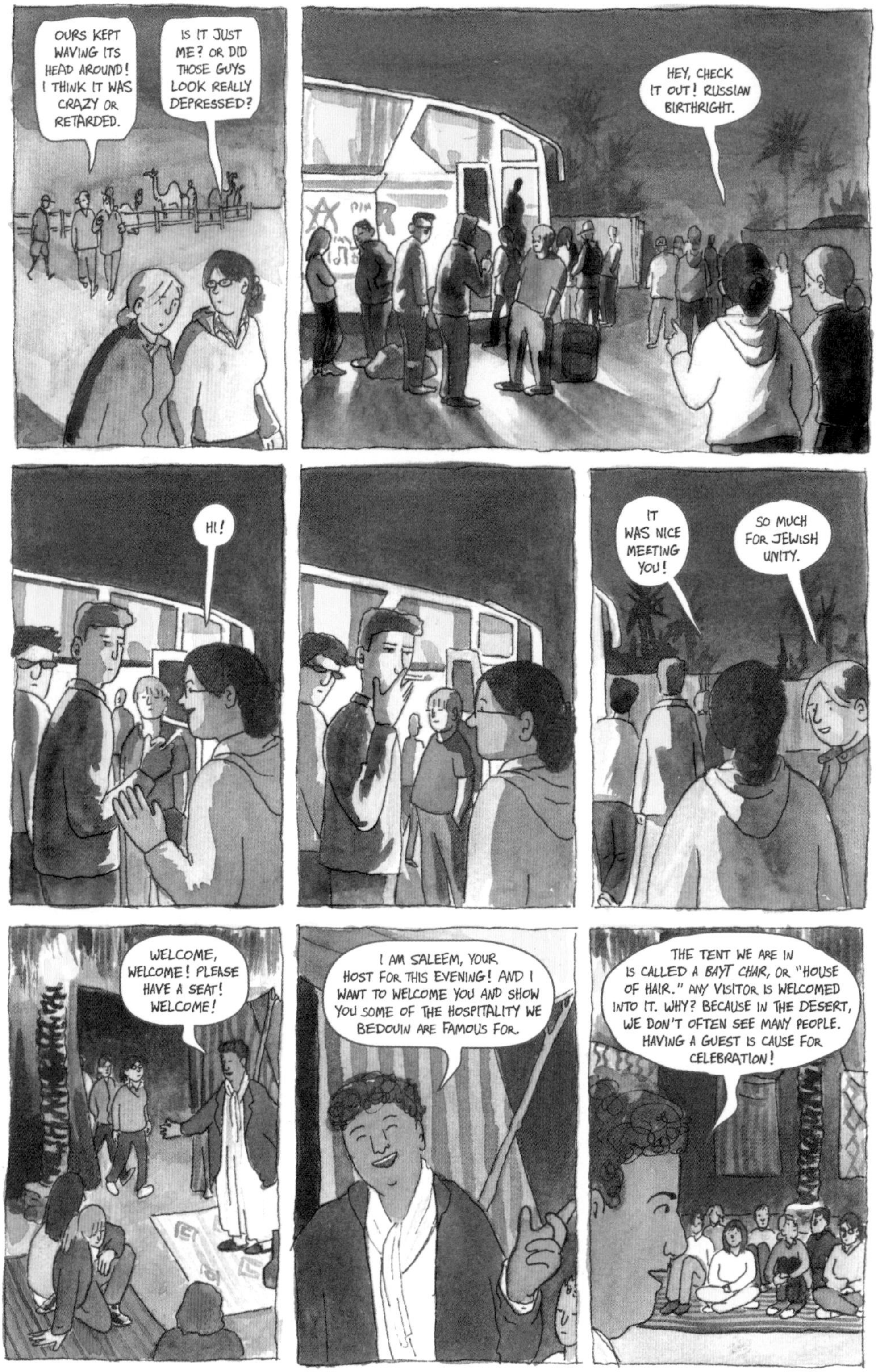
OURS KEPT WAVING ITS HEAD AROUND! I THINK IT WAS CRAZY OR RETARDED.
IS IT JUST ME? OR DID THOSE GUYS LOOK REALLY DEPRESSED?
HEY, CHECK IT OUT! RUSSIAN BIRTHRIGHT.
HI!
IT WAS NICE MEETING YOU!
SO MUCH FOR JEWISH UNITY.
WELCOME, WELCOME! PLEASE HAVE A SEAT! WELCOME!
I AM SALEEM, YOUR HOST FOR THIS EVENING! AND I WANT TO WELCOME YOU AND SHOW YOU SOME OF THE HOSPITALITY WE BEDOUIN ARE FAMOUS FOR.
THE TENT WE ARE IN IS CALLED A *BAYT CHAR*, OR "HOUSE OF HAIR." ANY VISITOR IS WELCOMED INTO IT. WHY? BECAUSE IN THE DESERT, WE DON'T OFTEN SEE MANY PEOPLE. HAVING A GUEST IS CAUSE FOR CELEBRATION!

117

118

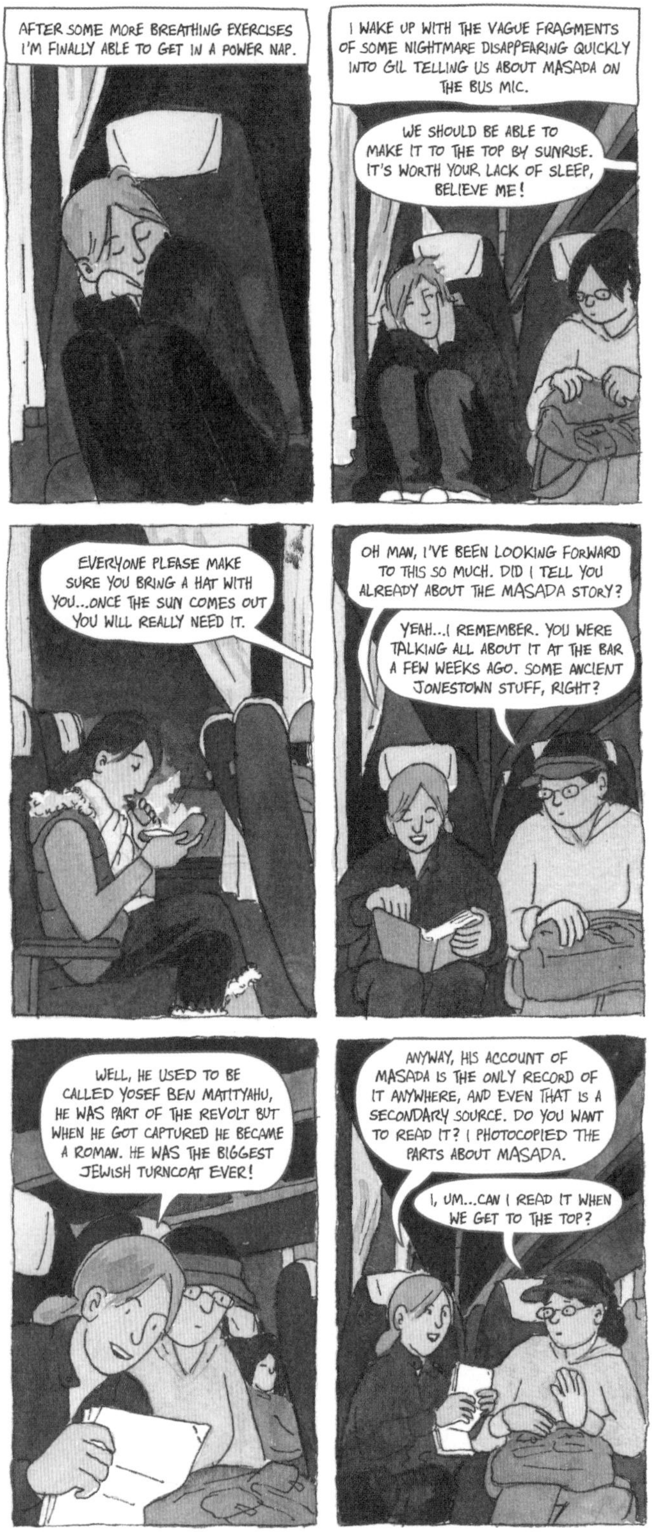
AFTER SOME MORE BREATHING EXERCISES I'M FINALLY ABLE TO GET IN A POWER NAP.
I WAKE UP WITH THE VAGUE FRAGMENTS OF SOME NIGHTMARE DISAPPEARING QUICKLY INTO GIL TELLING US ABOUT MASADA ON THE BUS MIC.
WE SHOULD BE ABLE TO MAKE IT TO THE TOP BY SUNRISE. IT'S WORTH YOUR LACK OF SLEEP, BELIEVE ME!
I QUICKLY FORGET ABOUT MY APPARENT ANTI-SEMITIC TENDENCIES AS I REMEMBER WHERE WE'RE HEADED AT SUCH AN UNGODLY HOUR.
MASADA!
EVERYONE PLEASE MAKE SURE YOU BRING A HAT WITH YOU...ONCE THE SUN COMES OUT YOU WILL REALLY NEED IT.
OH MAN, I'VE BEEN LOOKING FORWARD TO THIS SO MUCH. DID I TELL YOU ALREADY ABOUT THE MASADA STORY?
YEAH...I REMEMBER. YOU WERE TALKING ALL ABOUT IT AT THE BAR A FEW WEEKS AGO. SOME ANCIENT JONESTOWN STUFF, RIGHT?
WELL, NOT REALLY. BUT FASCINATING ANYWAY. IT WAS DURING THE FIRST JEWISH REVOLT AGAINST THE ROMANS IN THE FIRST CENTURY C.E. THE ONLY RECORD WE HAVE OF ANY OF THAT WHOLE WAR IS FROM THIS GUY JOSEPHUS.
XEROXES
WELL, HE USED TO BE CALLED YOSEF BEN MATTYAHU, HE WAS PART OF THE REVOLT BUT WHEN HE GOT CAPTURED HE BECAME A ROMAN. HE WAS THE BIGGEST JEWISH TURNCOAT EVER!
ANYWAY, HIS ACCOUNT OF MASADA IS THE ONLY RECORD OF IT ANYWHERE, AND EVEN THAT IS A SECONDARY SOURCE. DO YOU WANT TO READ IT? I PHOTOCOPIED THE PARTS ABOUT MASADA.
I, UM...CAN I READ IT WHEN WE GET TO THE TOP?
YEAH, NO PROBLEM! I WANTED TO GO BACK OVER IT ANYWAY BEFORE WE GO UP THERE.

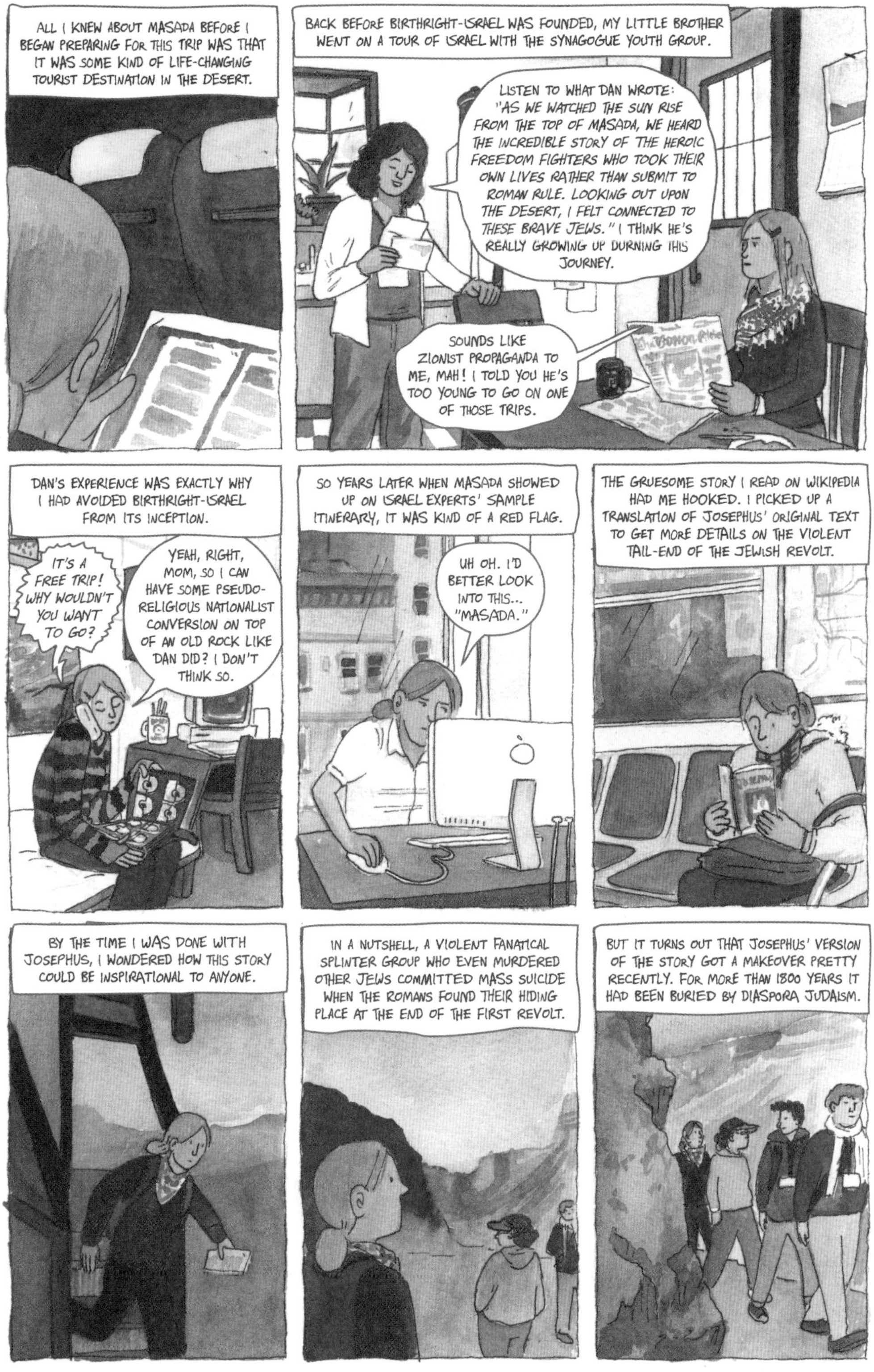

ALL I KNEW ABOUT MASADA BEFORE I BEGAN PREPARING FOR THIS TRIP WAS THAT IT WAS SOME KIND OF LIFE-CHANGING TOURIST DESTINATION IN THE DESERT.
BACK BEFORE BIRTHRIGHT-ISRAEL WAS FOUNDED, MY LITTLE BROTHER WENT ON A TOUR OF ISRAEL WITH THE SYNAGOGUE YOUTH GROUP.
LISTEN TO WHAT DAN WROTE: "AS WE WATCHED THE SUN RISE FROM THE TOP OF MASADA, WE HEARD THE INCREDIBLE STORY OF THE HEROIC FREEDOM FIGHTERS WHO TOOK THEIR OWN LIVES RATHER THAN SUBMIT TO ROMAN RULE. LOOKING OUT UPON THE DESERT, I FELT CONNECTED TO THESE BRAVE JEWS." I THINK HE'S REALLY GROWING UP DURNING THIS JOURNEY.
SOUNDS LIKE ZIONIST PROPAGANDA TO ME, MAH! I TOLD YOU HE'S TOO YOUNG TO GO ON ONE OF THOSE TRIPS.
DAN'S EXPERIENCE WAS EXACTLY WHY I HAD AVOIDED BIRTHRIGHT-ISRAEL FROM ITS INCEPTION.
IT'S A FREE TRIP! WHY WOULDN'T YOU WANT TO GO?
YEAH, RIGHT, MOM, SO I CAN HAVE SOME PSEUDO-RELIGIOUS NATIONALIST CONVERSION ON TOP OF AN OLD ROCK LIKE DAN DID? I DON'T THINK SO.
SO YEARS LATER WHEN MASADA SHOWED UP ON ISRAEL EXPERTS' SAMPLE ITINERARY, IT WAS KIND OF A RED FLAG.
UH OH. I'D BETTER LOOK INTO THIS... "MASADA."
THE GRUESOME STORY I READ ON WIKIPEDIA HAD ME HOOKED. I PICKED UP A TRANSLATION OF JOSEPHUS' ORIGINAL TEXT TO GET MORE DETAILS ON THE VIOLENT TAIL-END OF THE JEWISH REVOLT.
BY THE TIME I WAS DONE WITH JOSEPHUS, I WONDERED HOW THIS STORY COULD BE INSPIRATIONAL TO ANYONE.
IN A NUTSHELL, A VIOLENT FANATICAL SPLINTER GROUP WHO EVEN MURDERED OTHER JEWS COMMITTED MASS SUICIDE WHEN THE ROMANS FOUND THEIR HIDING PLACE AT THE END OF THE FIRST REVOLT.
BUT IT TURNS OUT THAT JOSEPHUS' VERSION OF THE STORY GOT A MAKEOVER PRETTY RECENTLY. FOR MORE THAN 1800 YEARS IT HAD BEEN BURIED BY DIASPORA JUDAISM.

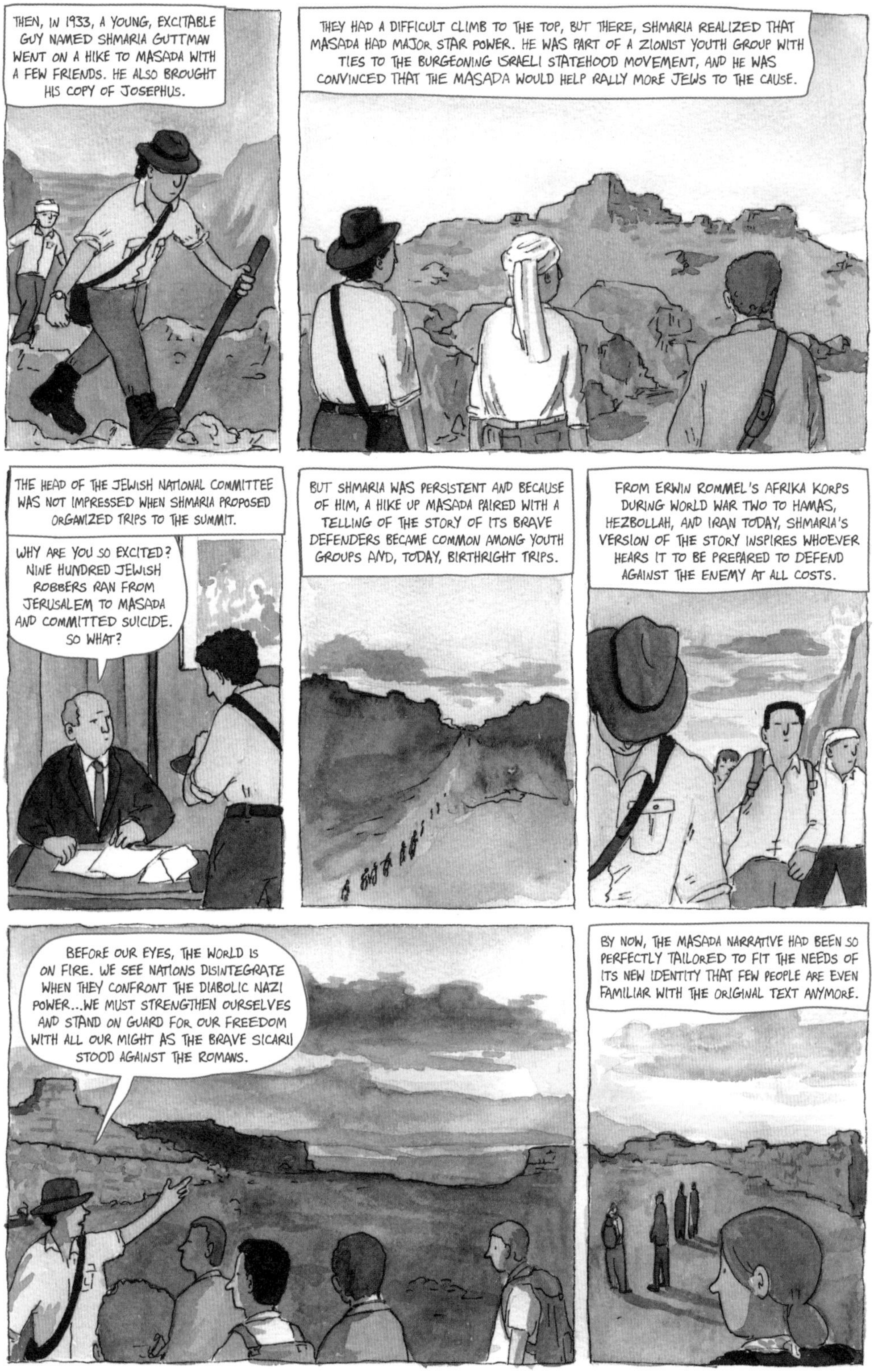
THEN, IN 1933, A YOUNG, EXCITABLE GUY NAMED SHMARIA GUTTMAN WENT ON A HIKE TO MASADA WITH A FEW FRIENDS. HE ALSO BROUGHT HIS COPY OF JOSEPHUS.
THEY HAD A DIFFICULT CLIMB TO THE TOP, BUT THERE, SHMARIA REALIZED THAT MASADA HAD MAJOR STAR POWER. HE WAS PART OF A ZIONIST YOUTH GROUP WITH TIES TO THE BURGEONING ISRAELI STATEHOOD MOVEMENT, AND HE WAS CONVINCED THAT THE MASADA WOULD HELP RALLY MORE JEWS TO THE CAUSE.
THE HEAD OF THE JEWISH NATIONAL COMMITTEE WAS NOT IMPRESSED WHEN SHMARIA PROPOSED ORGANIZED TRIPS TO THE SUMMIT.
WHY ARE YOU SO EXCITED? NINE HUNDRED JEWISH ROBBERS RAN FROM JERUSALEM TO MASADA AND COMMITTED SUICIDE. SO WHAT?
BUT SHMARIA WAS PERSISTENT AND BECAUSE OF HIM, A HIKE UP MASADA PAIRED WITH A TELLING OF THE STORY OF ITS BRAVE DEFENDERS BECAME COMMON AMONG YOUTH GROUPS AND, TODAY, BIRTHRIGHT TRIPS.
FROM ERWIN ROMMEL'S AFRIKA KORPS DURING WORLD WAR TWO TO HAMAS, HEZBOLLAH, AND IRAN TODAY, SHMARIA'S VERSION OF THE STORY INSPIRES WHOEVER HEARS IT TO BE PREPARED TO DEFEND AGAINST THE ENEMY AT ALL COSTS.
BEFORE OUR EYES, THE WORLD IS ON FIRE. WE SEE NATIONS DISINTEGRATE WHEN THEY CONFRONT THE DIABOLIC NAZI POWER...WE MUST STRENGTHEN OURSELVES AND STAND ON GUARD FOR OUR FREEDOM WITH ALL OUR MIGHT AS THE BRAVE SICARII STOOD AGAINST THE ROMANS.
BY NOW, THE MASADA NARRATIVE HAD BEEN SO PERFECTLY TAILORED TO FIT THE NEEDS OF ITS NEW IDENTITY THAT FEW PEOPLE ARE EVEN FAMILIAR WITH THE ORIGINAL TEXT ANYMORE.

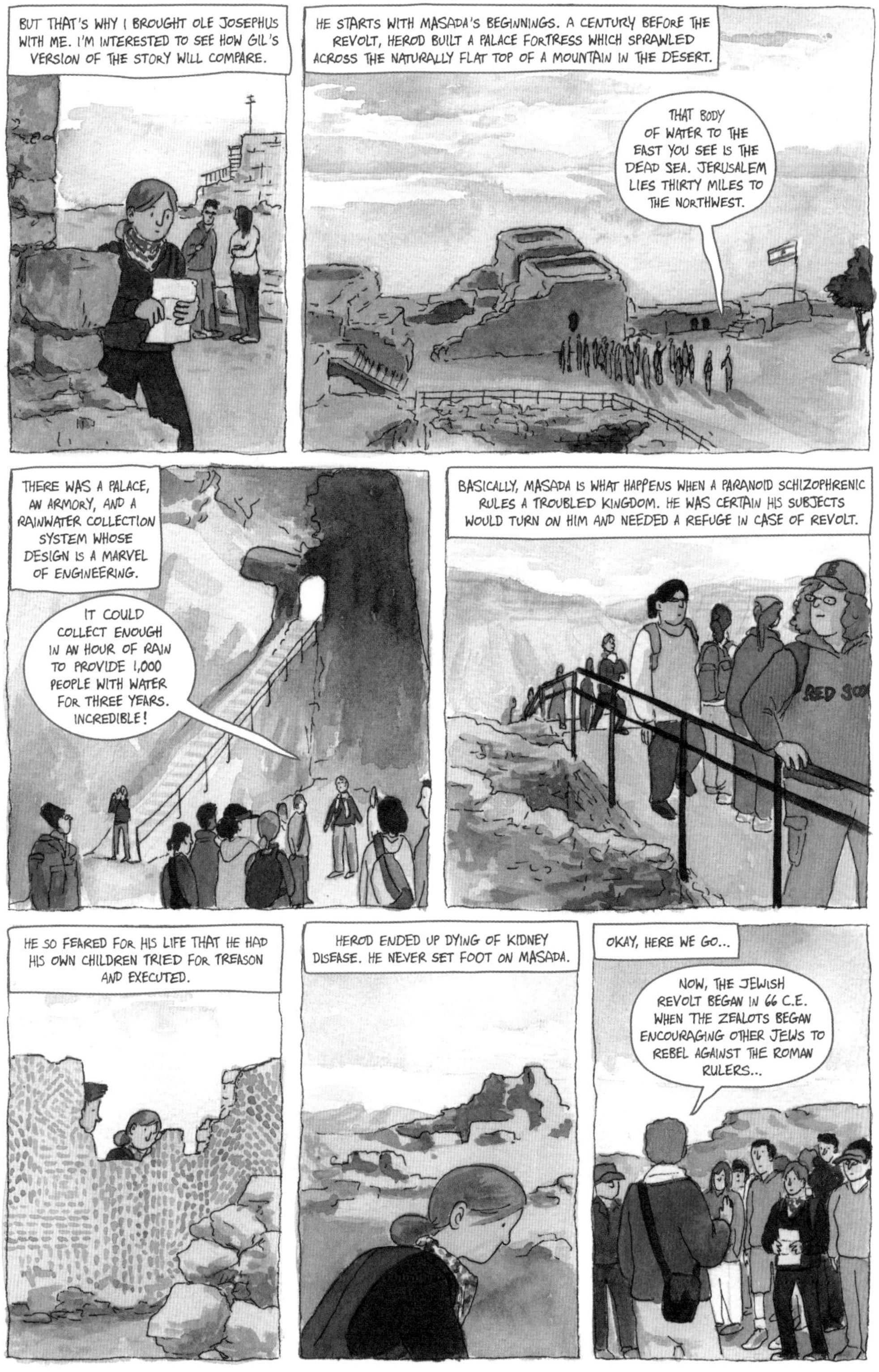
BUT THAT'S WHY I BROUGHT OLE JOSEPHUS WITH ME. I'M INTERESTED TO SEE HOW GIL'S VERSION OF THE STORY WILL COMPARE.
HE STARTS WITH MASADA'S BEGINNINGS. A CENTURY BEFORE THE REVOLT, HEROD BUILT A PALACE FORTRESS WHICH SPRAWLED ACROSS THE NATURALLY FLAT TOP OF A MOUNTAIN IN THE DESERT.
THAT BODY OF WATER TO THE EAST YOU SEE IS THE DEAD SEA. JERUSALEM LIES THIRTY MILES TO THE NORTHWEST.
THERE WAS A PALACE, AN ARMORY, AND A RAINWATER COLLECTION SYSTEM WHOSE DESIGN IS A MARVEL OF ENGINEERING.
IT COULD COLLECT ENOUGH IN AN HOUR OF RAIN TO PROVIDE 1,000 PEOPLE WITH WATER FOR THREE YEARS. INCREDIBLE!
BASICALLY, MASADA IS WHAT HAPPENS WHEN A PARANOID SCHIZOPHRENIC RULES A TROUBLED KINGDOM. HE WAS CERTAIN HIS SUBJECTS WOULD TURN ON HIM AND NEEDED A REFUGE IN CASE OF REVOLT.
HE SO FEARED FOR HIS LIFE THAT HE HAD HIS OWN CHILDREN TRIED FOR TREASON AND EXECUTED.
HEROD ENDED UP DYING OF KIDNEY DISEASE. HE NEVER SET FOOT ON MASADA.
OKAY, HERE WE GO...
NOW, THE JEWISH REVOLT BEGAN IN 66 C.E. WHEN THE ZEALOTS BEGAN ENCOURAGING OTHER JEWS TO REBEL AGAINST THE ROMAN RULERS...

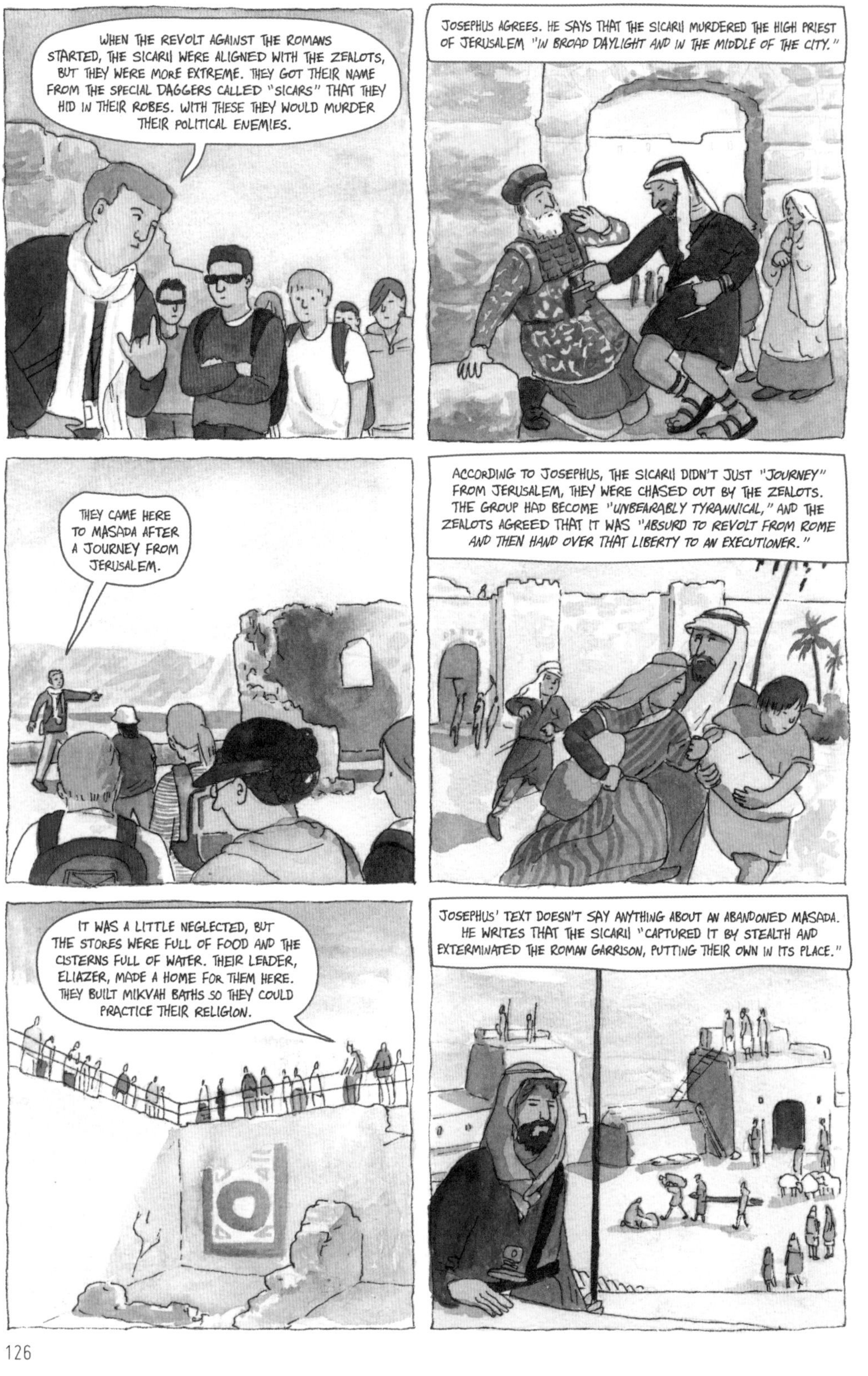
WHEN THE REVOLT AGAINST THE ROMANS STARTED, THE SICARII WERE ALIGNED WITH THE ZEALOTS, BUT THEY WERE MORE EXTREME. THEY GOT THEIR NAME FROM THE SPECIAL DAGGERS CALLED "SICARS" THAT THEY HID IN THEIR ROBES. WITH THESE THEY WOULD MURDER THEIR POLITICAL ENEMIES.
JOSEPHUS AGREES. HE SAYS THAT THE SICARII MURDERED THE HIGH PRIEST OF JERUSALEM "IN BROAD DAYLIGHT AND IN THE MIDDLE OF THE CITY."
THEY CAME HERE TO MASADA AFTER A JOURNEY FROM JERUSALEM.
ACCORDING TO JOSEPHUS, THE SICARII DIDN'T JUST "JOURNEY" FROM JERUSALEM, THEY WERE CHASED OUT BY THE ZEALOTS. THE GROUP HAD BECOME "UNBEARABLY TYRANNICAL," AND THE ZEALOTS AGREED THAT IT WAS "ABSURD TO REVOLT FROM ROME AND THEN HAND OVER THAT LIBERTY TO AN EXECUTIONER."
IT WAS A LITTLE NEGLECTED, BUT THE STORES WERE FULL OF FOOD AND THE CISTERNS FULL OF WATER. THEIR LEADER, ELIAZER, MADE A HOME FOR THEM HERE. THEY BUILT MIKVAH BATHS SO THEY COULD PRACTICE THEIR RELIGION.
JOSEPHUS' TEXT DOESN'T SAY ANYTHING ABOUT AN ABANDONED MASADA. HE WRITES THAT THE SICARII "CAPTURED IT BY STEALTH AND EXTERMINATED THE ROMAN GARRISON, PUTTING THEIR OWN IN ITS PLACE."

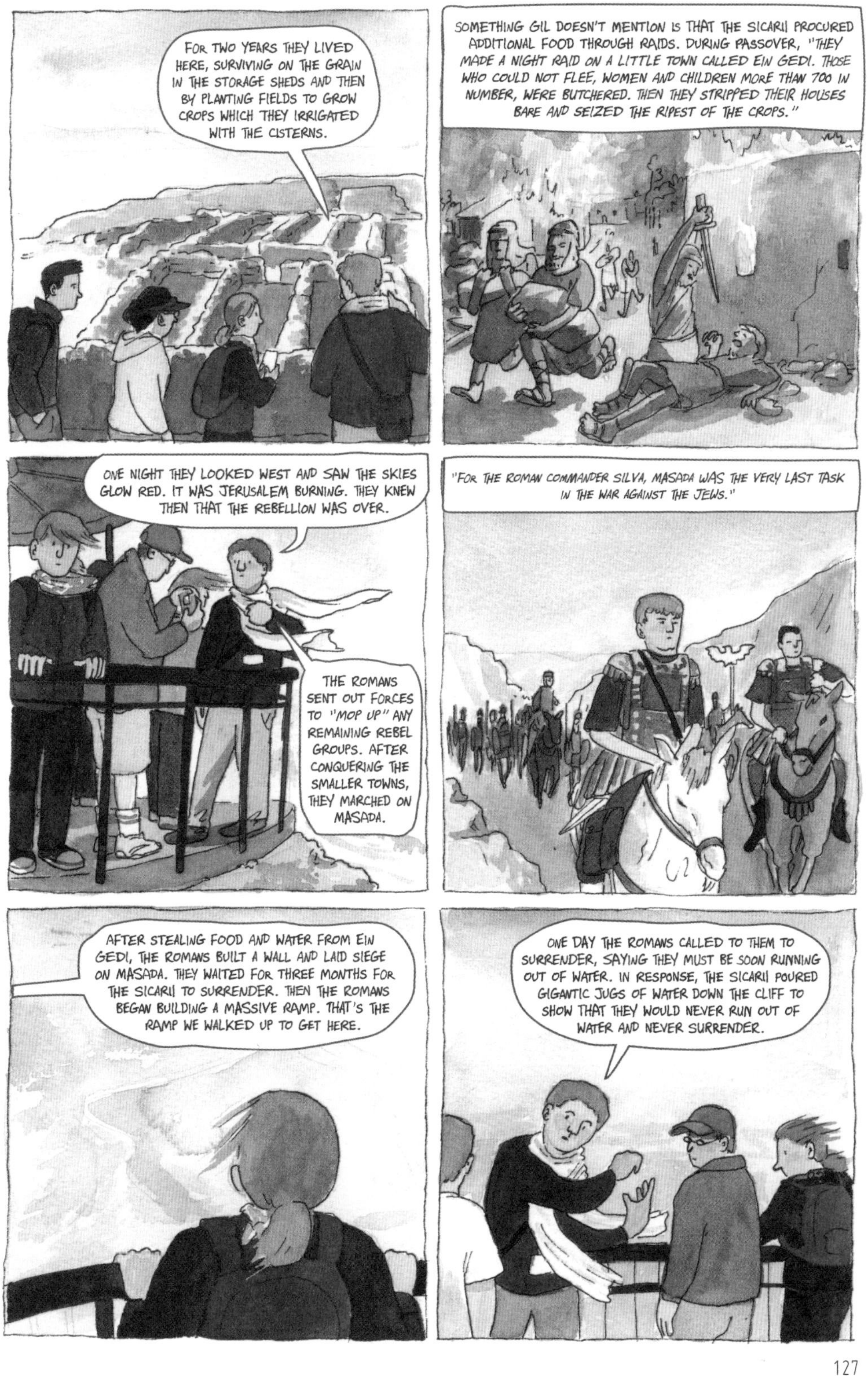

FOR TWO YEARS THEY LIVED HERE, SURVIVING ON THE GRAIN IN THE STORAGE SHEDS AND THEN BY PLANTING FIELDS TO GROW CROPS WHICH THEY IRRIGATED WITH THE CISTERNS.
SOMETHING GIL DOESN'T MENTION IS THAT THE SICARII PROCURED ADDITIONAL FOOD THROUGH RAIDS. DURING PASSOVER, "THEY MADE A NIGHT RAID ON A LITTLE TOWN CALLED EIN GEDI. THOSE WHO COULD NOT FLEE, WOMEN AND CHILDREN MORE THAN 700 IN NUMBER, WERE BUTCHERED. THEN THEY STRIPPED THEIR HOUSES BARE AND SEIZED THE RIPEST OF THE CROPS."
ONE NIGHT THEY LOOKED WEST AND SAW THE SKIES GLOW RED. IT WAS JERUSALEM BURNING. THEY KNEW THEN THAT THE REBELLION WAS OVER.
THE ROMANS SENT OUT FORCES TO "MOP UP" ANY REMAINING REBEL GROUPS. AFTER CONQUERING THE SMALLER TOWNS, THEY MARCHED ON MASADA.
"FOR THE ROMAN COMMANDER SILVA, MASADA WAS THE VERY LAST TASK IN THE WAR AGAINST THE JEWS."
AFTER STEALING FOOD AND WATER FROM EIN GEDI, THE ROMANS BUILT A WALL AND LAID SIEGE ON MASADA. THEY WAITED FOR THREE MONTHS FOR THE SICARII TO SURRENDER. THEN THE ROMANS BEGAN BUILDING A MASSIVE RAMP. THAT'S THE RAMP WE WALKED UP TO GET HERE.
ONE DAY THE ROMANS CALLED TO THEM TO SURRENDER, SAYING THEY MUST BE SOON RUNNING OUT OF WATER. IN RESPONSE, THE SICARII POURED GIGANTIC JUGS OF WATER DOWN THE CLIFF TO SHOW THAT THEY WOULD NEVER RUN OUT OF WATER AND NEVER SURRENDER.

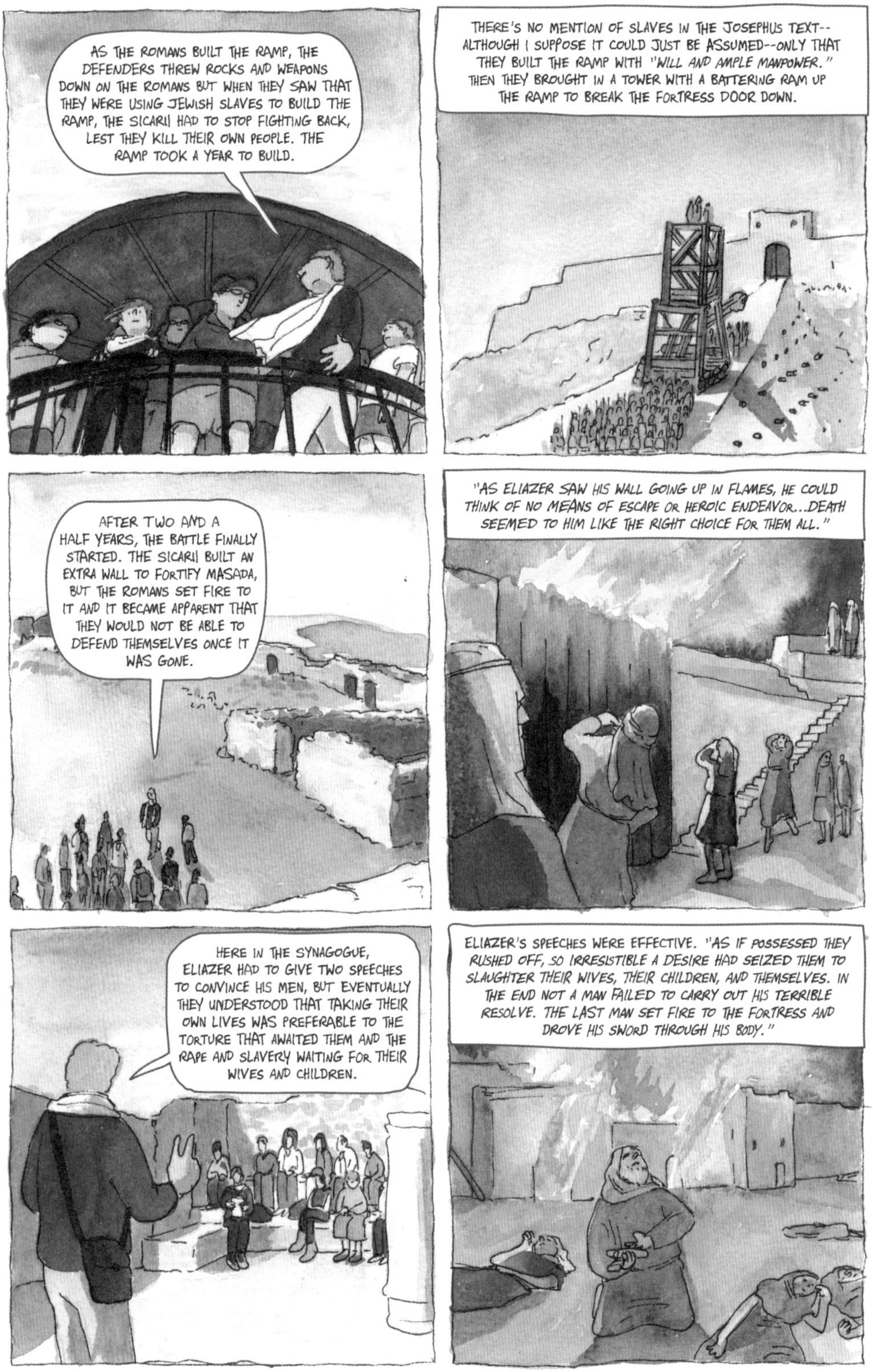
AS THE ROMANS BUILT THE RAMP, THE DEFENDERS THREW ROCKS AND WEAPONS DOWN ON THE ROMANS BUT WHEN THEY SAW THAT THEY WERE USING JEWISH SLAVES TO BUILD THE RAMP, THE SICARII HAD TO STOP FIGHTING BACK, LEST THEY KILL THEIR OWN PEOPLE. THE RAMP TOOK A YEAR TO BUILD.
THERE'S NO MENTION OF SLAVES IN THE JOSEPHUS TEXT--ALTHOUGH I SUPPOSE IT COULD JUST BE ASSUMED--ONLY THAT THEY BUILT THE RAMP WITH "WILL AND AMPLE MANPOWER." THEN THEY BROUGHT IN A TOWER WITH A BATTERING RAM UP THE RAMP TO BREAK THE FORTRESS DOOR DOWN.
AFTER TWO AND A HALF YEARS, THE BATTLE FINALLY STARTED. THE SICARII BUILT AN EXTRA WALL TO FORTIFY MASADA, BUT THE ROMANS SET FIRE TO IT AND IT BECAME APPARENT THAT THEY WOULD NOT BE ABLE TO DEFEND THEMSELVES ONCE IT WAS GONE.
"AS ELIAZER SAW HIS WALL GOING UP IN FLAMES, HE COULD THINK OF NO MEANS OF ESCAPE OR HEROIC ENDEAVOR...DEATH SEEMED TO HIM LIKE THE RIGHT CHOICE FOR THEM ALL."
HERE IN THE SYNAGOGUE, ELIAZER HAD TO GIVE TWO SPEECHES TO CONVINCE HIS MEN, BUT EVENTUALLY THEY UNDERSTOOD THAT TAKING THEIR OWN LIVES WAS PREFERABLE TO THE TORTURE THAT AWAITED THEM AND THE RAPE AND SLAVERY WAITING FOR THEIR WIVES AND CHILDREN.
ELIAZER'S SPEECHES WERE EFFECTIVE. "AS IF POSSESSED THEY RUSHED OFF, SO IRRESISTIBLE A DESIRE HAD SEIZED THEM TO SLAUGHTER THEIR WIVES, THEIR CHILDREN, AND THEMSELVES. IN THE END NOT A MAN FAILED TO CARRY OUT HIS TERRIBLE RESOLVE. THE LAST MAN SET FIRE TO THE FORTRESS AND DROVE HIS SWORD THROUGH HIS BODY."

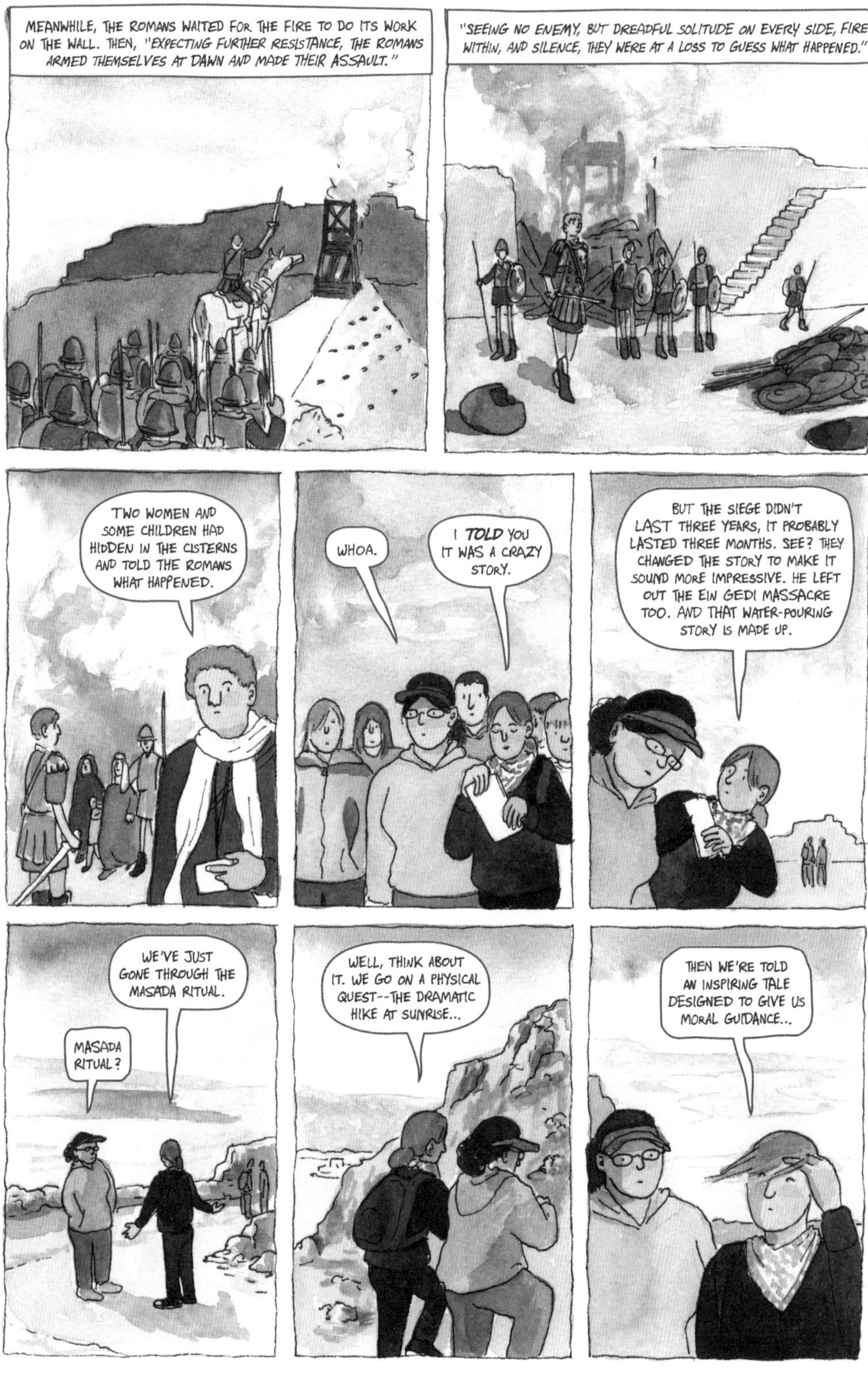
MEANWHILE, THE ROMANS WAITED FOR THE FIRE TO DO ITS WORK ON THE WALL. THEN, "EXPECTING FURTHER RESISTANCE, THE ROMANS ARMED THEMSELVES AT DAWN AND MADE THEIR ASSAULT."
"SEEING NO ENEMY, BUT DREADFUL SOLITUDE ON EVERY SIDE, FIRE WITHIN, AND SILENCE, THEY WERE AT A LOSS TO GUESS WHAT HAPPENED."
TWO WOMEN AND SOME CHILDREN HAD HIDDEN IN THE CISTERNS AND TOLD THE ROMANS WHAT HAPPENED.
WHOA.
I **TOLD** YOU IT WAS A CRAZY STORY.
BUT THE SIEGE DIDN'T LAST THREE YEARS, IT PROBABLY LASTED THREE MONTHS. SEE? THEY CHANGED THE STORY TO MAKE IT SOUND MORE IMPRESSIVE. HE LEFT OUT THE EIN GEDI MASSACRE TOO. AND THAT WATER-POURING STORY IS MADE UP.
WE'VE JUST GONE THROUGH THE MASADA RITUAL.
MASADA RITUAL?
WELL, THINK ABOUT IT. WE GO ON A PHYSICAL QUEST--THE DRAMATIC HIKE AT SUNRISE...
THEN WE'RE TOLD AN INSPIRING TALE DESIGNED TO GIVE US MORAL GUIDANCE...

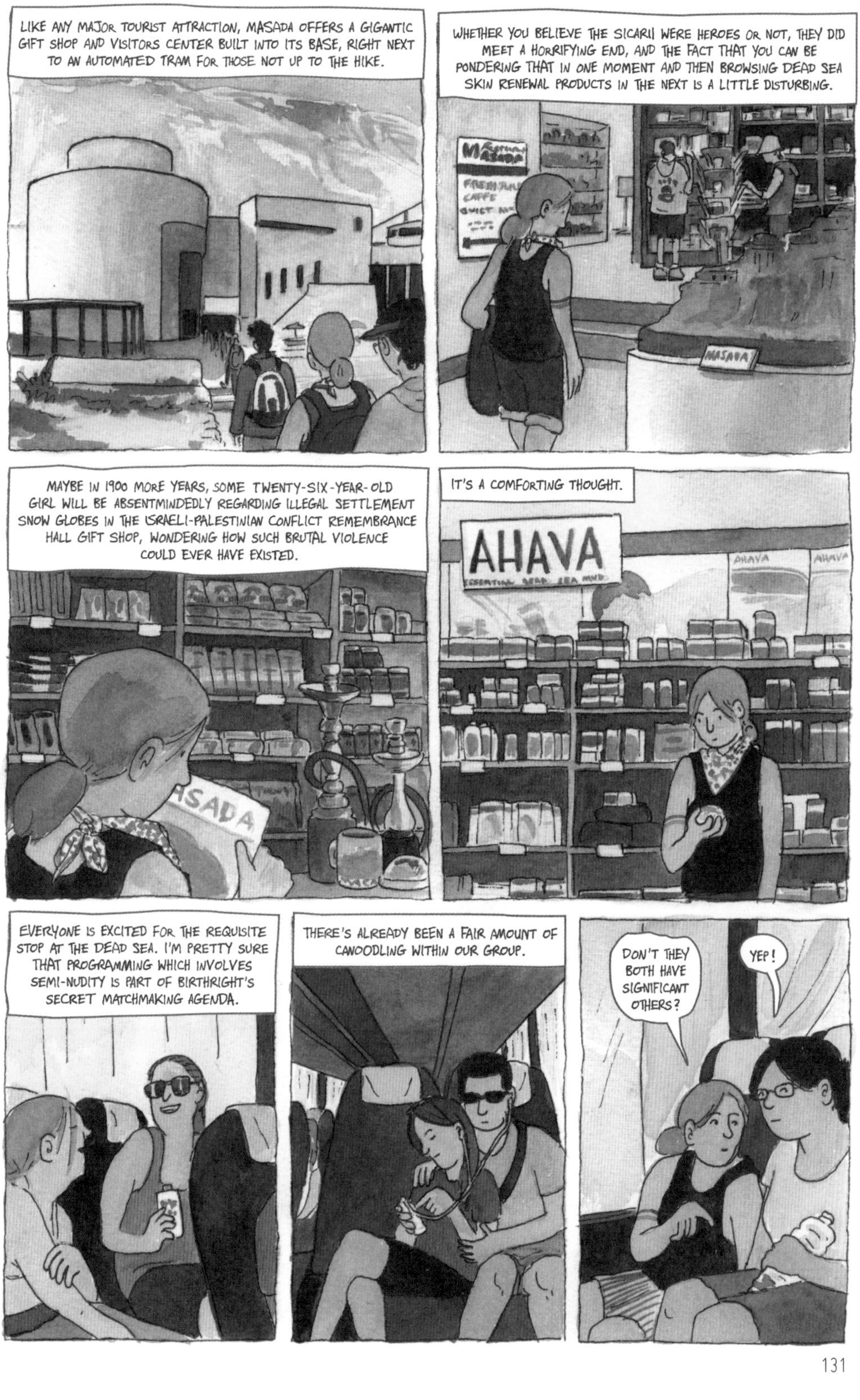
LIKE ANY MAJOR TOURIST ATTRACTION, MASADA OFFERS A GIGANTIC GIFT SHOP AND VISITORS CENTER BUILT INTO ITS BASE, RIGHT NEXT TO AN AUTOMATED TRAM FOR THOSE NOT UP TO THE HIKE.
WHETHER YOU BELIEVE THE SICARII WERE HEROES OR NOT, THEY DID MEET A HORRIFYING END, AND THE FACT THAT YOU CAN BE PONDERING THAT IN ONE MOMENT AND THEN BROWSING DEAD SEA SKIN RENEWAL PRODUCTS IN THE NEXT IS A LITTLE DISTURBING.
MASADA
MAYBE IN 1900 MORE YEARS, SOME TWENTY-SIX-YEAR-OLD GIRL WILL BE ABSENTMINDEDLY REGARDING ILLEGAL SETTLEMENT SNOW GLOBES IN THE ISRAELI-PALESTINIAN CONFLICT REMEMBRANCE HALL GIFT SHOP, WONDERING HOW SUCH BRUTAL VIOLENCE COULD EVER HAVE EXISTED.
ASADA
IT'S A COMFORTING THOUGHT.
AHAVA
AHAVA
AHAVA
EVERYONE IS EXCITED FOR THE REQUISITE STOP AT THE DEAD SEA. I'M PRETTY SURE THAT PROGRAMMING WHICH INVOLVES SEMI-NUDITY IS PART OF BIRTHRIGHT'S SECRET MATCHMAKING AGENDA.
THERE'S ALREADY BEEN A FAIR AMOUNT OF CANOODLING WITHIN OUR GROUP.
DON'T THEY BOTH HAVE SIGNIFICANT OTHERS?
YEP!

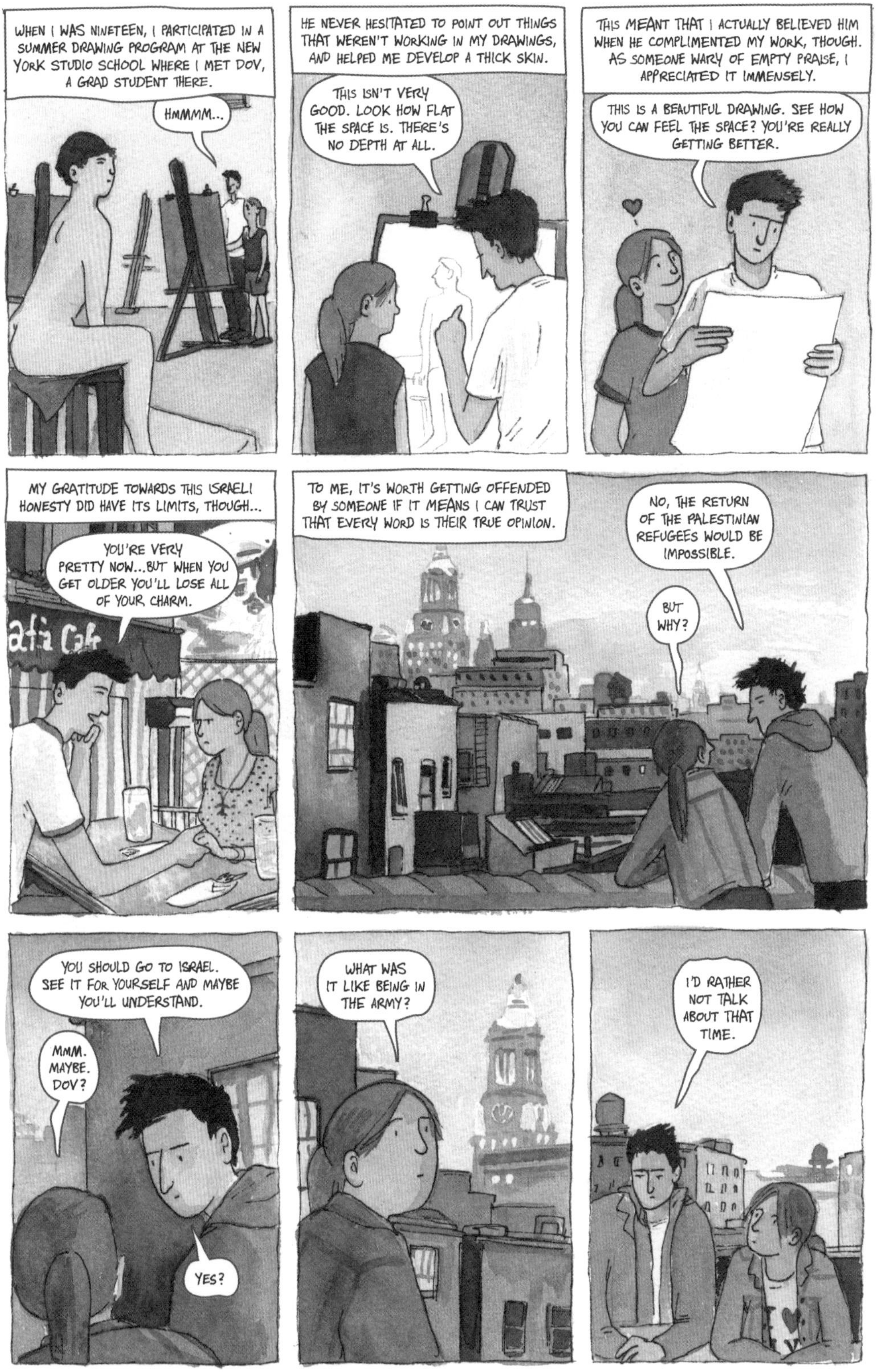
WHEN I WAS NINETEEN, I PARTICIPATED IN A SUMMER DRAWING PROGRAM AT THE NEW YORK STUDIO SCHOOL WHERE I MET DOV, A GRAD STUDENT THERE.
HMMMM...
HE NEVER HESITATED TO POINT OUT THINGS THAT WEREN'T WORKING IN MY DRAWINGS, AND HELPED ME DEVELOP A THICK SKIN.
THIS ISN'T VERY GOOD. LOOK HOW FLAT THE SPACE IS. THERE'S NO DEPTH AT ALL.
THIS MEANT THAT I ACTUALLY BELIEVED HIM WHEN HE COMPLIMENTED MY WORK, THOUGH. AS SOMEONE WARY OF EMPTY PRAISE, I APPRECIATED IT IMMENSELY.
THIS IS A BEAUTIFUL DRAWING. SEE HOW YOU CAN FEEL THE SPACE? YOU'RE REALLY GETTING BETTER.
MY GRATITUDE TOWARDS THIS ISRAELI HONESTY DID HAVE ITS LIMITS, THOUGH...
YOU'RE VERY PRETTY NOW...BUT WHEN YOU GET OLDER YOU'LL LOSE ALL OF YOUR CHARM.
afia Caf
TO ME, IT'S WORTH GETTING OFFENDED BY SOMEONE IF IT MEANS I CAN TRUST THAT EVERY WORD IS THEIR TRUE OPINION.
NO, THE RETURN OF THE PALESTINIAN REFUGEES WOULD BE IMPOSSIBLE.
BUT WHY?
YOU SHOULD GO TO ISRAEL. SEE IT FOR YOURSELF AND MAYBE YOU'LL UNDERSTAND.
MMM. MAYBE. DOV?
YES?
WHAT WAS IT LIKE BEING IN THE ARMY?
I'D RATHER NOT TALK ABOUT THAT TIME.

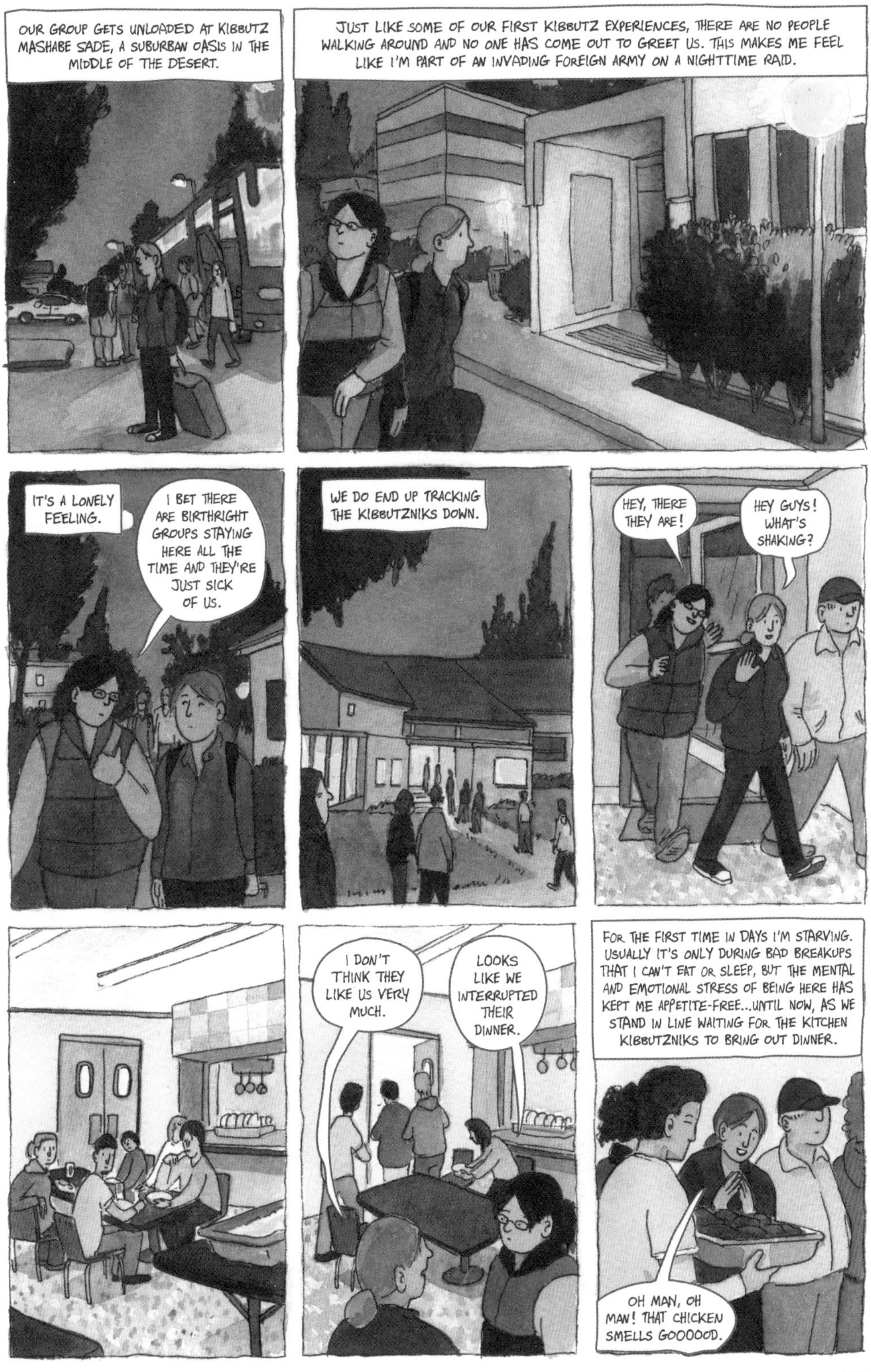
OUR GROUP GETS UNLOADED AT KIBBUTZ MASHABE SADE, A SUBURBAN OASIS IN THE MIDDLE OF THE DESERT.
JUST LIKE SOME OF OUR FIRST KIBBUTZ EXPERIENCES, THERE ARE NO PEOPLE WALKING AROUND AND NO ONE HAS COME OUT TO GREET US. THIS MAKES ME FEEL LIKE I'M PART OF AN INVADING FOREIGN ARMY ON A NIGHTTIME RAID.
IT'S A LONELY FEELING.
I BET THERE ARE BIRTHRIGHT GROUPS STAYING HERE ALL THE TIME AND THEY'RE JUST SICK OF US.
WE DO END UP TRACKING THE KIBBUTZNIKS DOWN.
HEY, THERE THEY ARE!
HEY GUYS! WHAT'S SHAKING?
I DON'T THINK THEY LIKE US VERY MUCH.
LOOKS LIKE WE INTERRUPTED THEIR DINNER.
FOR THE FIRST TIME IN DAYS I'M STARVING. USUALLY IT'S ONLY DURING BAD BREAKUPS THAT I CAN'T EAT OR SLEEP, BUT THE MENTAL AND EMOTIONAL STRESS OF BEING HERE HAS KEPT ME APPETITE-FREE...UNTIL NOW, AS WE STAND IN LINE WAITING FOR THE KITCHEN KIBBUTZNIKS TO BRING OUT DINNER.
OH MAN, OH MAN! THAT CHICKEN SMELLS GOOOOOD.

138

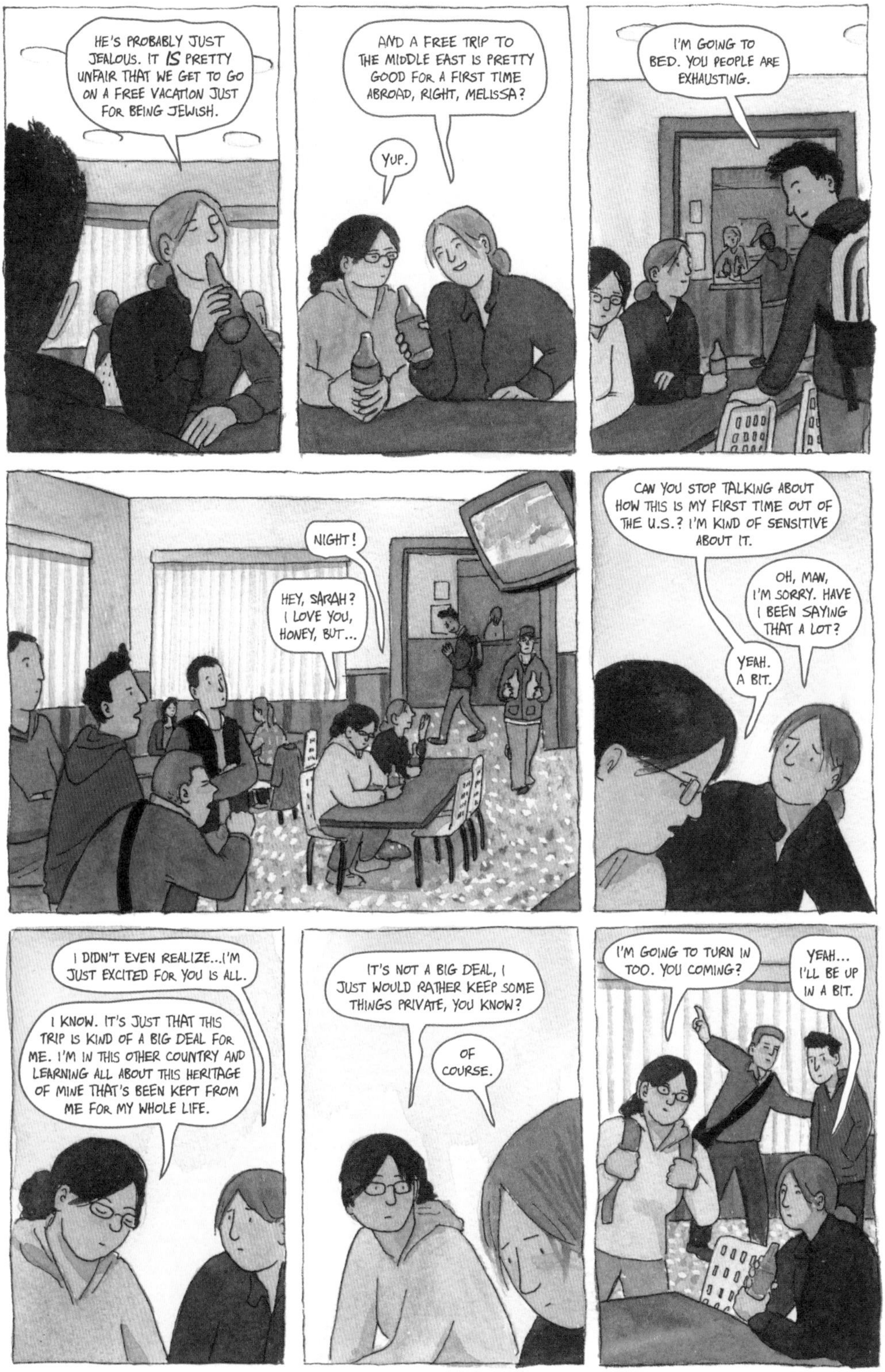
HE'S PROBABLY JUST JEALOUS. IT IS PRETTY UNFAIR THAT WE GET TO GO ON A FREE VACATION JUST FOR BEING JEWISH.
AND A FREE TRIP TO THE MIDDLE EAST IS PRETTY GOOD FOR A FIRST TIME ABROAD, RIGHT, MELISSA?
YUP.
I'M GOING TO BED. YOU PEOPLE ARE EXHAUSTING.
NIGHT!
HEY, SARAH? I LOVE YOU, HONEY, BUT...
CAN YOU STOP TALKING ABOUT HOW THIS IS MY FIRST TIME OUT OF THE U.S.? I'M KIND OF SENSITIVE ABOUT IT.
OH, MAN, I'M SORRY. HAVE I BEEN SAYING THAT A LOT?
YEAH. A BIT.
I DIDN'T EVEN REALIZE...I'M JUST EXCITED FOR YOU IS ALL.
I KNOW. IT'S JUST THAT THIS TRIP IS KIND OF A BIG DEAL FOR ME. I'M IN THIS OTHER COUNTRY AND LEARNING ALL ABOUT THIS HERITAGE OF MINE THAT'S BEEN KEPT FROM ME FOR MY WHOLE LIFE.
IT'S NOT A BIG DEAL, I JUST WOULD RATHER KEEP SOME THINGS PRIVATE, YOU KNOW?
OF COURSE.
I'M GOING TO TURN IN TOO. YOU COMING?
YEAH... I'LL BE UP IN A BIT.

142

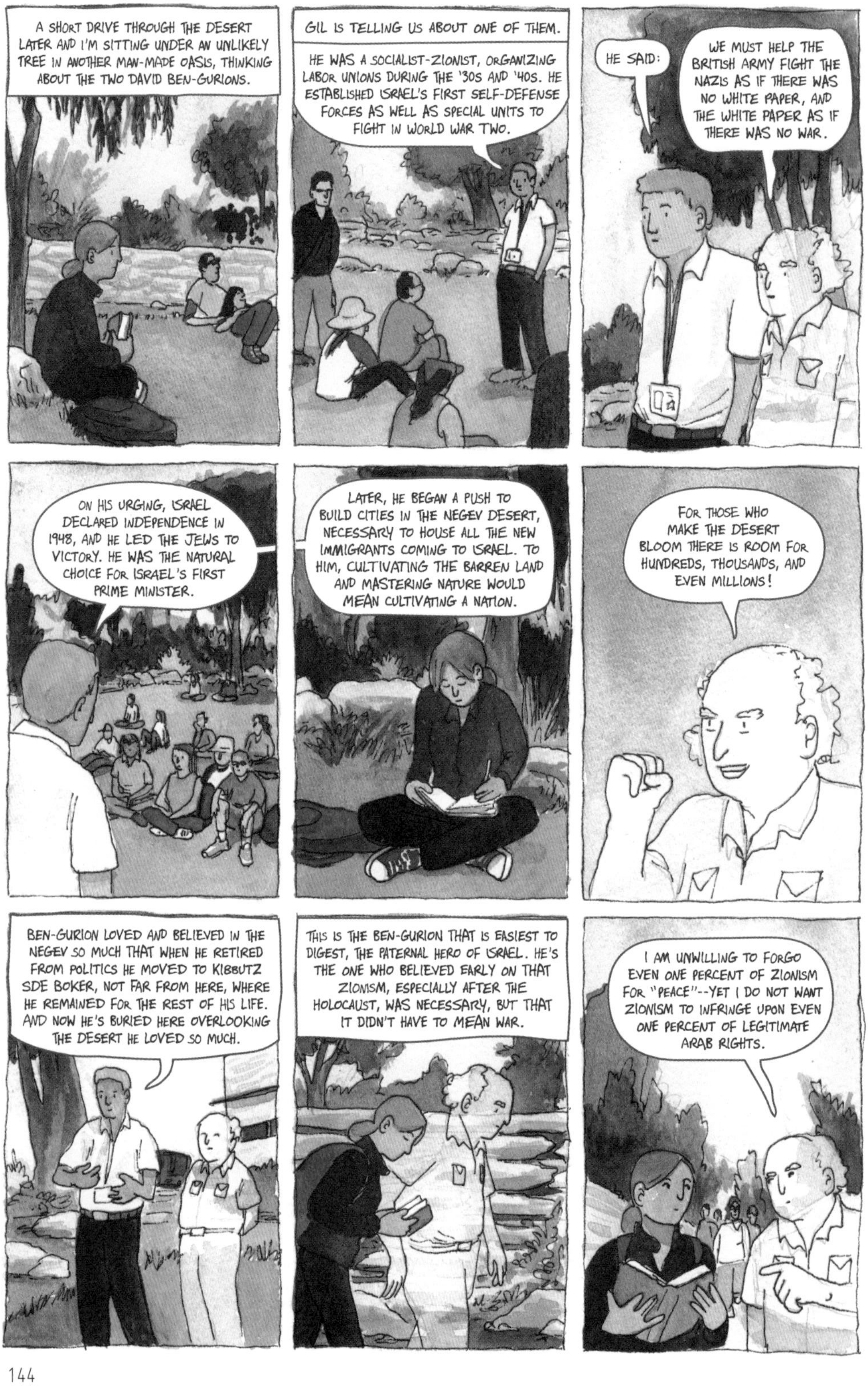
A SHORT DRIVE THROUGH THE DESERT LATER AND I'M SITTING UNDER AN UNLIKELY TREE IN ANOTHER MAN-MADE OASIS, THINKING ABOUT THE TWO DAVID BEN-GURIONS.
GIL IS TELLING US ABOUT ONE OF THEM.
HE WAS A SOCIALIST-ZIONIST, ORGANIZING LABOR UNIONS DURING THE '30S AND '40S. HE ESTABLISHED ISRAEL'S FIRST SELF-DEFENSE FORCES AS WELL AS SPECIAL UNITS TO FIGHT IN WORLD WAR TWO.
HE SAID:
WE MUST HELP THE BRITISH ARMY FIGHT THE NAZIS AS IF THERE WAS NO WHITE PAPER, AND THE WHITE PAPER AS IF THERE WAS NO WAR.
ON HIS URGING, ISRAEL DECLARED INDEPENDENCE IN 1948, AND HE LED THE JEWS TO VICTORY. HE WAS THE NATURAL CHOICE FOR ISRAEL'S FIRST PRIME MINISTER.
LATER, HE BEGAN A PUSH TO BUILD CITIES IN THE NEGEV DESERT, NECESSARY TO HOUSE ALL THE NEW IMMIGRANTS COMING TO ISRAEL. TO HIM, CULTIVATING THE BARREN LAND AND MASTERING NATURE WOULD MEAN CULTIVATING A NATION.
FOR THOSE WHO MAKE THE DESERT BLOOM THERE IS ROOM FOR HUNDREDS, THOUSANDS, AND EVEN MILLIONS!
BEN-GURION LOVED AND BELIEVED IN THE NEGEV SO MUCH THAT WHEN HE RETIRED FROM POLITICS HE MOVED TO KIBBUTZ SDE BOKER, NOT FAR FROM HERE, WHERE HE REMAINED FOR THE REST OF HIS LIFE. AND NOW HE'S BURIED HERE OVERLOOKING THE DESERT HE LOVED SO MUCH.
THIS IS THE BEN-GURION THAT IS EASIEST TO DIGEST, THE PATERNAL HERO OF ISRAEL. HE'S THE ONE WHO BELIEVED EARLY ON THAT ZIONISM, ESPECIALLY AFTER THE HOLOCAUST, WAS NECESSARY, BUT THAT IT DIDN'T HAVE TO MEAN WAR.
I AM UNWILLING TO FORGO EVEN ONE PERCENT OF ZIONISM FOR "PEACE"--YET I DO NOT WANT ZIONISM TO INFRINGE UPON EVEN ONE PERCENT OF LEGITIMATE ARAB RIGHTS.

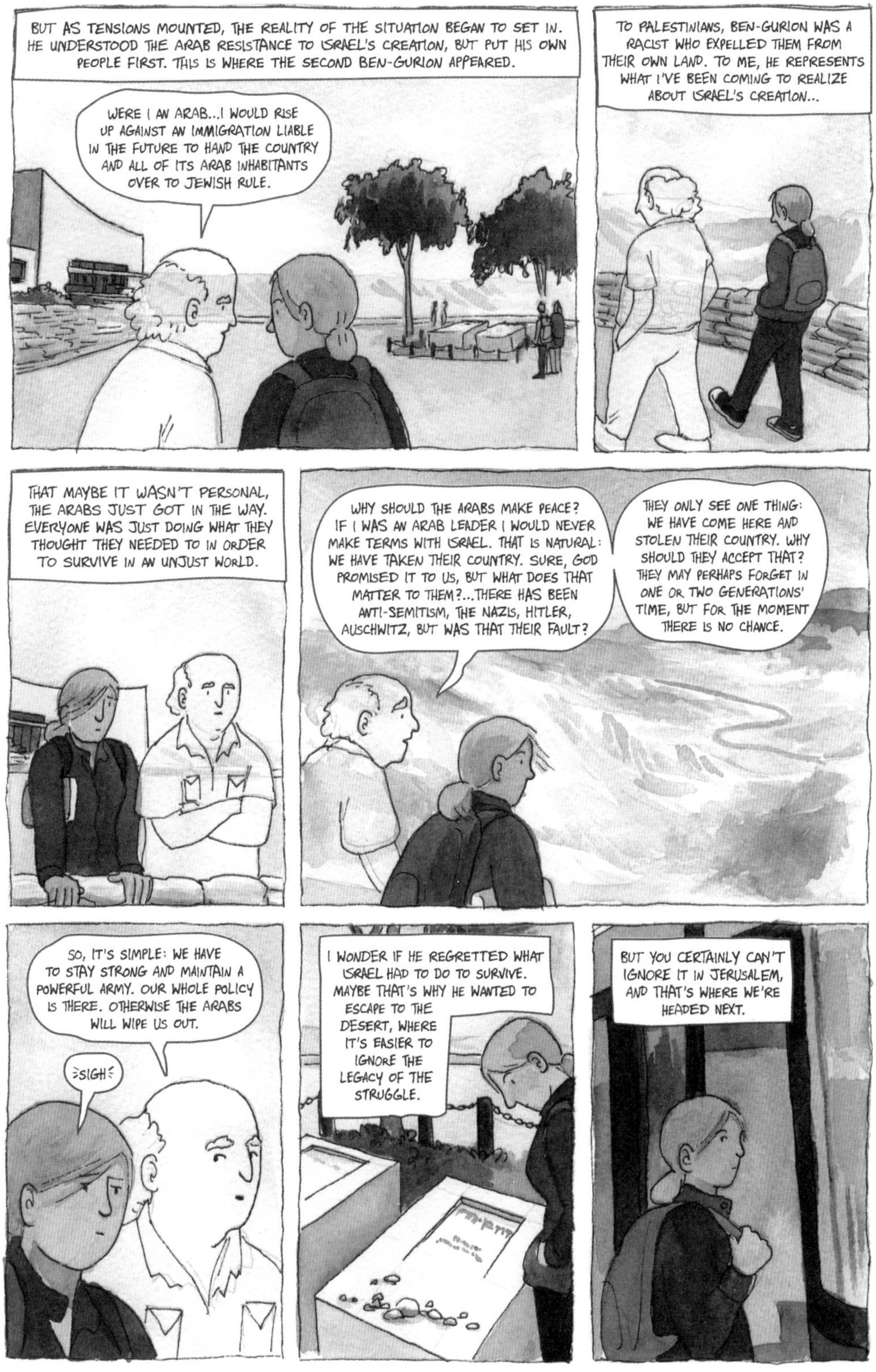

BUT AS TENSIONS MOUNTED, THE REALITY OF THE SITUATION BEGAN TO SET IN. HE UNDERSTOOD THE ARAB RESISTANCE TO ISRAEL'S CREATION, BUT PUT HIS OWN PEOPLE FIRST. THIS IS WHERE THE SECOND BEN-GURION APPEARED.
WERE I AN ARAB...I WOULD RISE UP AGAINST AN IMMIGRATION LIABLE IN THE FUTURE TO HAND THE COUNTRY AND ALL OF ITS ARAB INHABITANTS OVER TO JEWISH RULE.
TO PALESTINIANS, BEN-GURION WAS A RACIST WHO EXPELLED THEM FROM THEIR OWN LAND. TO ME, HE REPRESENTS WHAT I'VE BEEN COMING TO REALIZE ABOUT ISRAEL'S CREATION...
THAT MAYBE IT WASN'T PERSONAL, THE ARABS JUST GOT IN THE WAY. EVERYONE WAS JUST DOING WHAT THEY THOUGHT THEY NEEDED TO IN ORDER TO SURVIVE IN AN UNJUST WORLD.
WHY SHOULD THE ARABS MAKE PEACE? IF I WAS AN ARAB LEADER I WOULD NEVER MAKE TERMS WITH ISRAEL. THAT IS NATURAL: WE HAVE TAKEN THEIR COUNTRY. SURE, GOD PROMISED IT TO US, BUT WHAT DOES THAT MATTER TO THEM?...THERE HAS BEEN ANTI-SEMITISM, THE NAZIS, HITLER, AUSCHWITZ, BUT WAS THAT THEIR FAULT?
THEY ONLY SEE ONE THING: WE HAVE COME HERE AND STOLEN THEIR COUNTRY. WHY SHOULD THEY ACCEPT THAT? THEY MAY PERHAPS FORGET IN ONE OR TWO GENERATIONS' TIME, BUT FOR THE MOMENT THERE IS NO CHANCE.
SO, IT'S SIMPLE: WE HAVE TO STAY STRONG AND MAINTAIN A POWERFUL ARMY. OUR WHOLE POLICY IS THERE. OTHERWISE THE ARABS WILL WIPE US OUT.
SIGH
I WONDER IF HE REGRETTED WHAT ISRAEL HAD TO DO TO SURVIVE. MAYBE THAT'S WHY HE WANTED TO ESCAPE TO THE DESERT, WHERE IT'S EASIER TO IGNORE THE LEGACY OF THE STRUGGLE.
BUT YOU CERTAINLY CAN'T IGNORE IT IN JERUSALEM, AND THAT'S WHERE WE'RE HEADED NEXT.

CHAPTER SIX JERUSALEM

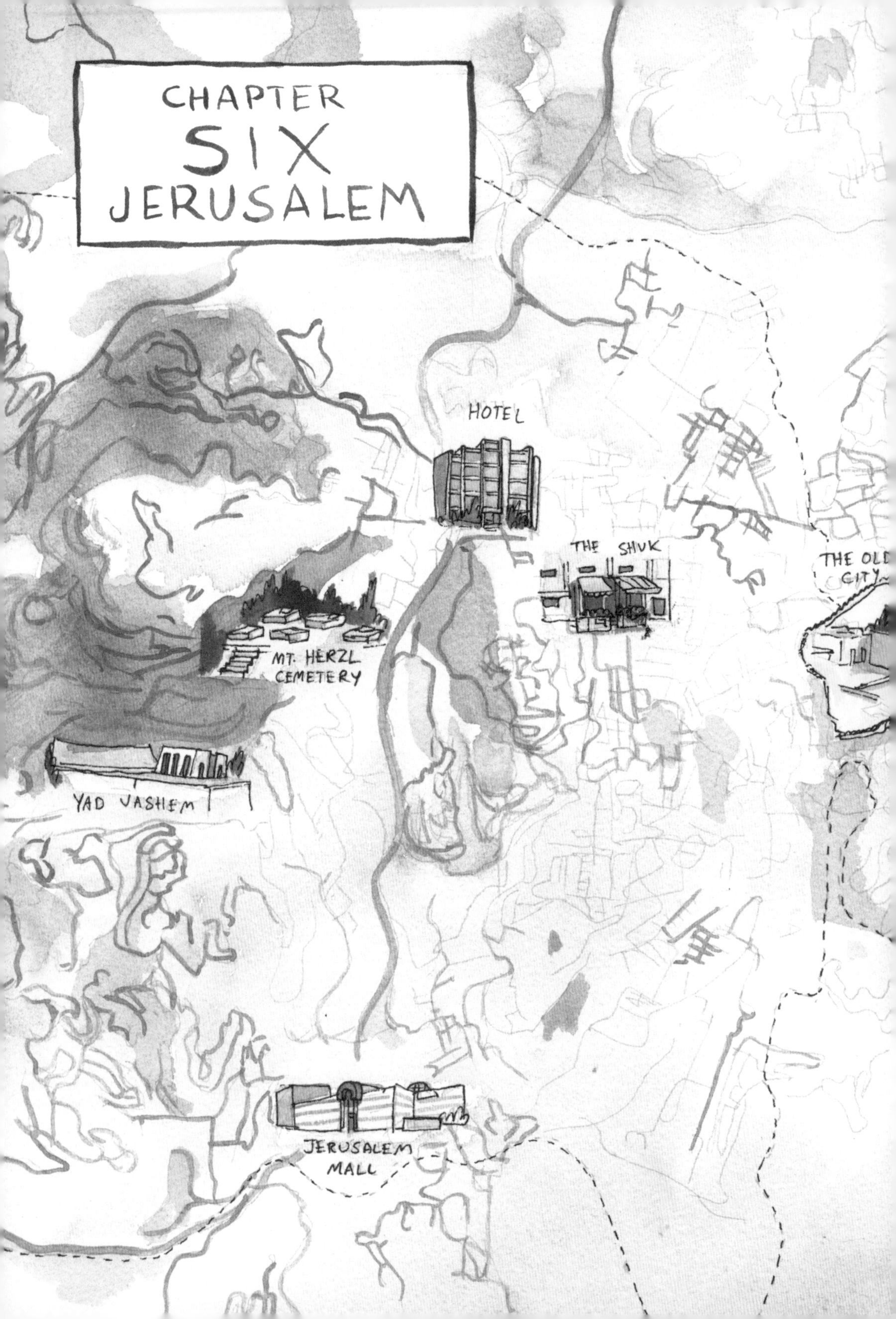
HOTEL
THE SHUK
THE OLD CITY
MT. HERZL CEMETERY
YAD VASHEM
JERUSALEM MALL

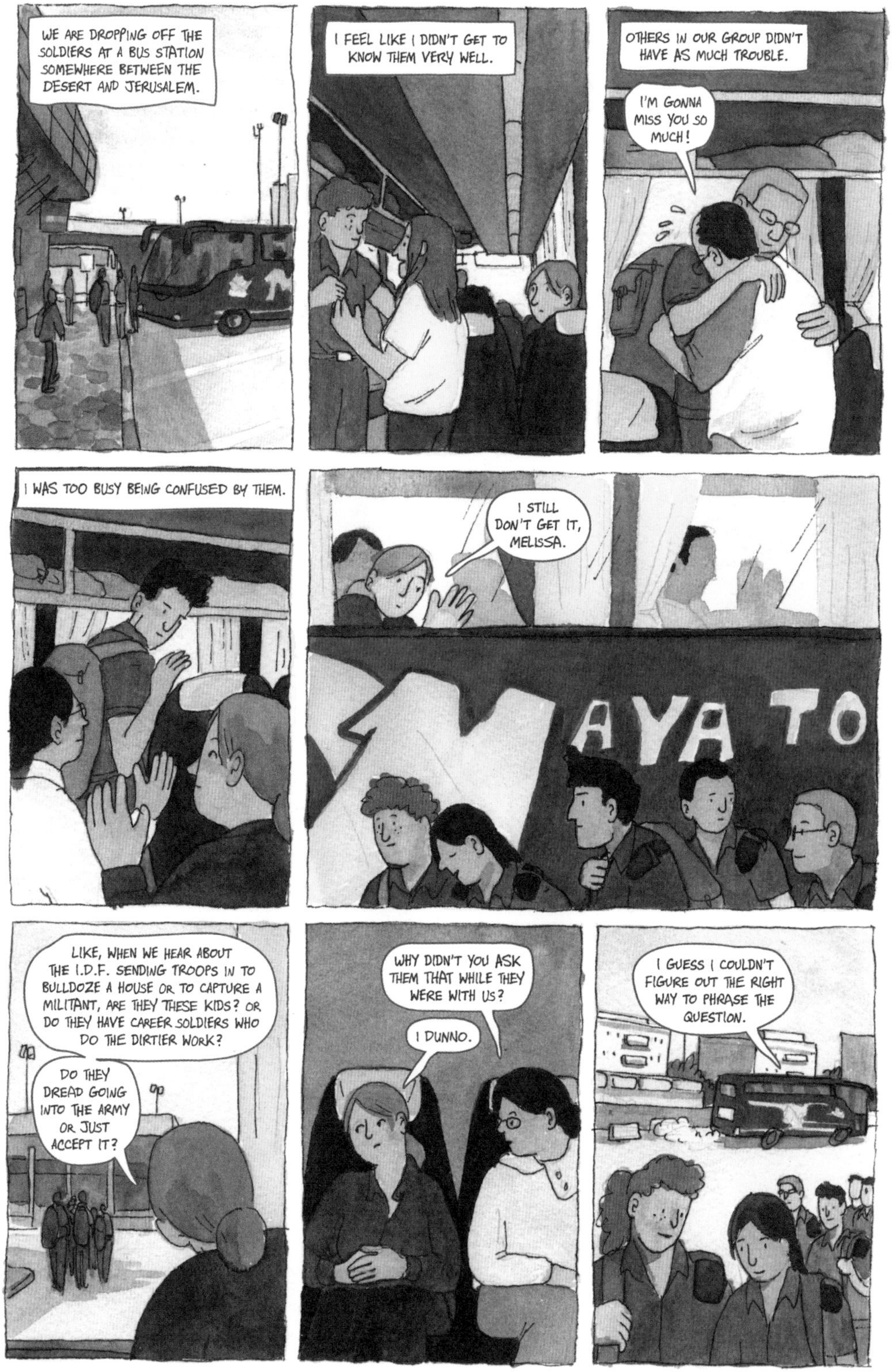
WE ARE DROPPING OFF THE SOLDIERS AT A BUS STATION SOMEWHERE BETWEEN THE DESERT AND JERUSALEM.
I FEEL LIKE I DIDN'T GET TO KNOW THEM VERY WELL.
OTHERS IN OUR GROUP DIDN'T HAVE AS MUCH TROUBLE.
I'M GONNA MISS YOU SO MUCH!
I WAS TOO BUSY BEING CONFUSED BY THEM.
I STILL DON'T GET IT, MELISSA.
AYA TO
LIKE, WHEN WE HEAR ABOUT THE I.D.F. SENDING TROOPS IN TO BULLDOZE A HOUSE OR TO CAPTURE A MILITANT, ARE THEY THESE KIDS? OR DO THEY HAVE CAREER SOLDIERS WHO DO THE DIRTIER WORK?
DO THEY DREAD GOING INTO THE ARMY OR JUST ACCEPT IT?
WHY DIDN'T YOU ASK THEM THAT WHILE THEY WERE WITH US?
I DUNNO.
I GUESS I COULDN'T FIGURE OUT THE RIGHT WAY TO PHRASE THE QUESTION.

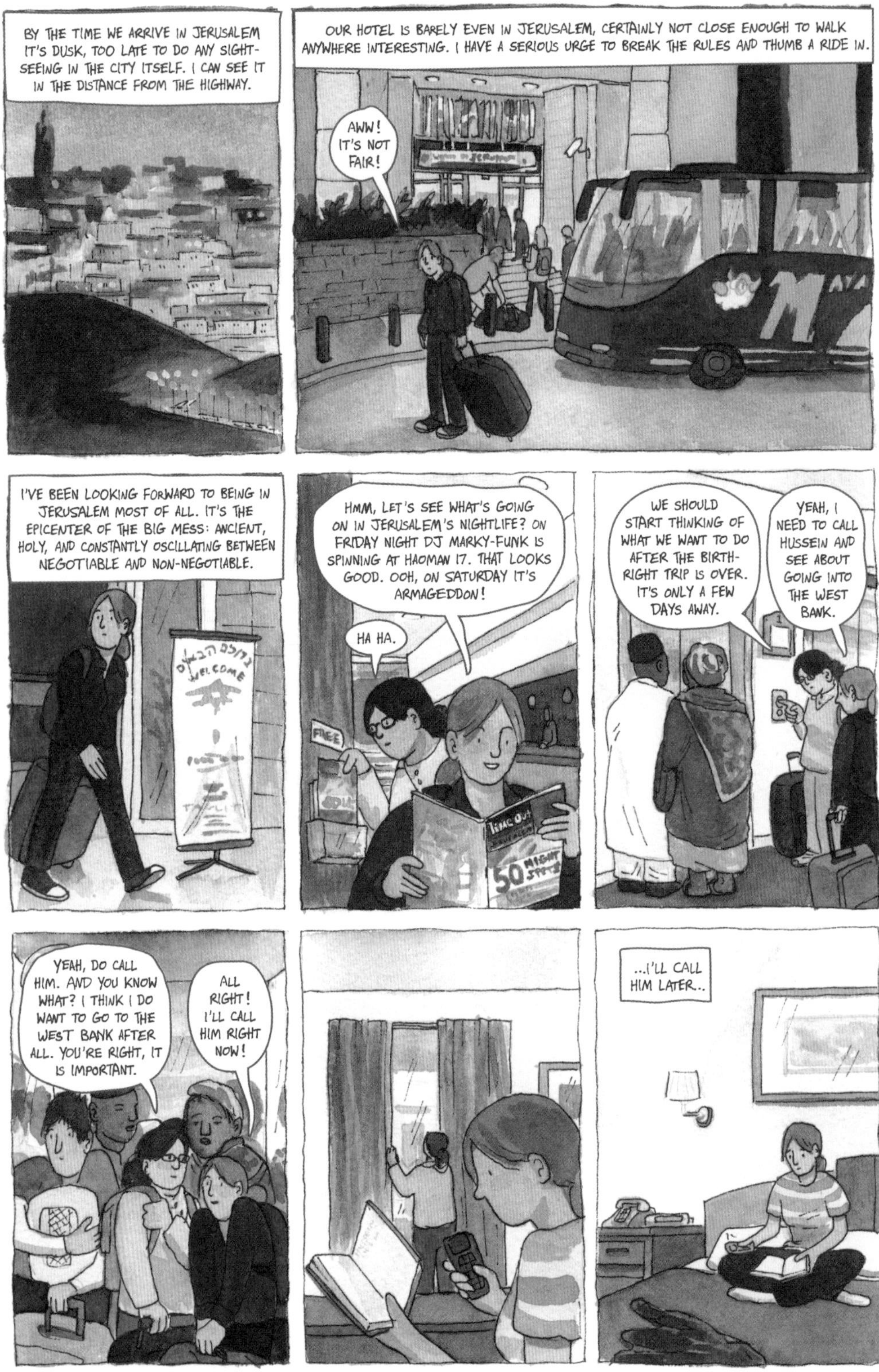

BY THE TIME WE ARRIVE IN JERUSALEM IT'S DUSK, TOO LATE TO DO ANY SIGHT-SEEING IN THE CITY ITSELF. I CAN SEE IT IN THE DISTANCE FROM THE HIGHWAY.
OUR HOTEL IS BARELY EVEN IN JERUSALEM, CERTAINLY NOT CLOSE ENOUGH TO WALK ANYWHERE INTERESTING. I HAVE A SERIOUS URGE TO BREAK THE RULES AND THUMB A RIDE IN.
AWW! IT'S NOT FAIR!
I'VE BEEN LOOKING FORWARD TO BEING IN JERUSALEM MOST OF ALL. IT'S THE EPICENTER OF THE BIG MESS: ANCIENT, HOLY, AND CONSTANTLY OSCILLATING BETWEEN NEGOTIABLE AND NON-NEGOTIABLE.
WELCOME
HMM, LET'S SEE WHAT'S GOING ON IN JERUSALEM'S NIGHTLIFE? ON FRIDAY NIGHT DJ MARKY-FUNK IS SPINNING AT HAOMAN 17. THAT LOOKS GOOD. OOH, ON SATURDAY IT'S ARMAGEDDON!
HA HA.
FREE
TIME OUT
50 NIGHT SPOTS
WE SHOULD START THINKING OF WHAT WE WANT TO DO AFTER THE BIRTH-RIGHT TRIP IS OVER. IT'S ONLY A FEW DAYS AWAY.
YEAH, I NEED TO CALL HUSSEIN AND SEE ABOUT GOING INTO THE WEST BANK.
YEAH, DO CALL HIM. AND YOU KNOW WHAT? I THINK I DO WANT TO GO TO THE WEST BANK AFTER ALL. YOU'RE RIGHT, IT IS IMPORTANT.
ALL RIGHT! I'LL CALL HIM RIGHT NOW!
...I'LL CALL HIM LATER...

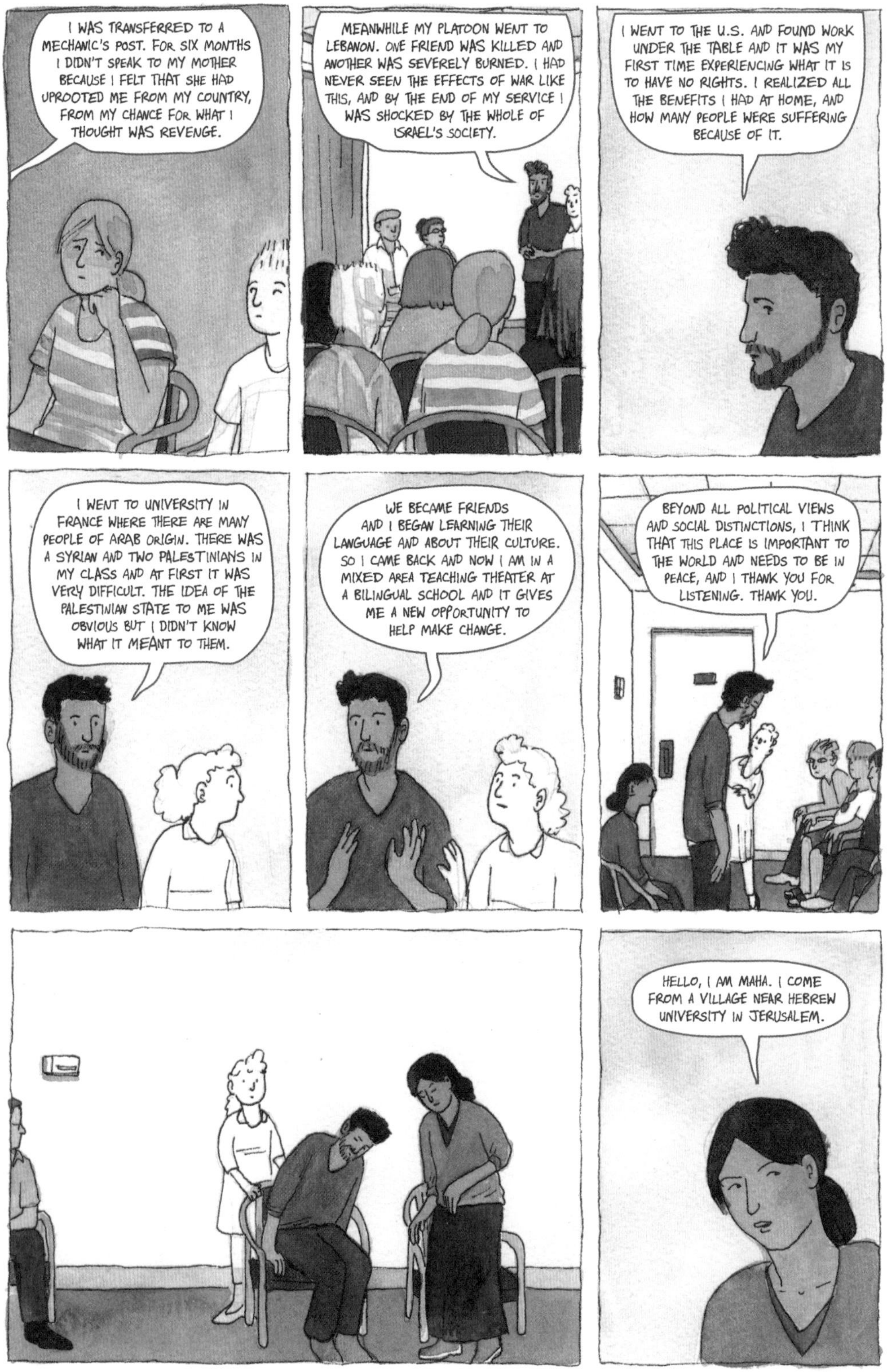
I WAS TRANSFERRED TO A MECHANIC'S POST. FOR SIX MONTHS I DIDN'T SPEAK TO MY MOTHER BECAUSE I FELT THAT SHE HAD UPROOTED ME FROM MY COUNTRY, FROM MY CHANCE FOR WHAT I THOUGHT WAS REVENGE.
MEANWHILE MY PLATOON WENT TO LEBANON. ONE FRIEND WAS KILLED AND ANOTHER WAS SEVERELY BURNED. I HAD NEVER SEEN THE EFFECTS OF WAR LIKE THIS, AND BY THE END OF MY SERVICE I WAS SHOCKED BY THE WHOLE OF ISRAEL'S SOCIETY.
I WENT TO THE U.S. AND FOUND WORK UNDER THE TABLE AND IT WAS MY FIRST TIME EXPERIENCING WHAT IT IS TO HAVE NO RIGHTS. I REALIZED ALL THE BENEFITS I HAD AT HOME, AND HOW MANY PEOPLE WERE SUFFERING BECAUSE OF IT.
I WENT TO UNIVERSITY IN FRANCE WHERE THERE ARE MANY PEOPLE OF ARAB ORIGIN. THERE WAS A SYRIAN AND TWO PALESTINIANS IN MY CLASS AND AT FIRST IT WAS VERY DIFFICULT. THE IDEA OF THE PALESTINIAN STATE TO ME WAS OBVIOUS BUT I DIDN'T KNOW WHAT IT MEANT TO THEM.
WE BECAME FRIENDS AND I BEGAN LEARNING THEIR LANGUAGE AND ABOUT THEIR CULTURE. SO I CAME BACK AND NOW I AM IN A MIXED AREA TEACHING THEATER AT A BILINGUAL SCHOOL AND IT GIVES ME A NEW OPPORTUNITY TO HELP MAKE CHANGE.
BEYOND ALL POLITICAL VIEWS AND SOCIAL DISTINCTIONS, I THINK THAT THIS PLACE IS IMPORTANT TO THE WORLD AND NEEDS TO BE IN PEACE, AND I THANK YOU FOR LISTENING. THANK YOU.
HELLO, I AM MAHA. I COME FROM A VILLAGE NEAR HEBREW UNIVERSITY IN JERUSALEM.

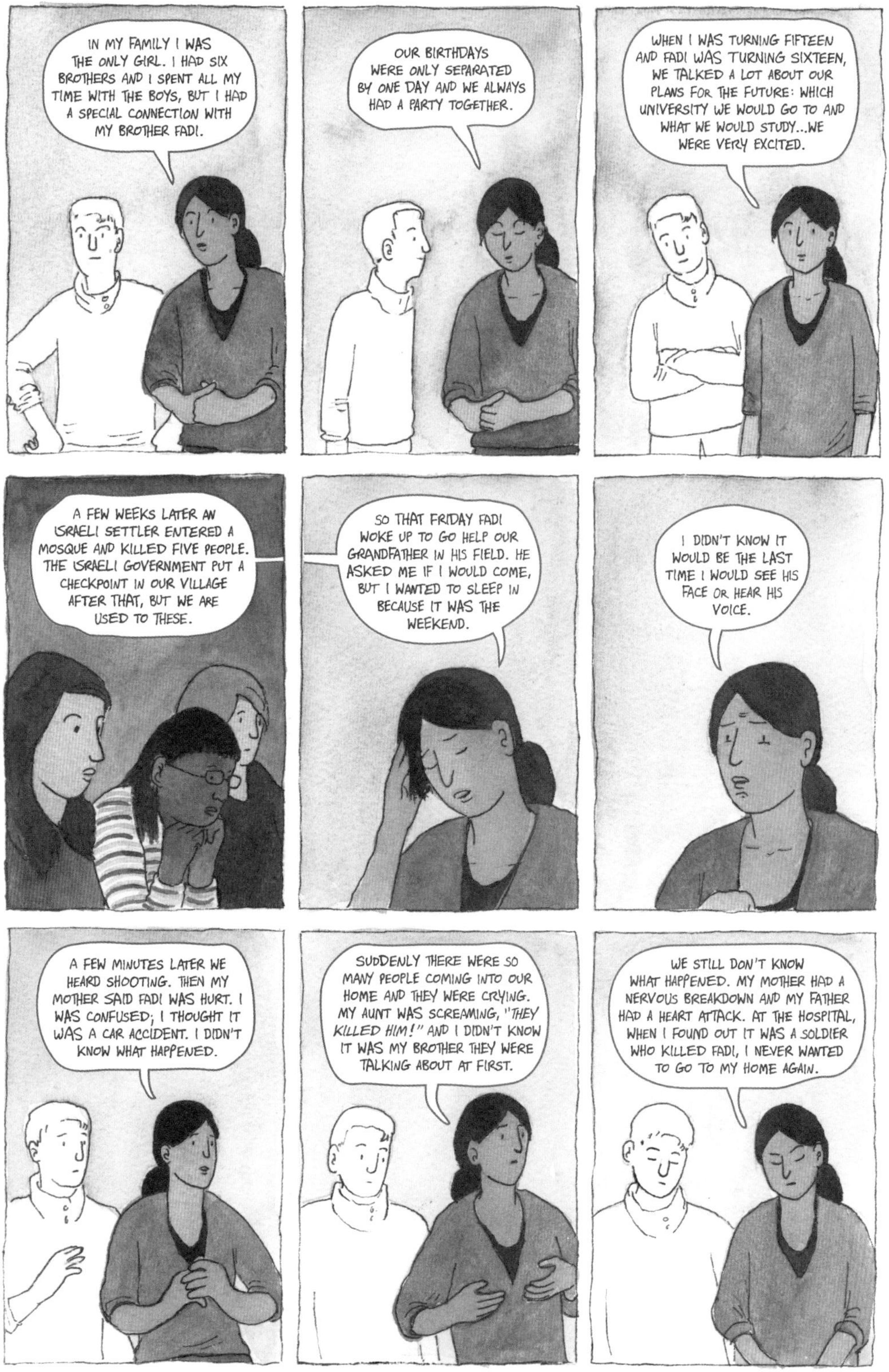
IN MY FAMILY I WAS THE ONLY GIRL. I HAD SIX BROTHERS AND I SPENT ALL MY TIME WITH THE BOYS, BUT I HAD A SPECIAL CONNECTION WITH MY BROTHER FADI.
OUR BIRTHDAYS WERE ONLY SEPARATED BY ONE DAY AND WE ALWAYS HAD A PARTY TOGETHER.
WHEN I WAS TURNING FIFTEEN AND FADI WAS TURNING SIXTEEN, WE TALKED A LOT ABOUT OUR PLANS FOR THE FUTURE: WHICH UNIVERSITY WE WOULD GO TO AND WHAT WE WOULD STUDY...WE WERE VERY EXCITED.
A FEW WEEKS LATER AN ISRAELI SETTLER ENTERED A MOSQUE AND KILLED FIVE PEOPLE. THE ISRAELI GOVERNMENT PUT A CHECKPOINT IN OUR VILLAGE AFTER THAT, BUT WE ARE USED TO THESE.
SO THAT FRIDAY FADI WOKE UP TO GO HELP OUR GRANDFATHER IN HIS FIELD. HE ASKED ME IF I WOULD COME, BUT I WANTED TO SLEEP IN BECAUSE IT WAS THE WEEKEND.
I DIDN'T KNOW IT WOULD BE THE LAST TIME I WOULD SEE HIS FACE OR HEAR HIS VOICE.
A FEW MINUTES LATER WE HEARD SHOOTING. THEN MY MOTHER SAID FADI WAS HURT. I WAS CONFUSED; I THOUGHT IT WAS A CAR ACCIDENT. I DIDN'T KNOW WHAT HAPPENED.
SUDDENLY THERE WERE SO MANY PEOPLE COMING INTO OUR HOME AND THEY WERE CRYING. MY AUNT WAS SCREAMING, "*THEY KILLED HIM!*" AND I DIDN'T KNOW IT WAS MY BROTHER THEY WERE TALKING ABOUT AT FIRST.
WE STILL DON'T KNOW WHAT HAPPENED. MY MOTHER HAD A NERVOUS BREAKDOWN AND MY FATHER HAD A HEART ATTACK. AT THE HOSPITAL, WHEN I FOUND OUT IT WAS A SOLDIER WHO KILLED FADI, I NEVER WANTED TO GO TO MY HOME AGAIN.

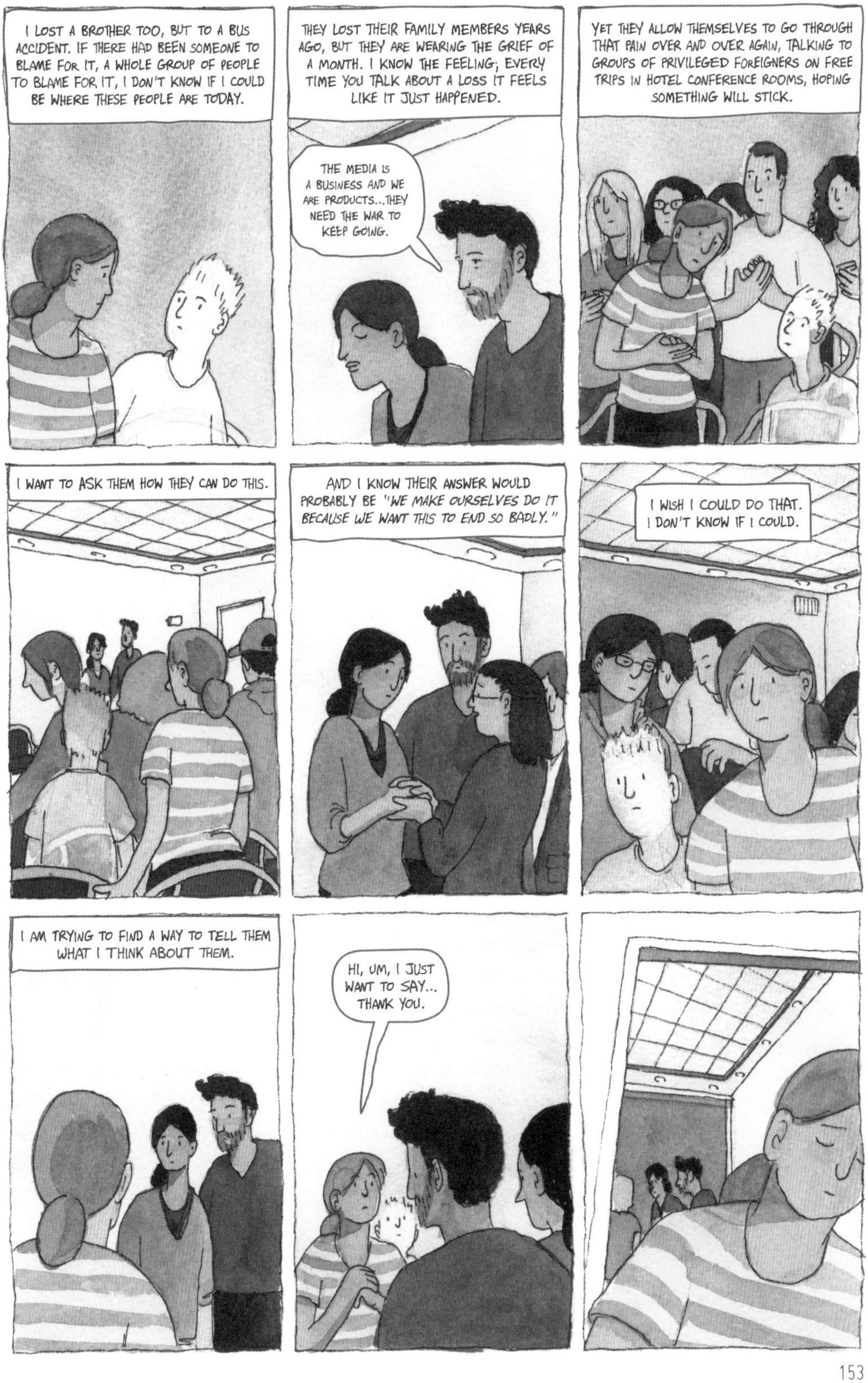
I LOST A BROTHER TOO, BUT TO A BUS ACCIDENT. IF THERE HAD BEEN SOMEONE TO BLAME FOR IT, A WHOLE GROUP OF PEOPLE TO BLAME FOR IT, I DON'T KNOW IF I COULD BE WHERE THESE PEOPLE ARE TODAY.
THEY LOST THEIR FAMILY MEMBERS YEARS AGO, BUT THEY ARE WEARING THE GRIEF OF A MONTH. I KNOW THE FEELING; EVERY TIME YOU TALK ABOUT A LOSS IT FEELS LIKE IT JUST HAPPENED.
THE MEDIA IS A BUSINESS AND WE ARE PRODUCTS... THEY NEED THE WAR TO KEEP GOING.
YET THEY ALLOW THEMSELVES TO GO THROUGH THAT PAIN OVER AND OVER AGAIN, TALKING TO GROUPS OF PRIVILEGED FOREIGNERS ON FREE TRIPS IN HOTEL CONFERENCE ROOMS, HOPING SOMETHING WILL STICK.
I WANT TO ASK THEM HOW THEY CAN DO THIS.
AND I KNOW THEIR ANSWER WOULD PROBABLY BE "WE MAKE OURSELVES DO IT BECAUSE WE WANT THIS TO END SO BADLY."
I WISH I COULD DO THAT. I DON'T KNOW IF I COULD.
I AM TRYING TO FIND A WAY TO TELL THEM WHAT I THINK ABOUT THEM.
HI, UM, I JUST WANT TO SAY... THANK YOU.

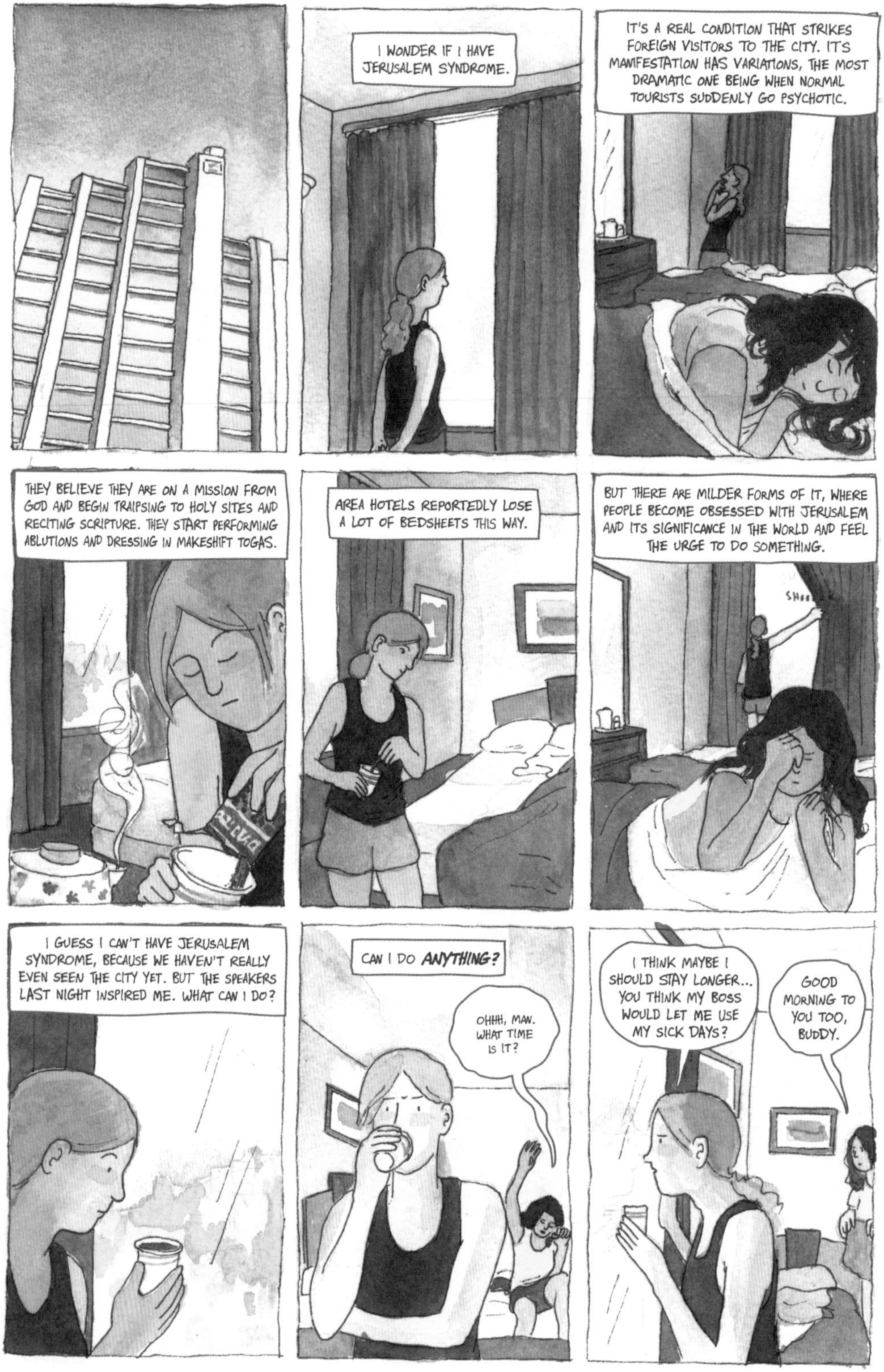
I WONDER IF I HAVE JERUSALEM SYNDROME.
IT'S A REAL CONDITION THAT STRIKES FOREIGN VISITORS TO THE CITY. ITS MANIFESTATION HAS VARIATIONS, THE MOST DRAMATIC ONE BEING WHEN NORMAL TOURISTS SUDDENLY GO PSYCHOTIC.
THEY BELIEVE THEY ARE ON A MISSION FROM GOD AND BEGIN TRAIPSING TO HOLY SITES AND RECITING SCRIPTURE. THEY START PERFORMING ABLUTIONS AND DRESSING IN MAKESHIFT TOGAS.
AREA HOTELS REPORTEDLY LOSE A LOT OF BEDSHEETS THIS WAY.
BUT THERE ARE MILDER FORMS OF IT, WHERE PEOPLE BECOME OBSESSED WITH JERUSALEM AND ITS SIGNIFICANCE IN THE WORLD AND FEEL THE URGE TO DO SOMETHING.
I GUESS I CAN'T HAVE JERUSALEM SYNDROME, BECAUSE WE HAVEN'T REALLY EVEN SEEN THE CITY YET. BUT THE SPEAKERS LAST NIGHT INSPIRED ME. WHAT CAN I DO?
CAN I DO ***ANYTHING?***
OHHH, MAN. WHAT TIME IS IT?
I THINK MAYBE I SHOULD STAY LONGER... YOU THINK MY BOSS WOULD LET ME USE MY SICK DAYS?
GOOD MORNING TO YOU TOO, BUDDY.

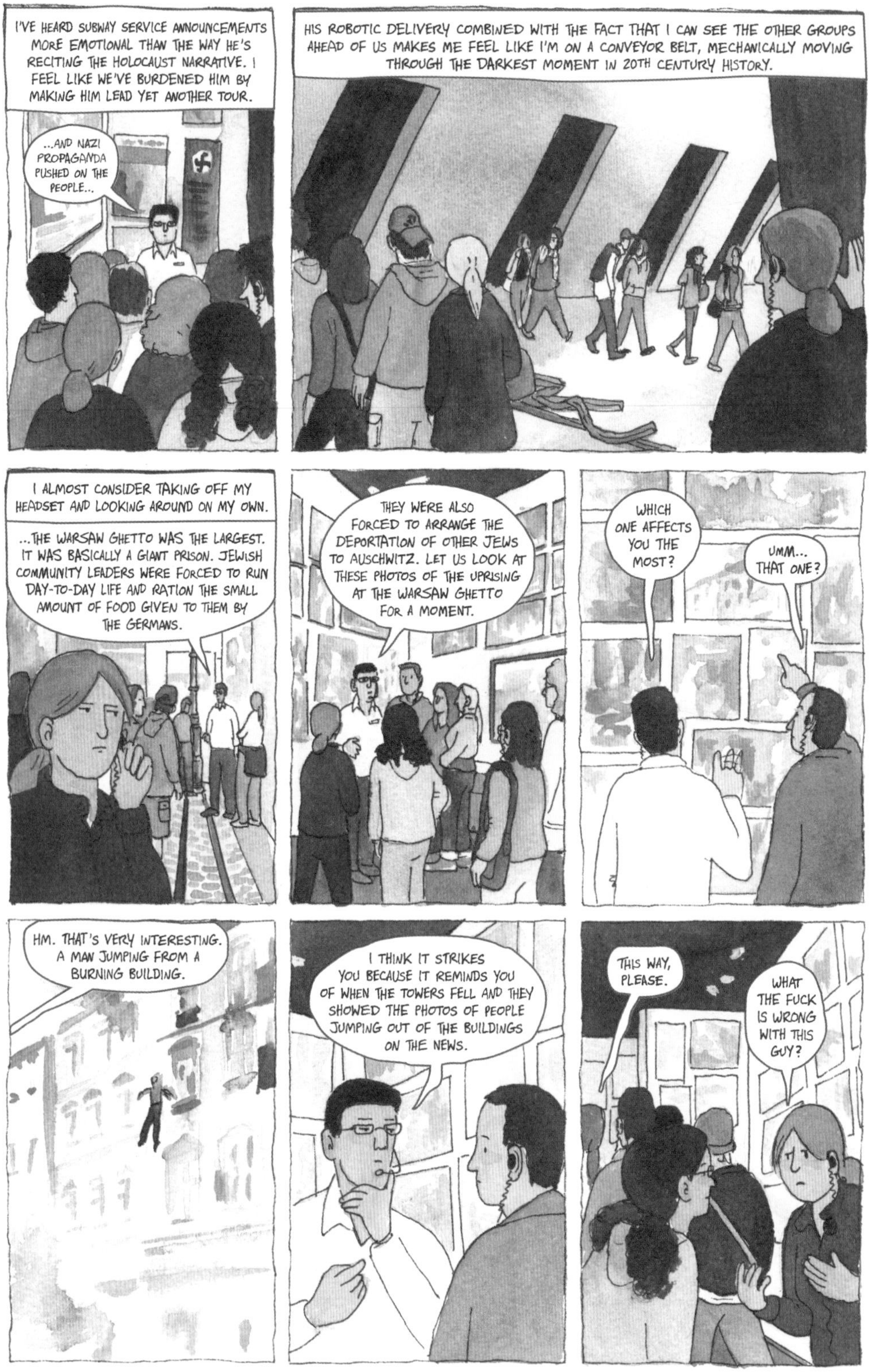
I'VE HEARD SUBWAY SERVICE ANNOUNCEMENTS MORE EMOTIONAL THAN THE WAY HE'S RECITING THE HOLOCAUST NARRATIVE. I FEEL LIKE WE'VE BURDENED HIM BY MAKING HIM LEAD YET ANOTHER TOUR.
...AND NAZI PROPAGANDA PUSHED ON THE PEOPLE...
HIS ROBOTIC DELIVERY COMBINED WITH THE FACT THAT I CAN SEE THE OTHER GROUPS AHEAD OF US MAKES ME FEEL LIKE I'M ON A CONVEYOR BELT, MECHANICALLY MOVING THROUGH THE DARKEST MOMENT IN 20TH CENTURY HISTORY.
I ALMOST CONSIDER TAKING OFF MY HEADSET AND LOOKING AROUND ON MY OWN.
...THE WARSAW GHETTO WAS THE LARGEST. IT WAS BASICALLY A GIANT PRISON. JEWISH COMMUNITY LEADERS WERE FORCED TO RUN DAY-TO-DAY LIFE AND RATION THE SMALL AMOUNT OF FOOD GIVEN TO THEM BY THE GERMANS.
THEY WERE ALSO FORCED TO ARRANGE THE DEPORTATION OF OTHER JEWS TO AUSCHWITZ. LET US LOOK AT THESE PHOTOS OF THE UPRISING AT THE WARSAW GHETTO FOR A MOMENT.
WHICH ONE AFFECTS YOU THE MOST?
UMM... THAT ONE?
HM. THAT'S VERY INTERESTING. A MAN JUMPING FROM A BURNING BUILDING.
I THINK IT STRIKES YOU BECAUSE IT REMINDS YOU OF WHEN THE TOWERS FELL AND THEY SHOWED THE PHOTOS OF PEOPLE JUMPING OUT OF THE BUILDINGS ON THE NEWS.
THIS WAY, PLEASE.
WHAT THE FUCK IS WRONG WITH THIS GUY?

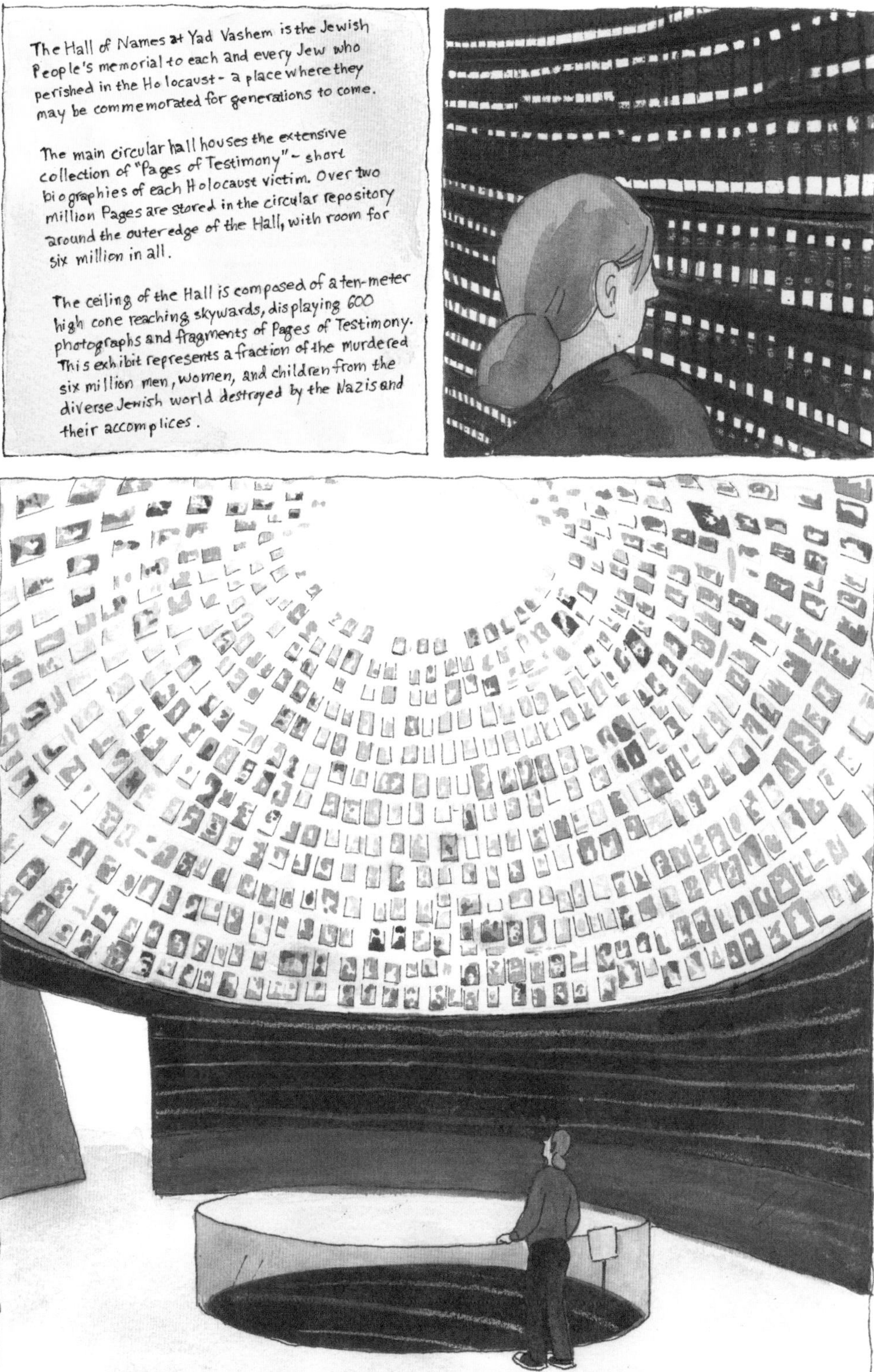
The Hall of Names at Yad Vashem is the Jewish People's memorial to each and every Jew who perished in the Holocaust - a place where they may be commemorated for generations to come.
The main circular hall houses the extensive collection of "Pages of Testimony" - short biographies of each Holocaust victim. Over two million Pages are stored in the circular repository around the outer edge of the Hall, with room for six million in all.
The ceiling of the Hall is composed of a ten-meter high cone reaching skywards, displaying 600 photographs and fragments of Pages of Testimony. This exhibit represents a fraction of the murdered six million men, women, and children from the diverse Jewish world destroyed by the Nazis and their accomplices.

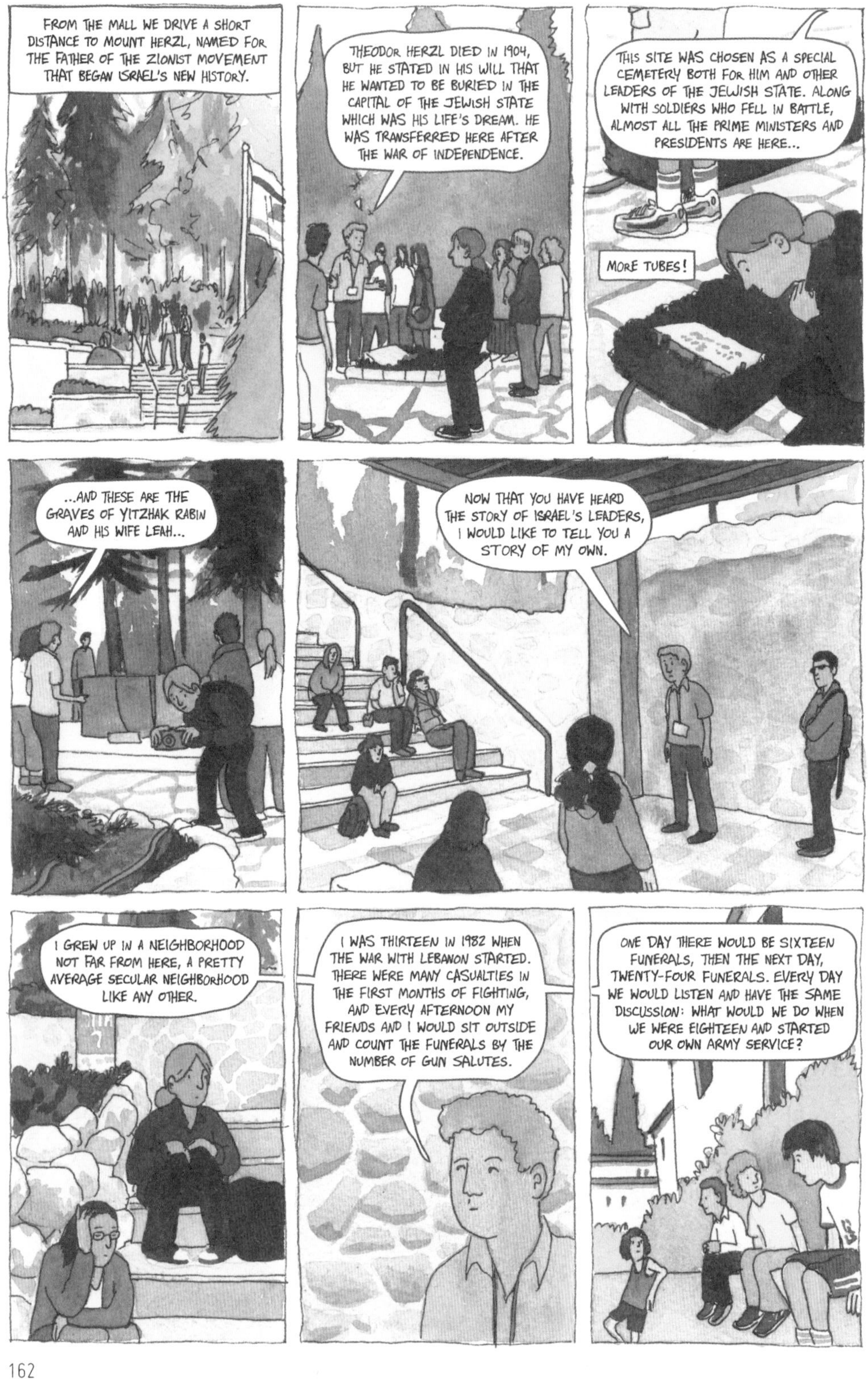
FROM THE MALL WE DRIVE A SHORT DISTANCE TO MOUNT HERZL, NAMED FOR THE FATHER OF THE ZIONIST MOVEMENT THAT BEGAN ISRAEL'S NEW HISTORY.
THEODOR HERZL DIED IN 1904, BUT HE STATED IN HIS WILL THAT HE WANTED TO BE BURIED IN THE CAPITAL OF THE JEWISH STATE WHICH WAS HIS LIFE'S DREAM. HE WAS TRANSFERRED HERE AFTER THE WAR OF INDEPENDENCE.
THIS SITE WAS CHOSEN AS A SPECIAL CEMETERY BOTH FOR HIM AND OTHER LEADERS OF THE JEWISH STATE. ALONG WITH SOLDIERS WHO FELL IN BATTLE, ALMOST ALL THE PRIME MINISTERS AND PRESIDENTS ARE HERE...
MORE TUBES!
...AND THESE ARE THE GRAVES OF YITZHAK RABIN AND HIS WIFE LEAH...
NOW THAT YOU HAVE HEARD THE STORY OF ISRAEL'S LEADERS, I WOULD LIKE TO TELL YOU A STORY OF MY OWN.
I GREW UP IN A NEIGHBORHOOD NOT FAR FROM HERE, A PRETTY AVERAGE SECULAR NEIGHBORHOOD LIKE ANY OTHER.
I WAS THIRTEEN IN 1982 WHEN THE WAR WITH LEBANON STARTED. THERE WERE MANY CASUALTIES IN THE FIRST MONTHS OF FIGHTING, AND EVERY AFTERNOON MY FRIENDS AND I WOULD SIT OUTSIDE AND COUNT THE FUNERALS BY THE NUMBER OF GUN SALUTES.
ONE DAY THERE WOULD BE SIXTEEN FUNERALS, THEN THE NEXT DAY, TWENTY-FOUR FUNERALS. EVERY DAY WE WOULD LISTEN AND HAVE THE SAME DISCUSSION: WHAT WOULD WE DO WHEN WE WERE EIGHTEEN AND STARTED OUR OWN ARMY SERVICE?

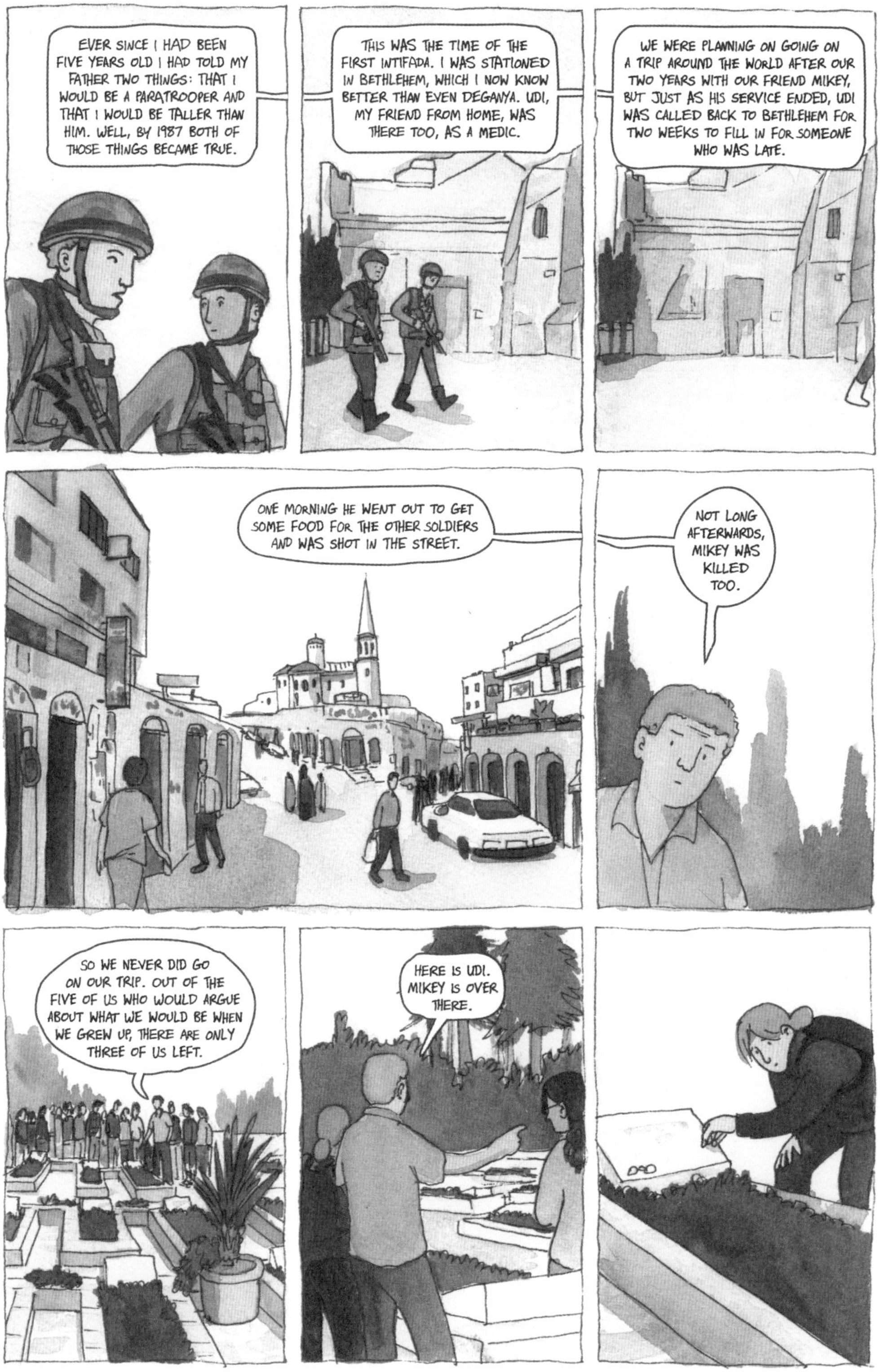
EVER SINCE I HAD BEEN FIVE YEARS OLD I HAD TOLD MY FATHER TWO THINGS: THAT I WOULD BE A PARATROOPER AND THAT I WOULD BE TALLER THAN HIM. WELL, BY 1987 BOTH OF THOSE THINGS BECAME TRUE.
THIS WAS THE TIME OF THE FIRST INTIFADA. I WAS STATIONED IN BETHLEHEM, WHICH I NOW KNOW BETTER THAN EVEN DEGANYA. UDI, MY FRIEND FROM HOME, WAS THERE TOO, AS A MEDIC.
WE WERE PLANNING ON GOING ON A TRIP AROUND THE WORLD AFTER OUR TWO YEARS WITH OUR FRIEND MIKEY, BUT JUST AS HIS SERVICE ENDED, UDI WAS CALLED BACK TO BETHLEHEM FOR TWO WEEKS TO FILL IN FOR SOMEONE WHO WAS LATE.
ONE MORNING HE WENT OUT TO GET SOME FOOD FOR THE OTHER SOLDIERS AND WAS SHOT IN THE STREET.
NOT LONG AFTERWARDS, MIKEY WAS KILLED TOO.
SO WE NEVER DID GO ON OUR TRIP. OUT OF THE FIVE OF US WHO WOULD ARGUE ABOUT WHAT WE WOULD BE WHEN WE GREW UP, THERE ARE ONLY THREE OF US LEFT.
HERE IS UDI. MIKEY IS OVER THERE.

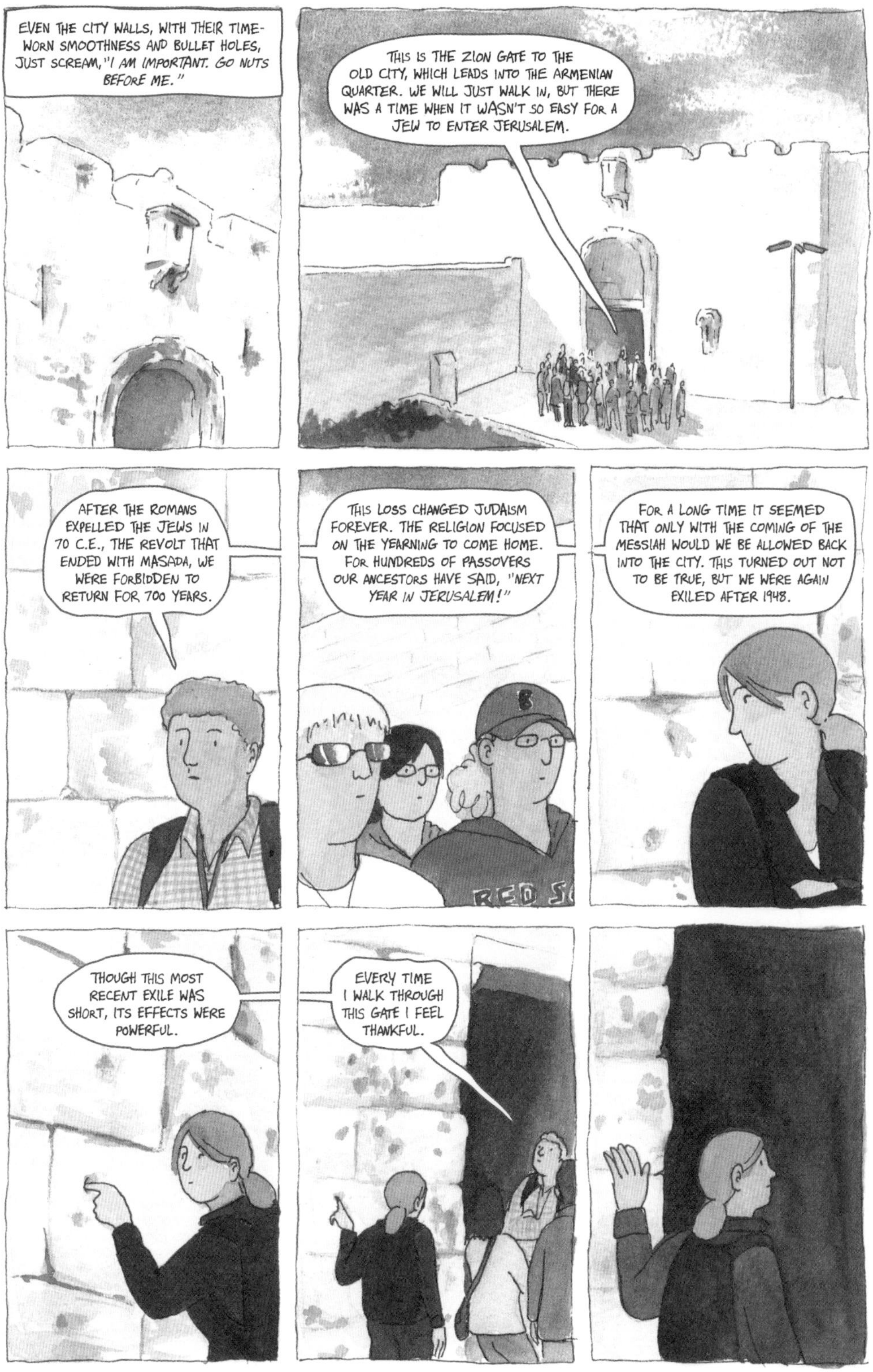
EVEN THE CITY WALLS, WITH THEIR TIME-WORN SMOOTHNESS AND BULLET HOLES, JUST SCREAM, "I AM IMPORTANT. GO NUTS BEFORE ME."
THIS IS THE ZION GATE TO THE OLD CITY, WHICH LEADS INTO THE ARMENIAN QUARTER. WE WILL JUST WALK IN, BUT THERE WAS A TIME WHEN IT WASN'T SO EASY FOR A JEW TO ENTER JERUSALEM.
AFTER THE ROMANS EXPELLED THE JEWS IN 70 C.E., THE REVOLT THAT ENDED WITH MASADA, WE WERE FORBIDDEN TO RETURN FOR 700 YEARS.
THIS LOSS CHANGED JUDAISM FOREVER. THE RELIGION FOCUSED ON THE YEARNING TO COME HOME. FOR HUNDREDS OF PASSOVERS OUR ANCESTORS HAVE SAID, "NEXT YEAR IN JERUSALEM!"
RED S
FOR A LONG TIME IT SEEMED THAT ONLY WITH THE COMING OF THE MESSIAH WOULD WE BE ALLOWED BACK INTO THE CITY. THIS TURNED OUT NOT TO BE TRUE, BUT WE WERE AGAIN EXILED AFTER 1948.
THOUGH THIS MOST RECENT EXILE WAS SHORT, ITS EFFECTS WERE POWERFUL.
EVERY TIME I WALK THROUGH THIS GATE I FEEL THANKFUL.

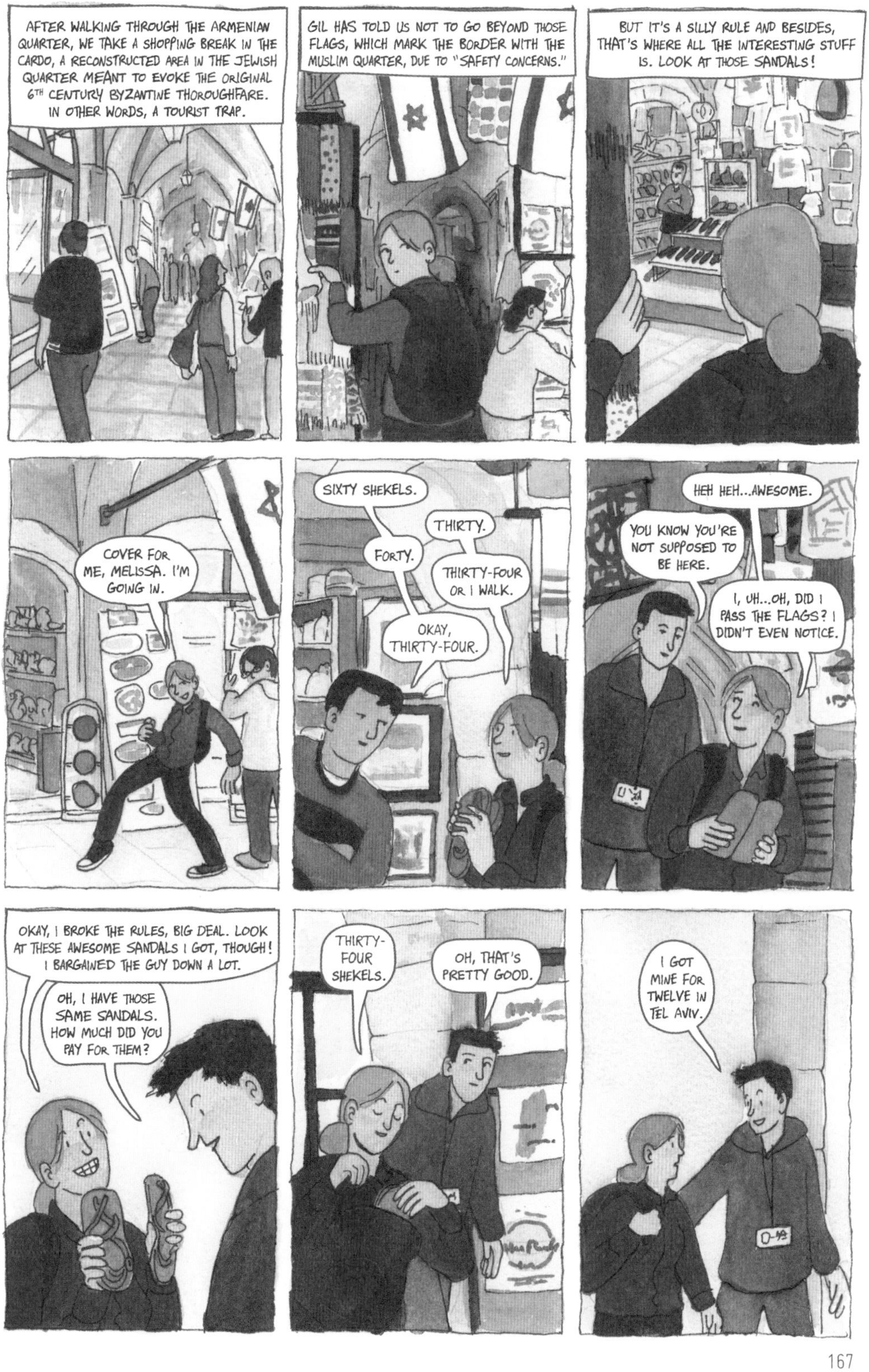
AFTER WALKING THROUGH THE ARMENIAN QUARTER, WE TAKE A SHOPPING BREAK IN THE CARDO, A RECONSTRUCTED AREA IN THE JEWISH QUARTER MEANT TO EVOKE THE ORIGINAL 6TH CENTURY BYZANTINE THOROUGHFARE. IN OTHER WORDS, A TOURIST TRAP.
GIL HAS TOLD US NOT TO GO BEYOND THOSE FLAGS, WHICH MARK THE BORDER WITH THE MUSLIM QUARTER, DUE TO "SAFETY CONCERNS."
BUT IT'S A SILLY RULE AND BESIDES, THAT'S WHERE ALL THE INTERESTING STUFF IS. LOOK AT THOSE SANDALS!
COVER FOR ME, MELISSA. I'M GOING IN.
SIXTY SHEKELS.
FORTY.
THIRTY.
THIRTY-FOUR OR I WALK.
OKAY, THIRTY-FOUR.
HEH HEH...AWESOME.
YOU KNOW YOU'RE NOT SUPPOSED TO BE HERE.
I, UH...OH, DID I PASS THE FLAGS? I DIDN'T EVEN NOTICE.
OKAY, I BROKE THE RULES, BIG DEAL. LOOK AT THESE AWESOME SANDALS I GOT, THOUGH! I BARGAINED THE GUY DOWN A LOT.
OH, I HAVE THOSE SAME SANDALS. HOW MUCH DID YOU PAY FOR THEM?
THIRTY-FOUR SHEKELS.
OH, THAT'S PRETTY GOOD.
I GOT MINE FOR TWELVE IN TEL AVIV.

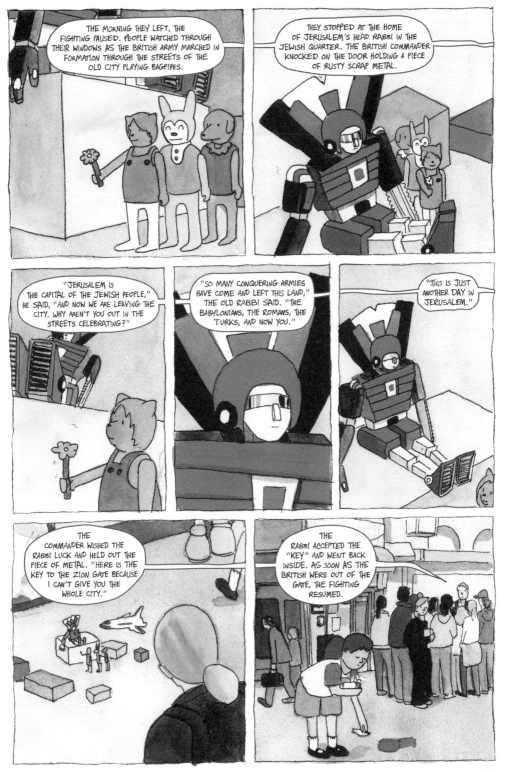

169

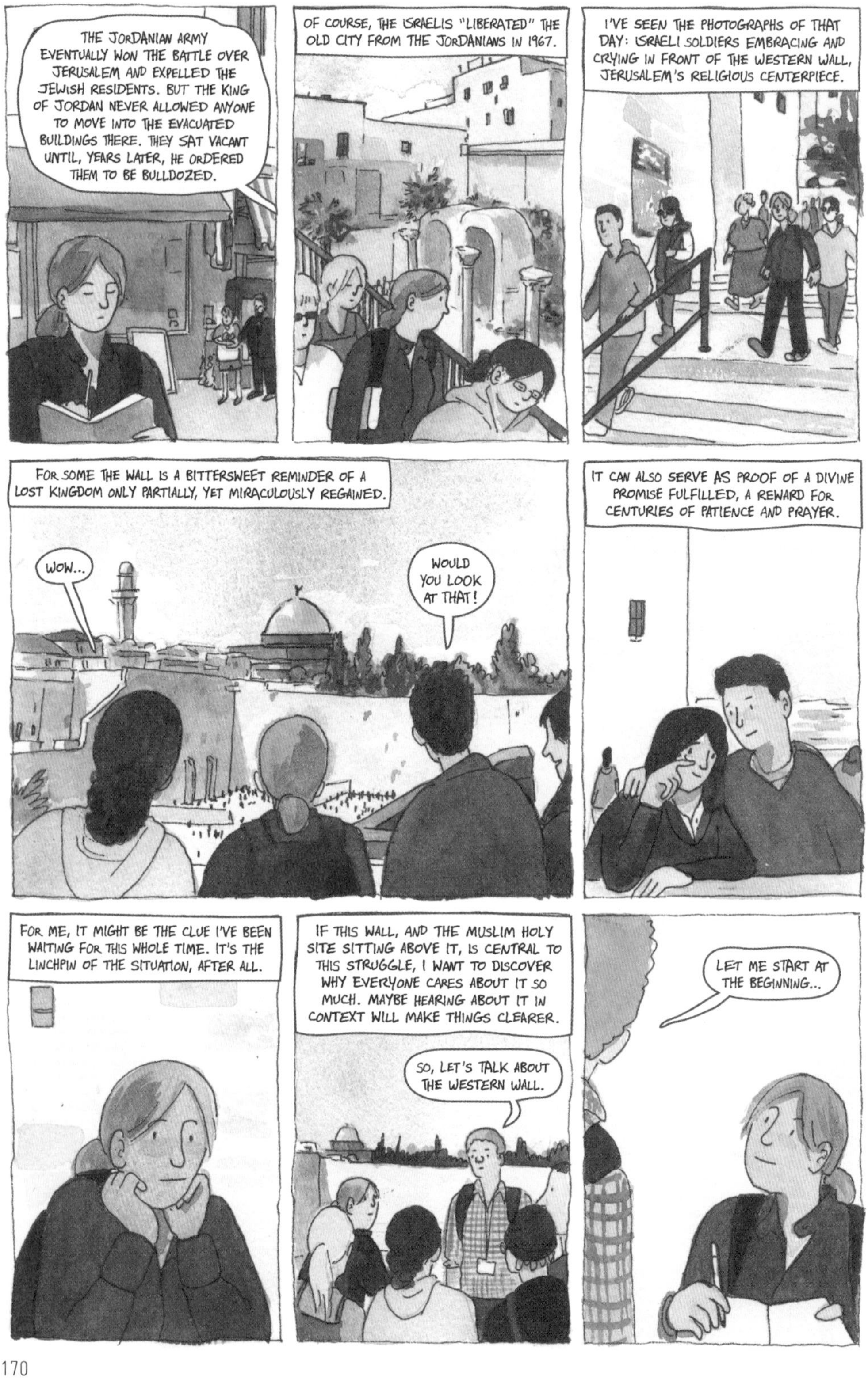
THE JORDANIAN ARMY EVENTUALLY WON THE BATTLE OVER JERUSALEM AND EXPELLED THE JEWISH RESIDENTS. BUT THE KING OF JORDAN NEVER ALLOWED ANYONE TO MOVE INTO THE EVACUATED BUILDINGS THERE. THEY SAT VACANT UNTIL, YEARS LATER, HE ORDERED THEM TO BE BULLDOZED.
OF COURSE, THE ISRAELIS "LIBERATED" THE OLD CITY FROM THE JORDANIANS IN 1967.
I'VE SEEN THE PHOTOGRAPHS OF THAT DAY: ISRAELI SOLDIERS EMBRACING AND CRYING IN FRONT OF THE WESTERN WALL, JERUSALEM'S RELIGIOUS CENTERPIECE.
FOR SOME THE WALL IS A BITTERSWEET REMINDER OF A LOST KINGDOM ONLY PARTIALLY, YET MIRACULOUSLY REGAINED.
WOW...
WOULD YOU LOOK AT THAT!
IT CAN ALSO SERVE AS PROOF OF A DIVINE PROMISE FULFILLED, A REWARD FOR CENTURIES OF PATIENCE AND PRAYER.
FOR ME, IT MIGHT BE THE CLUE I'VE BEEN WAITING FOR THIS WHOLE TIME. IT'S THE LINCHPIN OF THE SITUATION, AFTER ALL.
IF THIS WALL, AND THE MUSLIM HOLY SITE SITTING ABOVE IT, IS CENTRAL TO THIS STRUGGLE, I WANT TO DISCOVER WHY EVERYONE CARES ABOUT IT SO MUCH. MAYBE HEARING ABOUT IT IN CONTEXT WILL MAKE THINGS CLEARER.
SO, LET'S TALK ABOUT THE WESTERN WALL.
LET ME START AT THE BEGINNING...

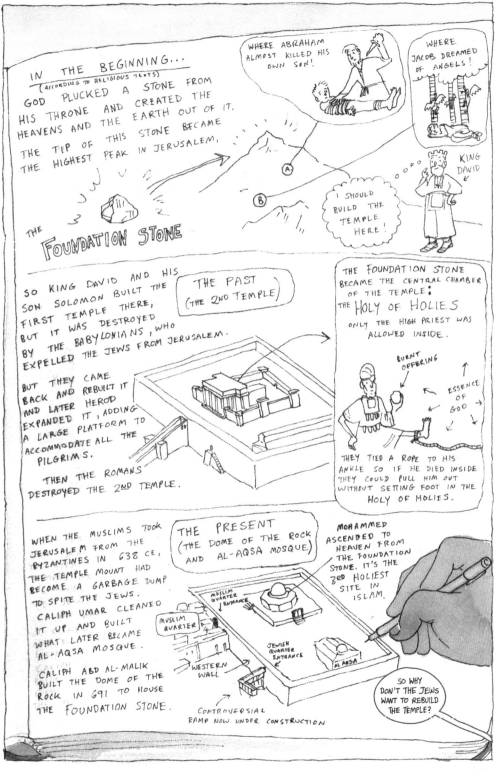

IN THE BEGINNING...
(ACCORDING TO RELIGIOUS TEXTS)
GOD PLUCKED A STONE FROM HIS THRONE AND CREATED THE HEAVENS AND THE EARTH OUT OF IT. THE TIP OF THIS STONE BECAME THE HIGHEST PEAK IN JERUSALEM.

THE FOUNDATION STONE

WHERE ABRAHAM ALMOST KILLED HIS OWN SON!

WHERE JACOB DREAMED OF ANGELS!

A.

B.

KING DAVID

I SHOULD BUILD THE TEMPLE HERE!

SO KING DAVID AND HIS SON SOLOMON BUILT THE FIRST TEMPLE THERE, BUT IT WAS DESTROYED BY THE BABYLONIANS, WHO EXPELLED THE JEWS FROM JERUSALEM.

BUT THEY CAME BACK AND REBUILT IT AND LATER HEROD EXPANDED IT, ADDING A LARGE PLATFORM TO ACCOMMODATE ALL THE PILGRIMS.

THEN THE ROMANS DESTROYED THE 2ND TEMPLE.

THE PAST
(THE 2ND TEMPLE)

THE FOUNDATION STONE BECAME THE CENTRAL CHAMBER OF THE TEMPLE: THE HOLY OF HOLIES ONLY THE HIGH PRIEST WAS ALLOWED INSIDE.

BURNT OFFERING

ESSENCE OF GOD

THEY TIED A ROPE TO HIS ANKLE SO IF HE DIED INSIDE THEY COULD PULL HIM OUT WITHOUT SETTING FOOT IN THE HOLY OF HOLIES.

WHEN THE MUSLIMS TOOK JERUSALEM FROM THE BYZANTINES IN 638 CE, THE TEMPLE MOUNT HAD BECOME A GARBAGE DUMP TO SPITE THE JEWS. CALIPH UMAR CLEANED IT UP AND BUILT WHAT LATER BECAME AL-AQSA MOSQUE.

CALIPH ABD AL-MALIK BUILT THE DOME OF THE ROCK IN 691 TO HOUSE THE FOUNDATION STONE.

THE PRESENT
(THE DOME OF THE ROCK AND AL-AQSA MOSQUE)

MOHAMMED ASCENDED TO HEAVEN FROM THE FOUNDATION STONE. IT'S THE 3RD HOLIEST SITE IN ISLAM.

MUSLIM QUARTER ENTRANCE

MUSLIM QUARTER

JEWISH QUARTER ENTRANCE

WESTERN WALL

AL AQSA

CONTROVERSIAL RAMP NOW UNDER CONSTRUCTION

SO WHY DON'T THE JEWS WANT TO REBUILD THE TEMPLE?

171

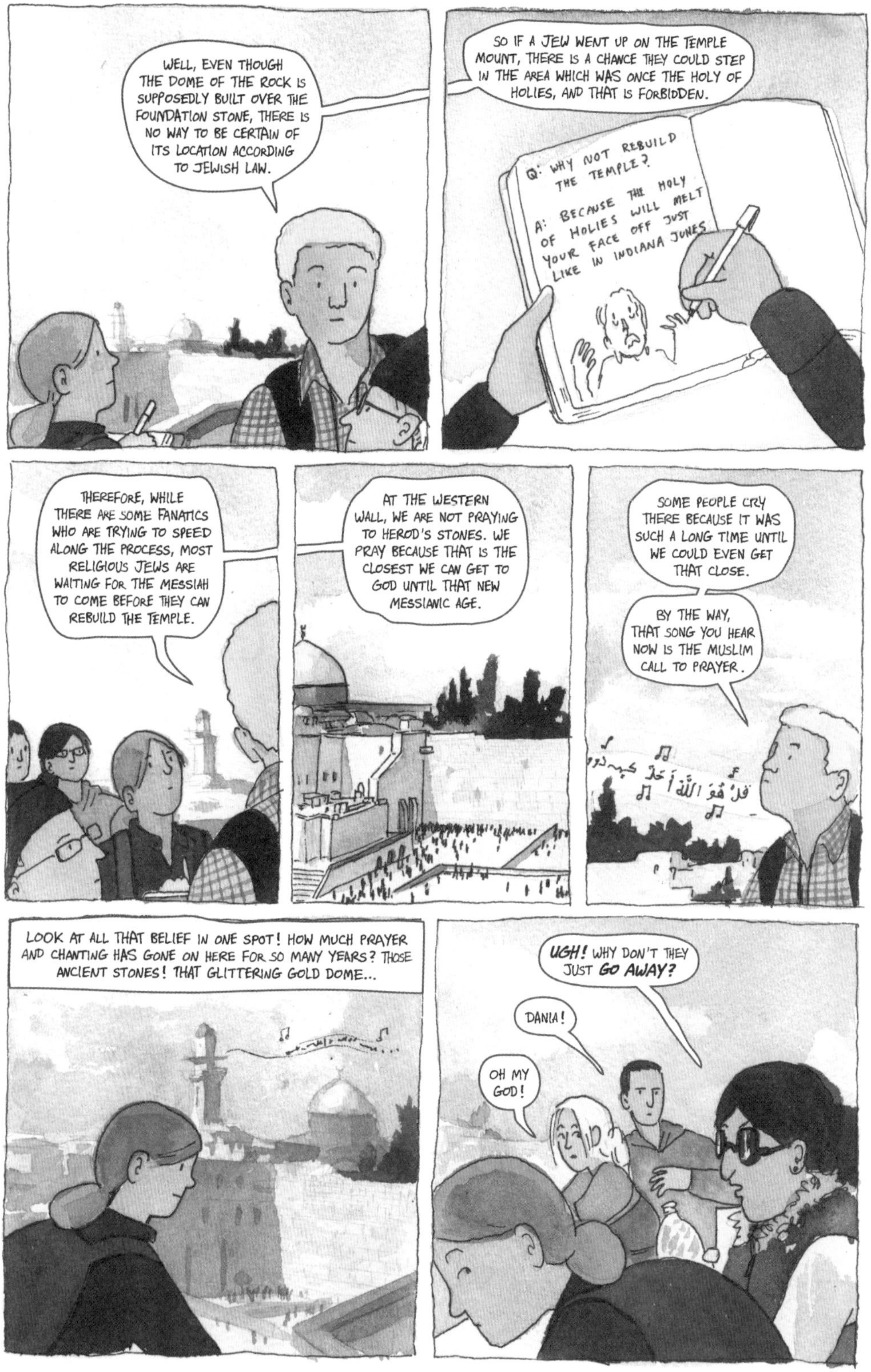
WELL, EVEN THOUGH THE DOME OF THE ROCK IS SUPPOSEDLY BUILT OVER THE FOUNDATION STONE, THERE IS NO WAY TO BE CERTAIN OF ITS LOCATION ACCORDING TO JEWISH LAW.
SO IF A JEW WENT UP ON THE TEMPLE MOUNT, THERE IS A CHANCE THEY COULD STEP IN THE AREA WHICH WAS ONCE THE HOLY OF HOLIES, AND THAT IS FORBIDDEN.
Q: WHY NOT REBUILD THE TEMPLE?
A: BECAUSE THE HOLY OF HOLIES WILL MELT YOUR FACE OFF JUST LIKE IN INDIANA JONES
THEREFORE, WHILE THERE ARE SOME FANATICS WHO ARE TRYING TO SPEED ALONG THE PROCESS, MOST RELIGIOUS JEWS ARE WAITING FOR THE MESSIAH TO COME BEFORE THEY CAN REBUILD THE TEMPLE.
AT THE WESTERN WALL, WE ARE NOT PRAYING TO HEROD'S STONES. WE PRAY BECAUSE THAT IS THE CLOSEST WE CAN GET TO GOD UNTIL THAT NEW MESSIANIC AGE.
SOME PEOPLE CRY THERE BECAUSE IT WAS SUCH A LONG TIME UNTIL WE COULD EVEN GET THAT CLOSE.
BY THE WAY, THAT SONG YOU HEAR NOW IS THE MUSLIM CALL TO PRAYER.
LOOK AT ALL THAT BELIEF IN ONE SPOT! HOW MUCH PRAYER AND CHANTING HAS GONE ON HERE FOR SO MANY YEARS? THOSE ANCIENT STONES! THAT GLITTERING GOLD DOME...
UGH! WHY DON'T THEY JUST GO AWAY?
DANIA!
OH MY GOD!

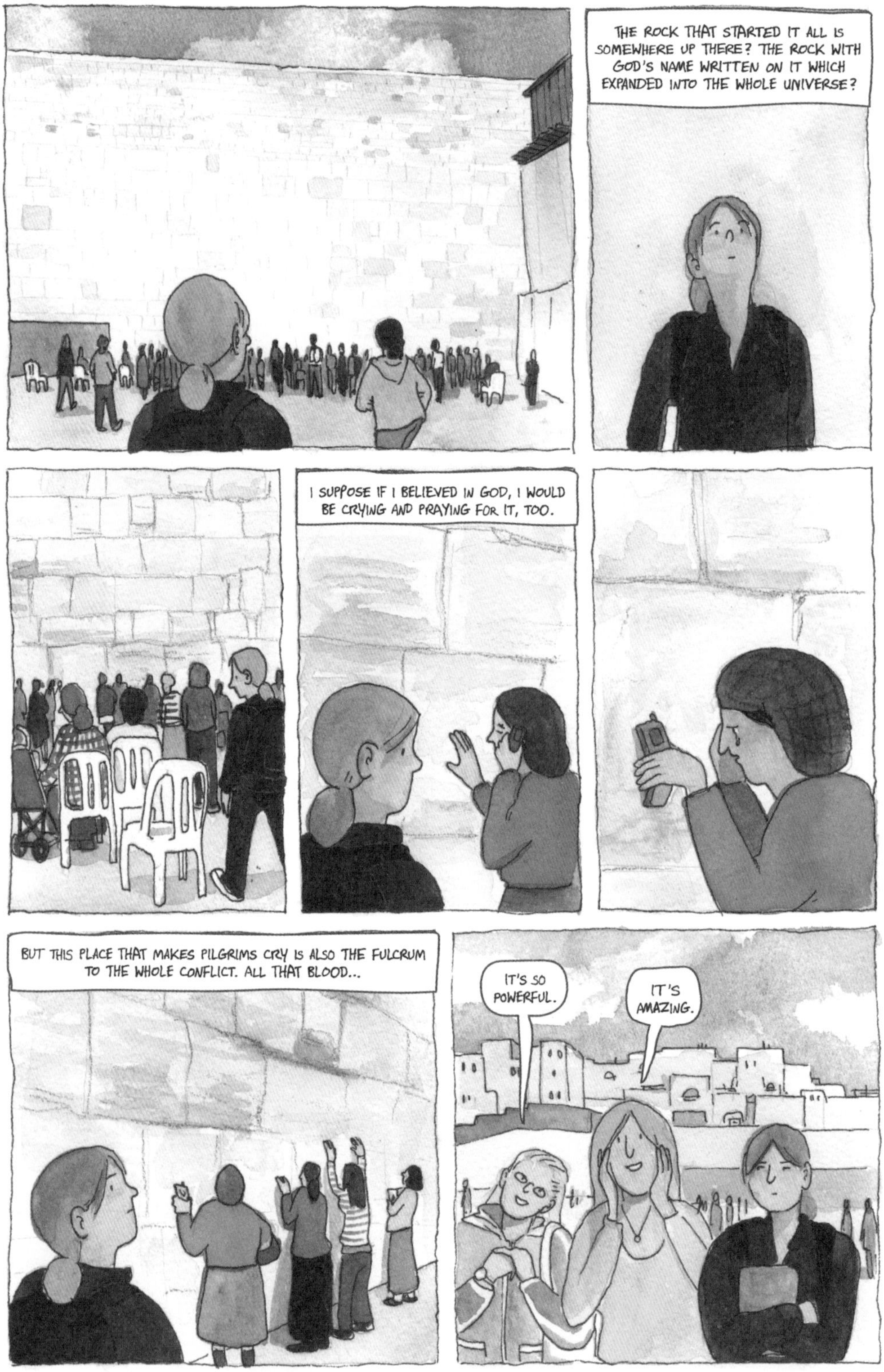
THE ROCK THAT STARTED IT ALL IS SOMEWHERE UP THERE? THE ROCK WITH GOD'S NAME WRITTEN ON IT WHICH EXPANDED INTO THE WHOLE UNIVERSE?
I SUPPOSE IF I BELIEVED IN GOD, I WOULD BE CRYING AND PRAYING FOR IT, TOO.
BUT THIS PLACE THAT MAKES PILGRIMS CRY IS ALSO THE FULCRUM TO THE WHOLE CONFLICT. ALL THAT BLOOD...
IT'S SO POWERFUL.
IT'S AMAZING.

BUT WHO AM I TO JUDGE SOMEONE ELSE'S HOLY SITE? IT FEELS ALMOST LIKE AN ACT OF VIOLENCE TO BECOME ANGRY AT A PLACE CONSIDERED INSPIRING AND DIVINE TO MILLIONS OF PEOPLE.

I'D BETTER WRITE A LITTLE PRAYER AND STICK IT IN THE CRACKS IN THE WALL LIKE EVERYONE ELSE AND STOP INTRUDING ON SACRED AIRSPACE.

OF ALL THE TIMES AND PLACES TO WISH FOR PEACE, THIS ONE SEEMS LIKE THE MOST APPROPRIATE.

NOW JUST TO TEAR IT OUT AND--

SHIT.

LET THERE BE PEACE BETWEEN THE ISRAELIS AND PALESTINIANS

JUST WONDERFUL. NOW I'VE CURSED PEACE IN THE MIDDLE EAST.

AS I START TO CRY, I'M CONFUSED.

175

176

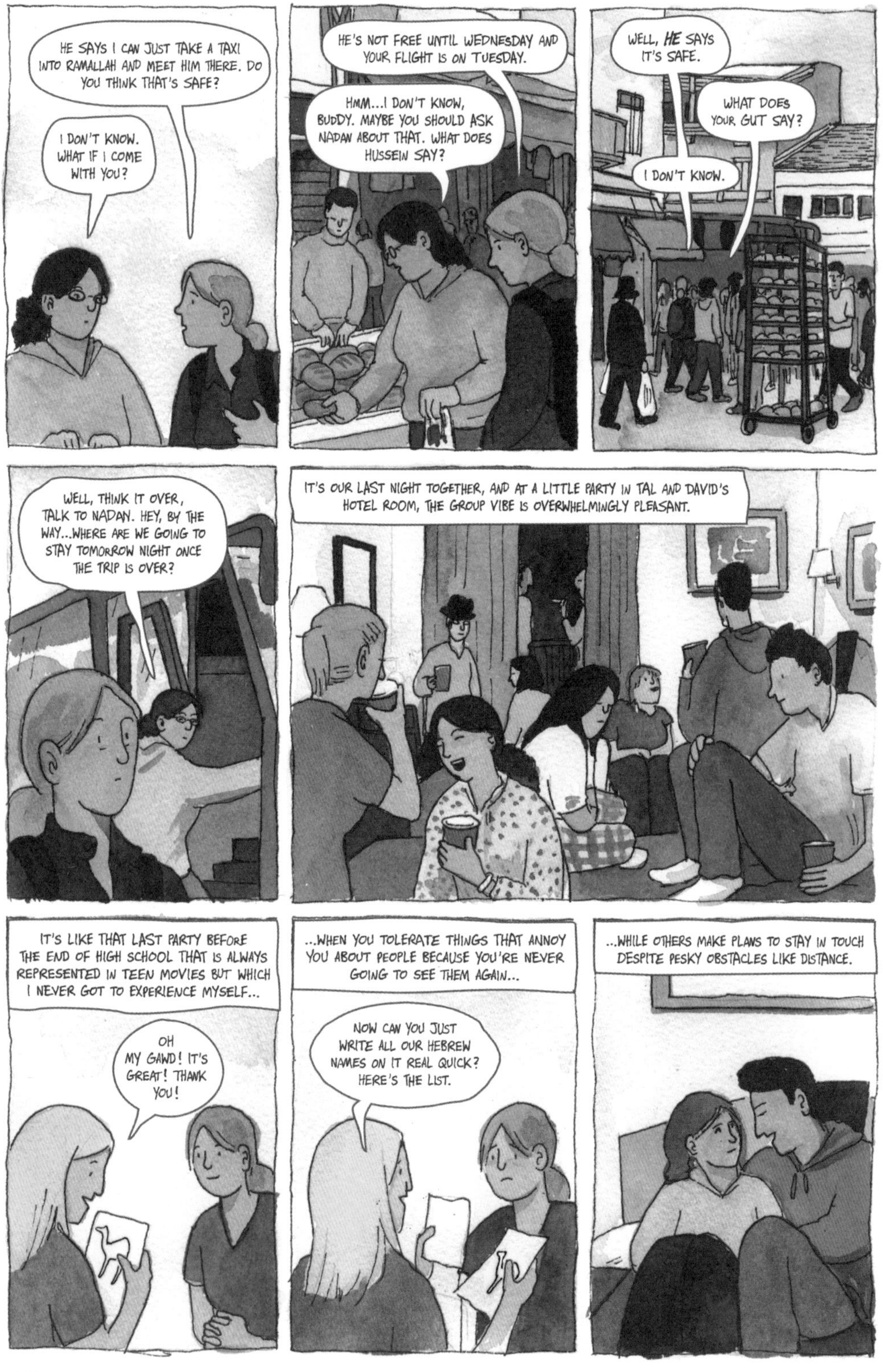
HE SAYS I CAN JUST TAKE A TAXI INTO RAMALLAH AND MEET HIM THERE. DO YOU THINK THAT'S SAFE?
I DON'T KNOW. WHAT IF I COME WITH YOU?
HE'S NOT FREE UNTIL WEDNESDAY AND YOUR FLIGHT IS ON TUESDAY.
HMM...I DON'T KNOW, BUDDY. MAYBE YOU SHOULD ASK NADAN ABOUT THAT. WHAT DOES HUSSEIN SAY?
WELL, HE SAYS IT'S SAFE.
WHAT DOES YOUR GUT SAY?
I DON'T KNOW.
WELL, THINK IT OVER, TALK TO NADAN. HEY, BY THE WAY...WHERE ARE WE GOING TO STAY TOMORROW NIGHT ONCE THE TRIP IS OVER?
IT'S OUR LAST NIGHT TOGETHER, AND AT A LITTLE PARTY IN TAL AND DAVID'S HOTEL ROOM, THE GROUP VIBE IS OVERWHELMINGLY PLEASANT.
IT'S LIKE THAT LAST PARTY BEFORE THE END OF HIGH SCHOOL THAT IS ALWAYS REPRESENTED IN TEEN MOVIES BUT WHICH I NEVER GOT TO EXPERIENCE MYSELF...
OH MY GAWD! IT'S GREAT! THANK YOU!
...WHEN YOU TOLERATE THINGS THAT ANNOY YOU ABOUT PEOPLE BECAUSE YOU'RE NEVER GOING TO SEE THEM AGAIN...
NOW CAN YOU JUST WRITE ALL OUR HEBREW NAMES ON IT REAL QUICK? HERE'S THE LIST.
...WHILE OTHERS MAKE PLANS TO STAY IN TOUCH DESPITE PESKY OBSTACLES LIKE DISTANCE.

CHAPTER SEVEN
POST BIRTHRIGHT

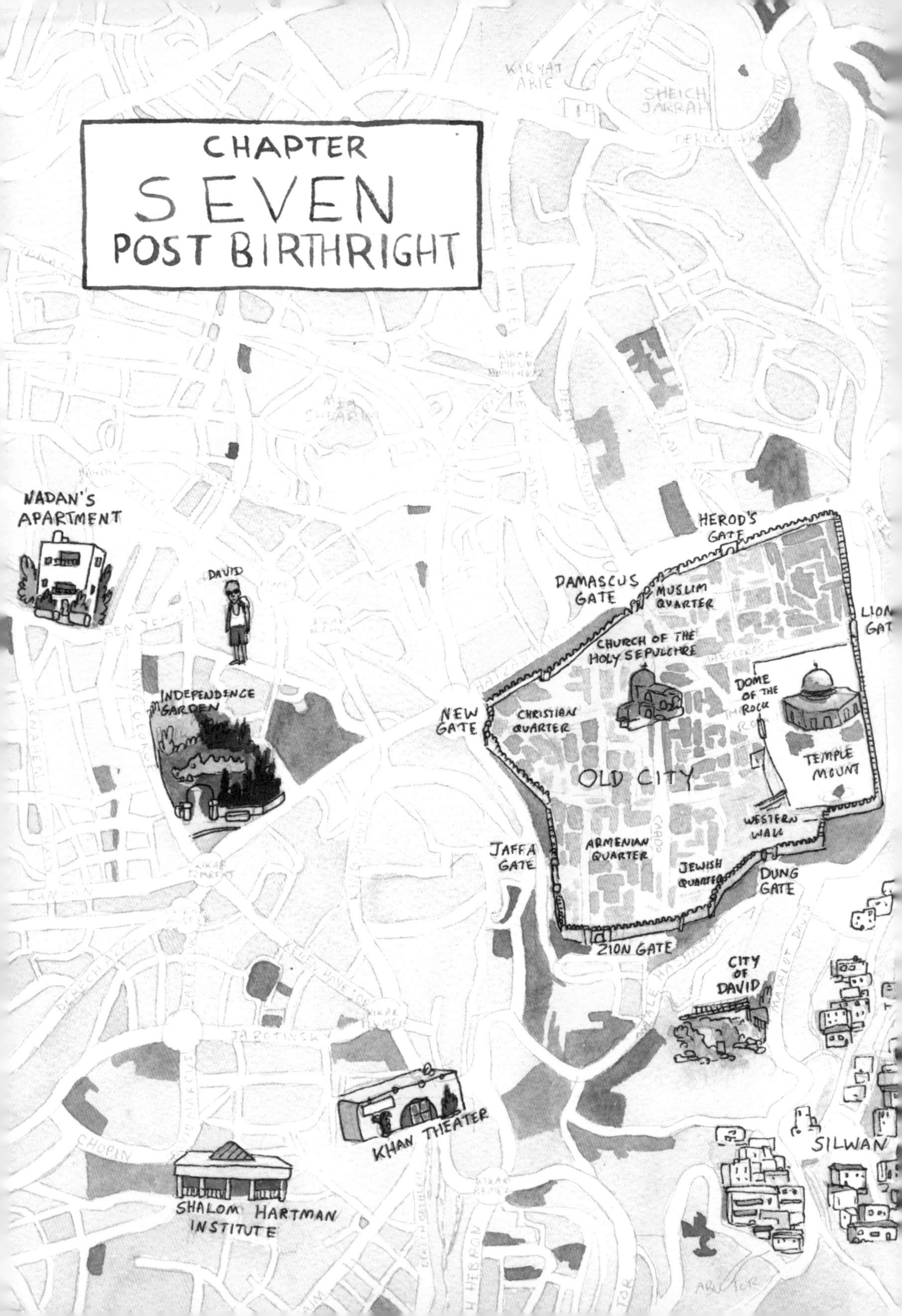

KIRYAT ARIE
SHEICH JARRAH
NADAN'S APARTMENT
DAVID
INDEPENDENCE GARDEN
HEROD'S GATE
DAMASCUS GATE
MUSLIM QUARTER
CHURCH OF THE HOLY SEPULCHRE
NEW GATE
CHRISTIAN QUARTER
DOME OF THE ROCK
OLD CITY
TEMPLE MOUNT
WESTERN WALL
JAFFA GATE
ARMENIAN QUARTER
JEWISH QUARTER
DUNG GATE
ZION GATE
CITY OF DAVID
JABOTINSKY
KHAN THEATER
SILWAN
SHALOM HARTMAN INSTITUTE

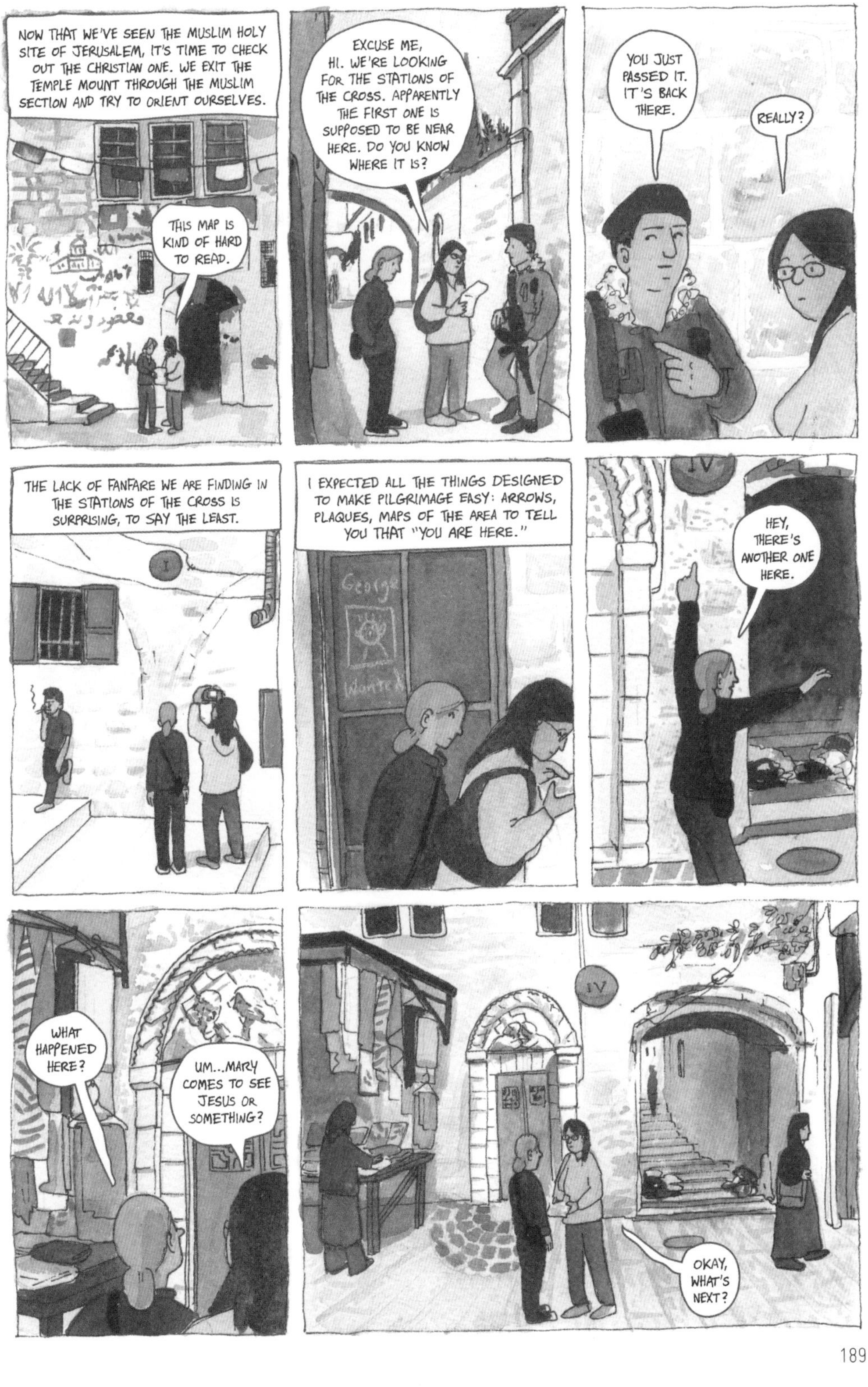
NOW THAT WE'VE SEEN THE MUSLIM HOLY SITE OF JERUSALEM, IT'S TIME TO CHECK OUT THE CHRISTIAN ONE. WE EXIT THE TEMPLE MOUNT THROUGH THE MUSLIM SECTION AND TRY TO ORIENT OURSELVES.
THIS MAP IS KIND OF HARD TO READ.
EXCUSE ME, HI. WE'RE LOOKING FOR THE STATIONS OF THE CROSS. APPARENTLY THE FIRST ONE IS SUPPOSED TO BE NEAR HERE. DO YOU KNOW WHERE IT IS?
YOU JUST PASSED IT. IT'S BACK THERE.
REALLY?
THE LACK OF FANFARE WE ARE FINDING IN THE STATIONS OF THE CROSS IS SURPRISING, TO SAY THE LEAST.
I
I EXPECTED ALL THE THINGS DESIGNED TO MAKE PILGRIMAGE EASY: ARROWS, PLAQUES, MAPS OF THE AREA TO TELL YOU THAT "YOU ARE HERE."
George
Wanted
IV
HEY, THERE'S ANOTHER ONE HERE.
WHAT HAPPENED HERE?
UM...MARY COMES TO SEE JESUS OR SOMETHING?
IV
OKAY, WHAT'S NEXT?

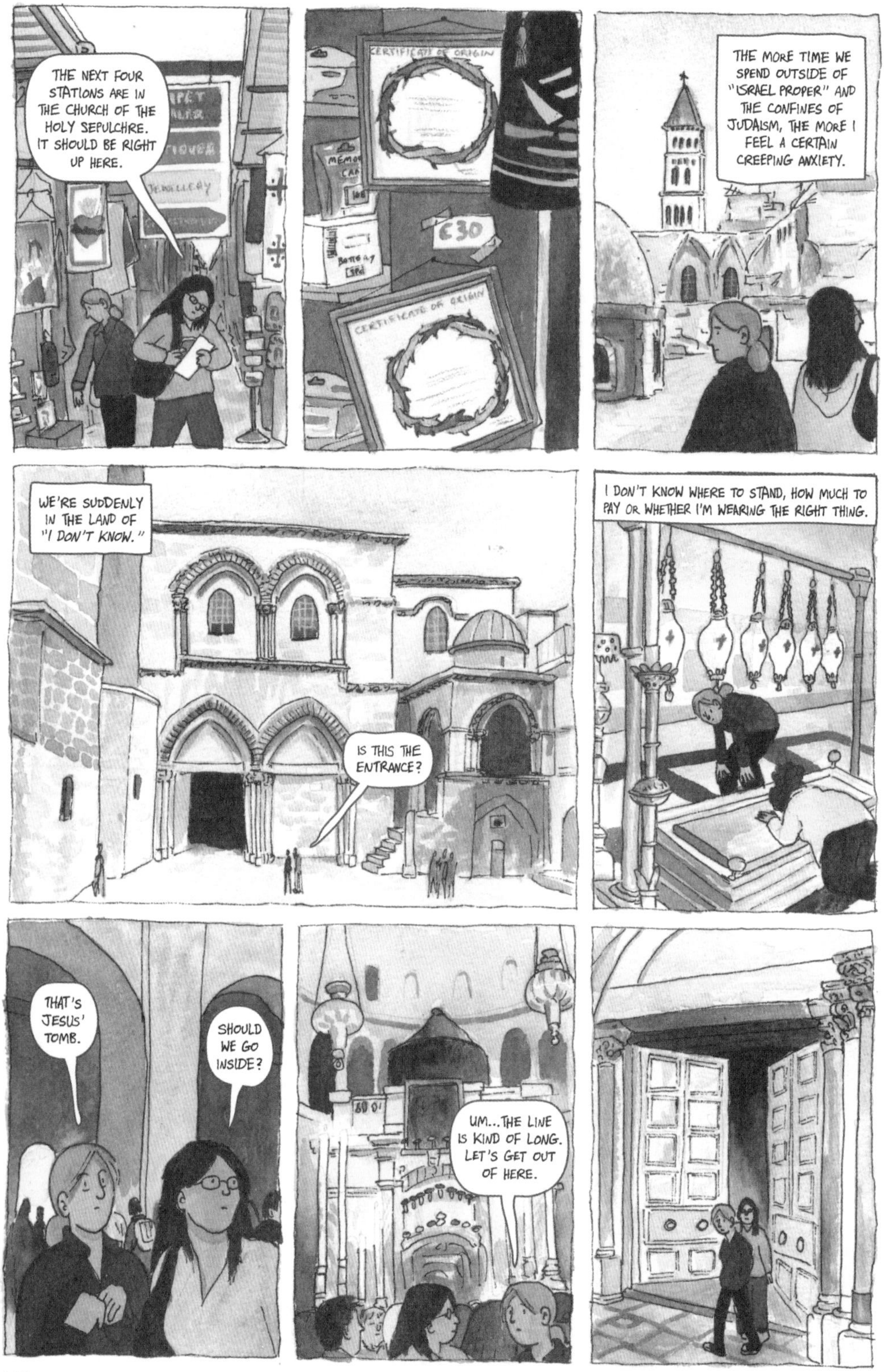
THE NEXT FOUR STATIONS ARE IN THE CHURCH OF THE HOLY SEPULCHRE. IT SHOULD BE RIGHT UP HERE.
CERTIFICATE OF ORIGIN
€30
CERTIFICATE OF ORIGIN
THE MORE TIME WE SPEND OUTSIDE OF "ISRAEL PROPER" AND THE CONFINES OF JUDAISM, THE MORE I FEEL A CERTAIN CREEPING ANXIETY.
WE'RE SUDDENLY IN THE LAND OF "I DON'T KNOW."
IS THIS THE ENTRANCE?
I DON'T KNOW WHERE TO STAND, HOW MUCH TO PAY OR WHETHER I'M WEARING THE RIGHT THING.
THAT'S JESUS' TOMB.
SHOULD WE GO INSIDE?
UM...THE LINE IS KIND OF LONG. LET'S GET OUT OF HERE.

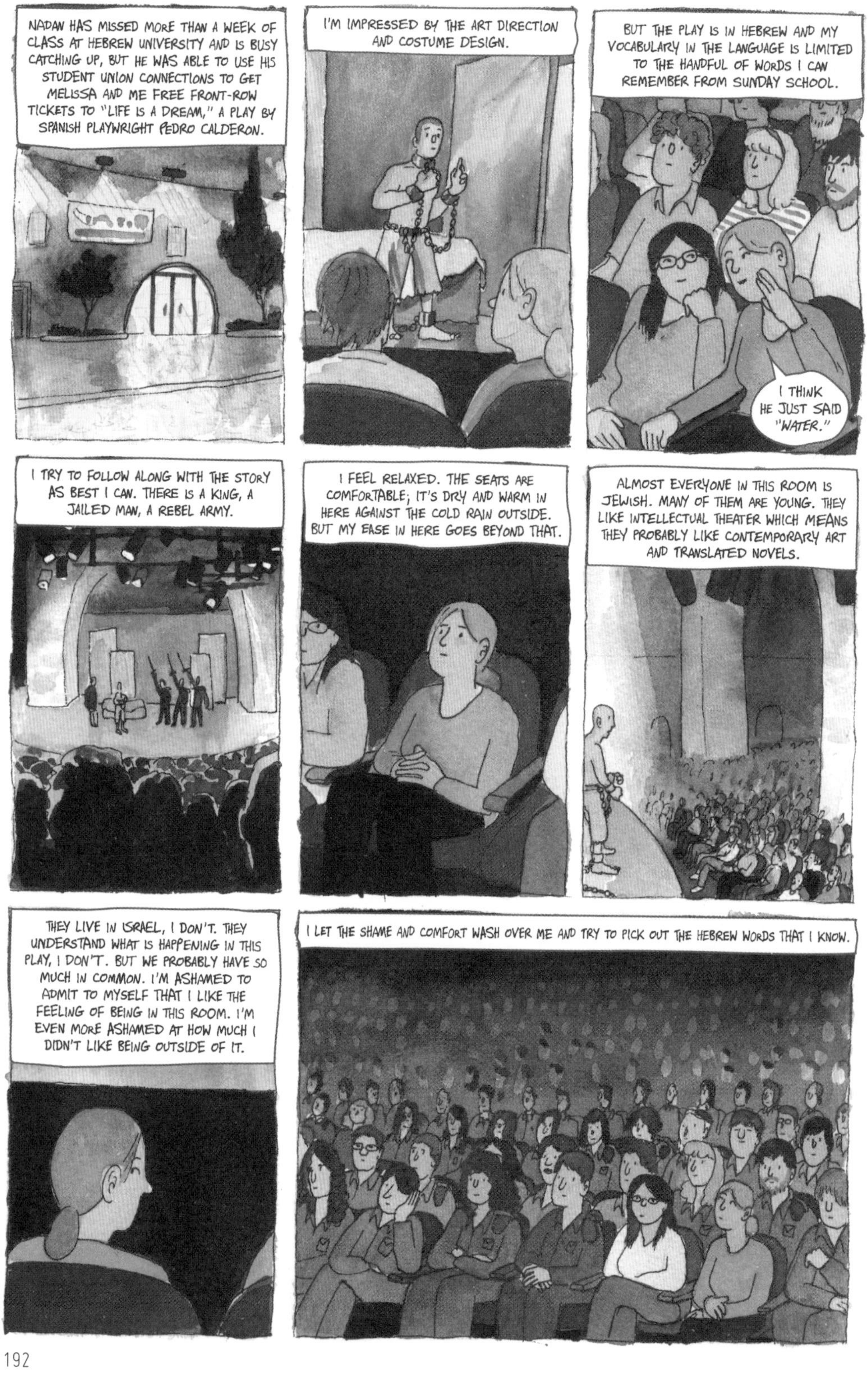
NADAN HAS MISSED MORE THAN A WEEK OF CLASS AT HEBREW UNIVERSITY AND IS BUSY CATCHING UP, BUT HE WAS ABLE TO USE HIS STUDENT UNION CONNECTIONS TO GET MELISSA AND ME FREE FRONT-ROW TICKETS TO "LIFE IS A DREAM," A PLAY BY SPANISH PLAYWRIGHT PEDRO CALDERON.
I'M IMPRESSED BY THE ART DIRECTION AND COSTUME DESIGN.
BUT THE PLAY IS IN HEBREW AND MY VOCABULARY IN THE LANGUAGE IS LIMITED TO THE HANDFUL OF WORDS I CAN REMEMBER FROM SUNDAY SCHOOL.
I THINK HE JUST SAID "WATER."
I TRY TO FOLLOW ALONG WITH THE STORY AS BEST I CAN. THERE IS A KING, A JAILED MAN, A REBEL ARMY.
I FEEL RELAXED. THE SEATS ARE COMFORTABLE; IT'S DRY AND WARM IN HERE AGAINST THE COLD RAIN OUTSIDE. BUT MY EASE IN HERE GOES BEYOND THAT.
ALMOST EVERYONE IN THIS ROOM IS JEWISH. MANY OF THEM ARE YOUNG. THEY LIKE INTELLECTUAL THEATER WHICH MEANS THEY PROBABLY LIKE CONTEMPORARY ART AND TRANSLATED NOVELS.
THEY LIVE IN ISRAEL, I DON'T. THEY UNDERSTAND WHAT IS HAPPENING IN THIS PLAY, I DON'T. BUT WE PROBABLY HAVE SO MUCH IN COMMON. I'M ASHAMED TO ADMIT TO MYSELF THAT I LIKE THE FEELING OF BEING IN THIS ROOM. I'M EVEN MORE ASHAMED AT HOW MUCH I DIDN'T LIKE BEING OUTSIDE OF IT.
I LET THE SHAME AND COMFORT WASH OVER ME AND TRY TO PICK OUT THE HEBREW WORDS THAT I KNOW.

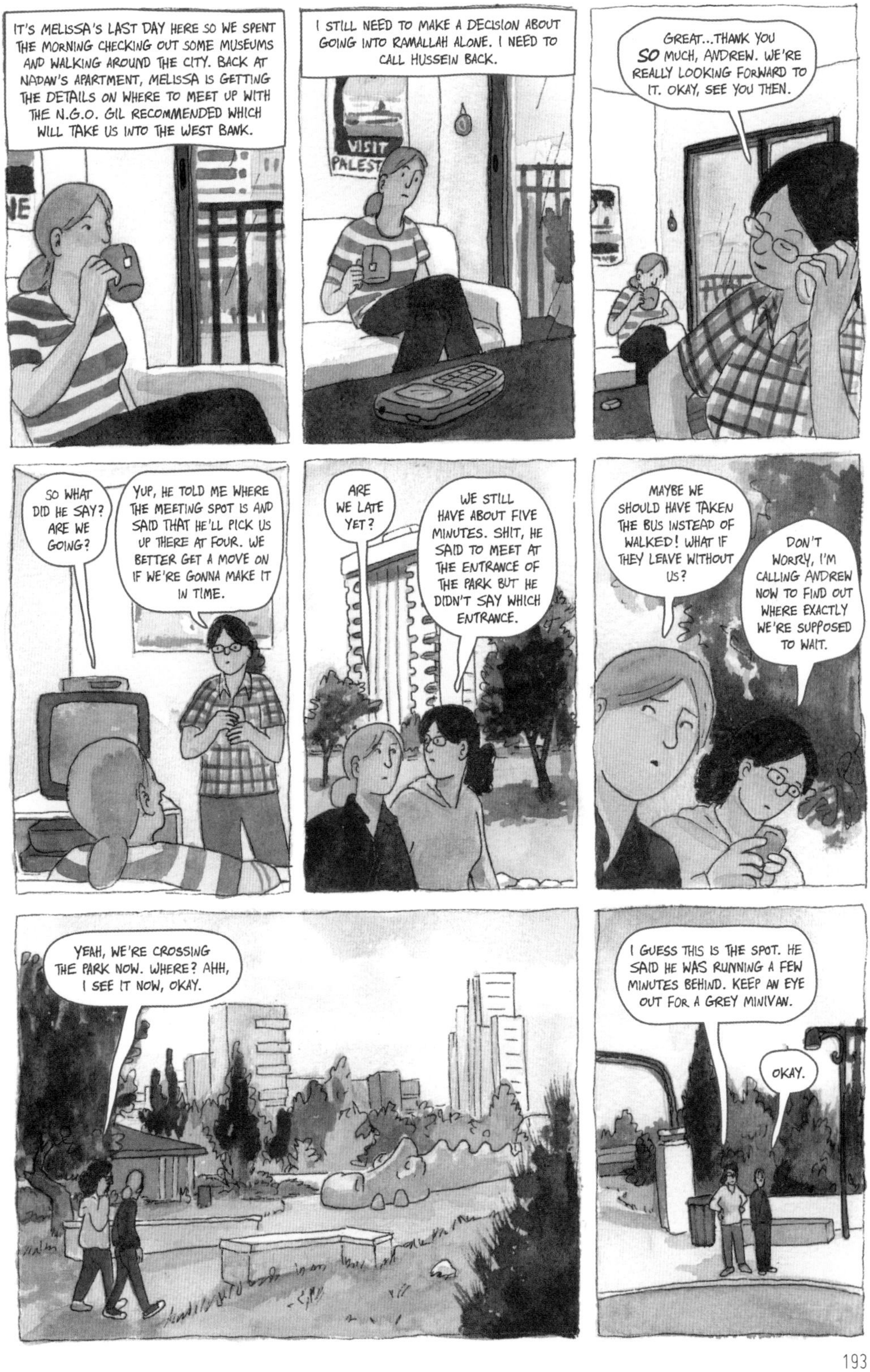
IT'S MELISSA'S LAST DAY HERE SO WE SPENT THE MORNING CHECKING OUT SOME MUSEUMS AND WALKING AROUND THE CITY. BACK AT NADAN'S APARTMENT, MELISSA IS GETTING THE DETAILS ON WHERE TO MEET UP WITH THE N.G.O. GIL RECOMMENDED WHICH WILL TAKE US INTO THE WEST BANK.
I STILL NEED TO MAKE A DECISION ABOUT GOING INTO RAMALLAH ALONE. I NEED TO CALL HUSSEIN BACK.
VISIT PALEST
GREAT...THANK YOU SO MUCH, ANDREW. WE'RE REALLY LOOKING FORWARD TO IT. OKAY, SEE YOU THEN.
SO WHAT DID HE SAY? ARE WE GOING?
YUP, HE TOLD ME WHERE THE MEETING SPOT IS AND SAID THAT HE'LL PICK US UP THERE AT FOUR. WE BETTER GET A MOVE ON IF WE'RE GONNA MAKE IT IN TIME.
ARE WE LATE YET?
WE STILL HAVE ABOUT FIVE MINUTES. SHIT, HE SAID TO MEET AT THE ENTRANCE OF THE PARK BUT HE DIDN'T SAY WHICH ENTRANCE.
MAYBE WE SHOULD HAVE TAKEN THE BUS INSTEAD OF WALKED! WHAT IF THEY LEAVE WITHOUT US?
DON'T WORRY, I'M CALLING ANDREW NOW TO FIND OUT WHERE EXACTLY WE'RE SUPPOSED TO WAIT.
YEAH, WE'RE CROSSING THE PARK NOW. WHERE? AHH, I SEE IT NOW, OKAY.
I GUESS THIS IS THE SPOT. HE SAID HE WAS RUNNING A FEW MINUTES BEHIND. KEEP AN EYE OUT FOR A GREY MINIVAN.
OKAY.

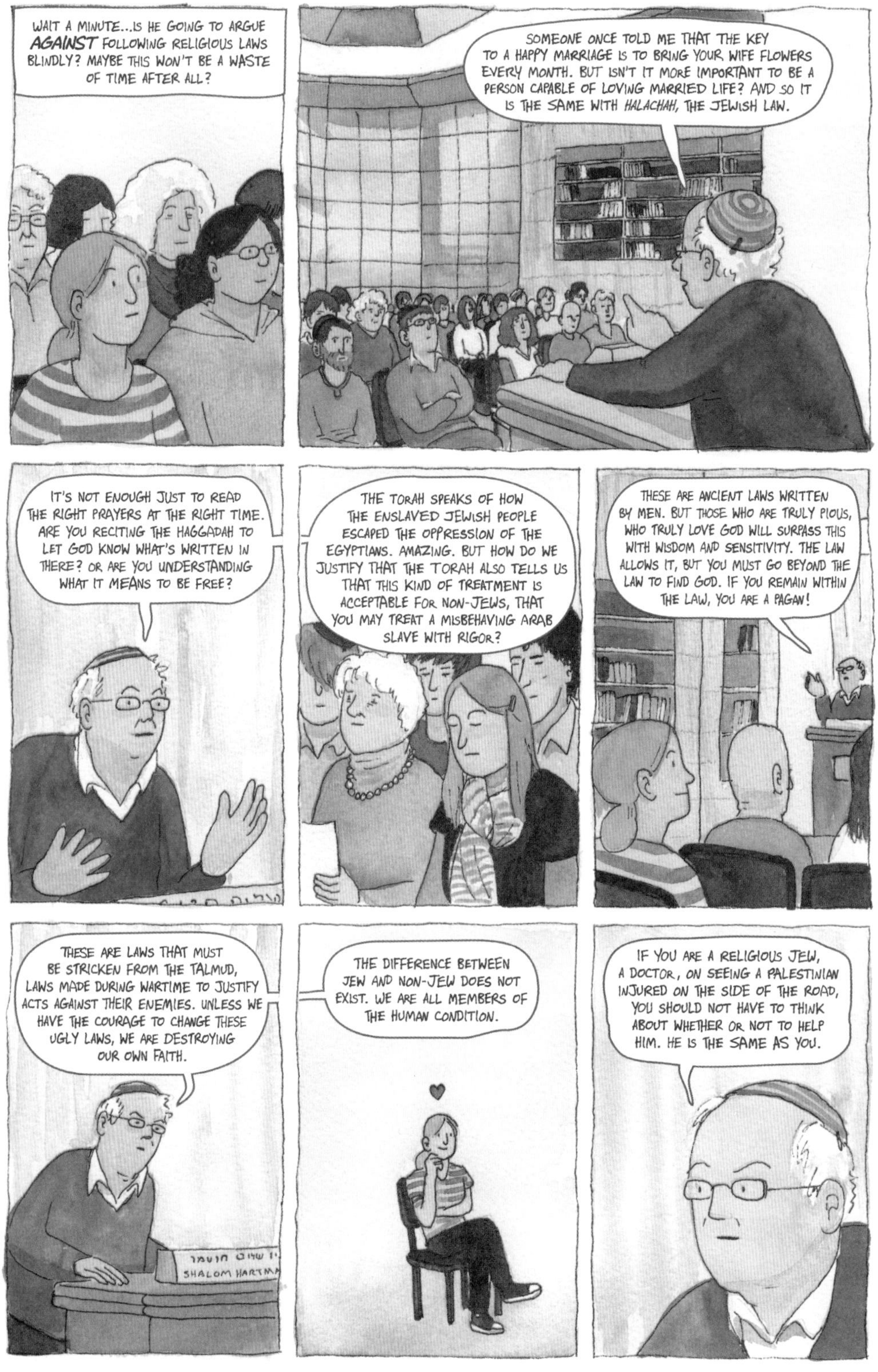
WAIT A MINUTE...IS HE GOING TO ARGUE AGAINST FOLLOWING RELIGIOUS LAWS BLINDLY? MAYBE THIS WON'T BE A WASTE OF TIME AFTER ALL?
SOMEONE ONCE TOLD ME THAT THE KEY TO A HAPPY MARRIAGE IS TO BRING YOUR WIFE FLOWERS EVERY MONTH. BUT ISN'T IT MORE IMPORTANT TO BE A PERSON CAPABLE OF LOVING MARRIED LIFE? AND SO IT IS THE SAME WITH HALACHAH, THE JEWISH LAW.
IT'S NOT ENOUGH JUST TO READ THE RIGHT PRAYERS AT THE RIGHT TIME. ARE YOU RECITING THE HAGGADAH TO LET GOD KNOW WHAT'S WRITTEN IN THERE? OR ARE YOU UNDERSTANDING WHAT IT MEANS TO BE FREE?
THE TORAH SPEAKS OF HOW THE ENSLAVED JEWISH PEOPLE ESCAPED THE OPPRESSION OF THE EGYPTIANS. AMAZING. BUT HOW DO WE JUSTIFY THAT THE TORAH ALSO TELLS US THAT THIS KIND OF TREATMENT IS ACCEPTABLE FOR NON-JEWS, THAT YOU MAY TREAT A MISBEHAVING ARAB SLAVE WITH RIGOR?
THESE ARE ANCIENT LAWS WRITTEN BY MEN. BUT THOSE WHO ARE TRULY PIOUS, WHO TRULY LOVE GOD WILL SURPASS THIS WITH WISDOM AND SENSITIVITY. THE LAW ALLOWS IT, BUT YOU MUST GO BEYOND THE LAW TO FIND GOD. IF YOU REMAIN WITHIN THE LAW, YOU ARE A PAGAN!
THESE ARE LAWS THAT MUST BE STRICKEN FROM THE TALMUD, LAWS MADE DURING WARTIME TO JUSTIFY ACTS AGAINST THEIR ENEMIES. UNLESS WE HAVE THE COURAGE TO CHANGE THESE UGLY LAWS, WE ARE DESTROYING OUR OWN FAITH.
SHALOM HARTMA
THE DIFFERENCE BETWEEN JEW AND NON-JEW DOES NOT EXIST. WE ARE ALL MEMBERS OF THE HUMAN CONDITION.
IF YOU ARE A RELIGIOUS JEW, A DOCTOR, ON SEEING A PALESTINIAN INJURED ON THE SIDE OF THE ROAD, YOU SHOULD NOT HAVE TO THINK ABOUT WHETHER OR NOT TO HELP HIM. HE IS THE SAME AS YOU.

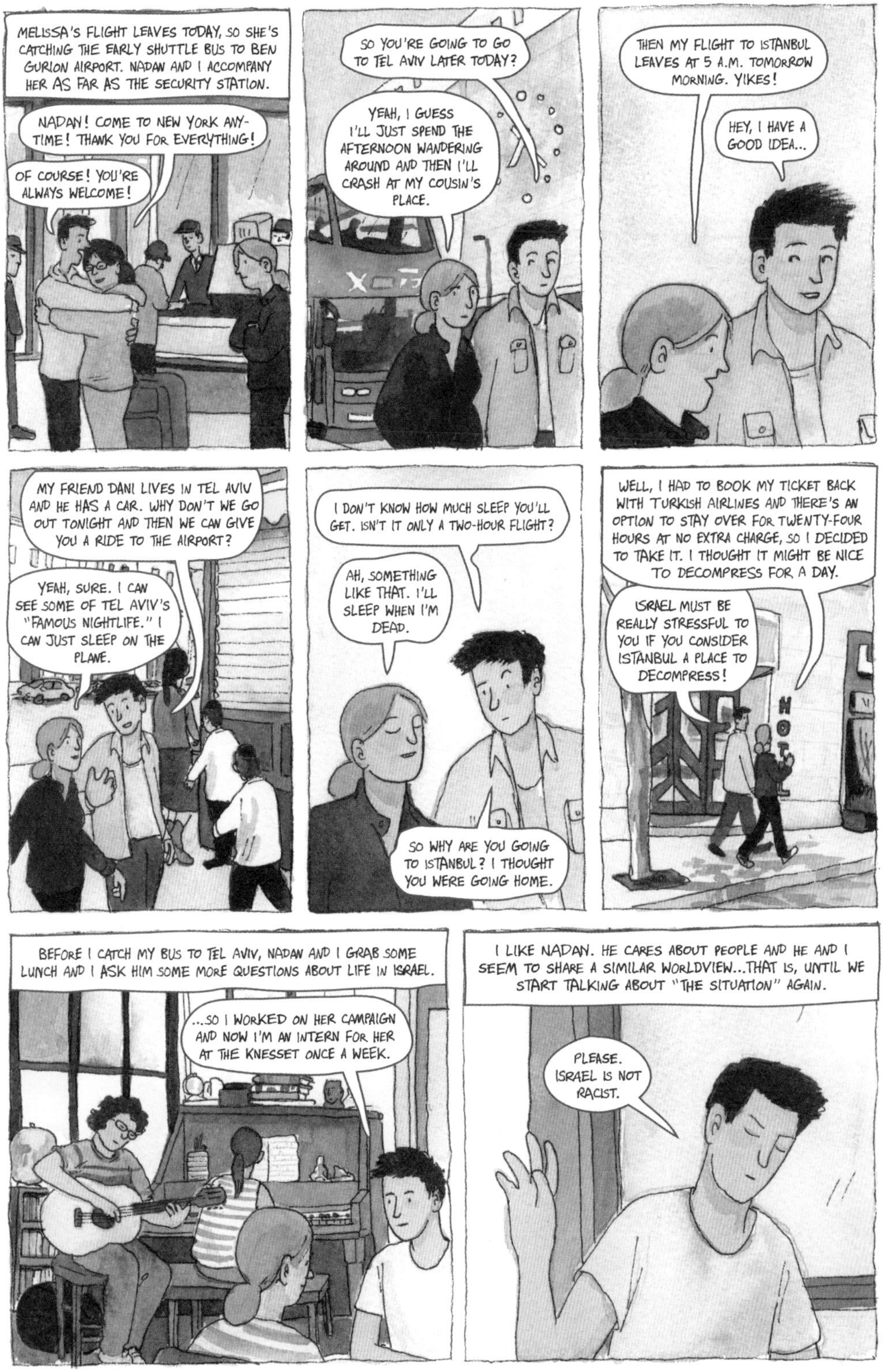
MELISSA'S FLIGHT LEAVES TODAY, SO SHE'S CATCHING THE EARLY SHUTTLE BUS TO BEN GURION AIRPORT. NADAN AND I ACCOMPANY HER AS FAR AS THE SECURITY STATION.
NADAN! COME TO NEW YORK ANY-TIME! THANK YOU FOR EVERYTHING!
OF COURSE! YOU'RE ALWAYS WELCOME!
SO YOU'RE GOING TO GO TO TEL AVIV LATER TODAY?
YEAH, I GUESS I'LL JUST SPEND THE AFTERNOON WANDERING AROUND AND THEN I'LL CRASH AT MY COUSIN'S PLACE.
THEN MY FLIGHT TO ISTANBUL LEAVES AT 5 A.M. TOMORROW MORNING. YIKES!
HEY, I HAVE A GOOD IDEA...
MY FRIEND DANI LIVES IN TEL AVIV AND HE HAS A CAR. WHY DON'T WE GO OUT TONIGHT AND THEN WE CAN GIVE YOU A RIDE TO THE AIRPORT?
YEAH, SURE. I CAN SEE SOME OF TEL AVIV'S "FAMOUS NIGHTLIFE." I CAN JUST SLEEP ON THE PLANE.
I DON'T KNOW HOW MUCH SLEEP YOU'LL GET. ISN'T IT ONLY A TWO-HOUR FLIGHT?
AH, SOMETHING LIKE THAT. I'LL SLEEP WHEN I'M DEAD.
SO WHY ARE YOU GOING TO ISTANBUL? I THOUGHT YOU WERE GOING HOME.
WELL, I HAD TO BOOK MY TICKET BACK WITH TURKISH AIRLINES AND THERE'S AN OPTION TO STAY OVER FOR TWENTY-FOUR HOURS AT NO EXTRA CHARGE, SO I DECIDED TO TAKE IT. I THOUGHT IT MIGHT BE NICE TO DECOMPRESS FOR A DAY.
ISRAEL MUST BE REALLY STRESSFUL TO YOU IF YOU CONSIDER ISTANBUL A PLACE TO DECOMPRESS!
HOTEL
BEFORE I CATCH MY BUS TO TEL AVIV, NADAN AND I GRAB SOME LUNCH AND I ASK HIM SOME MORE QUESTIONS ABOUT LIFE IN ISRAEL.
...SO I WORKED ON HER CAMPAIGN AND NOW I'M AN INTERN FOR HER AT THE KNESSET ONCE A WEEK.
I LIKE NADAN. HE CARES ABOUT PEOPLE AND HE AND I SEEM TO SHARE A SIMILAR WORLDVIEW...THAT IS, UNTIL WE START TALKING ABOUT "THE SITUATION" AGAIN.
PLEASE. ISRAEL IS NOT RACIST.

203

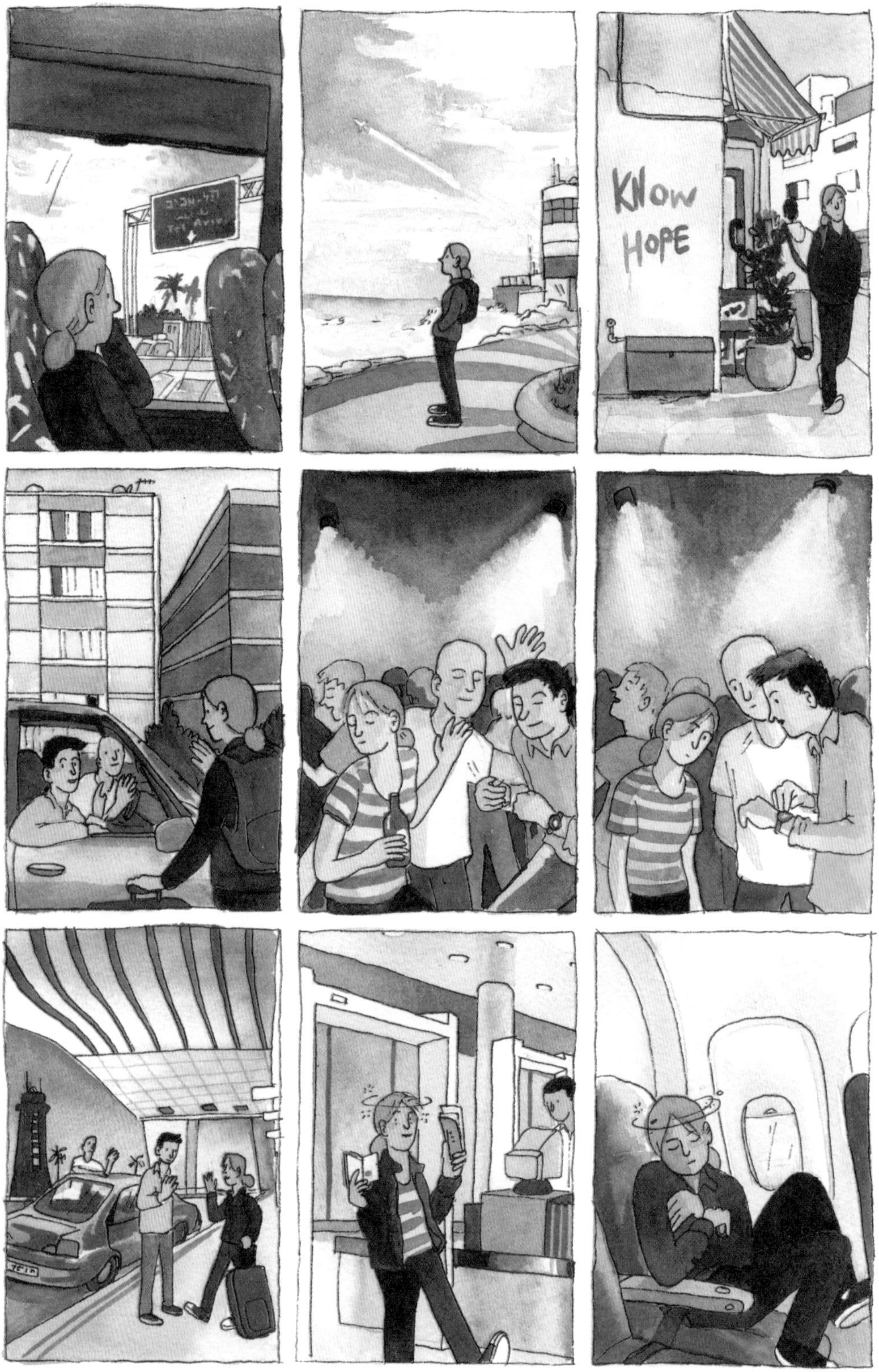
KNOW HOPE

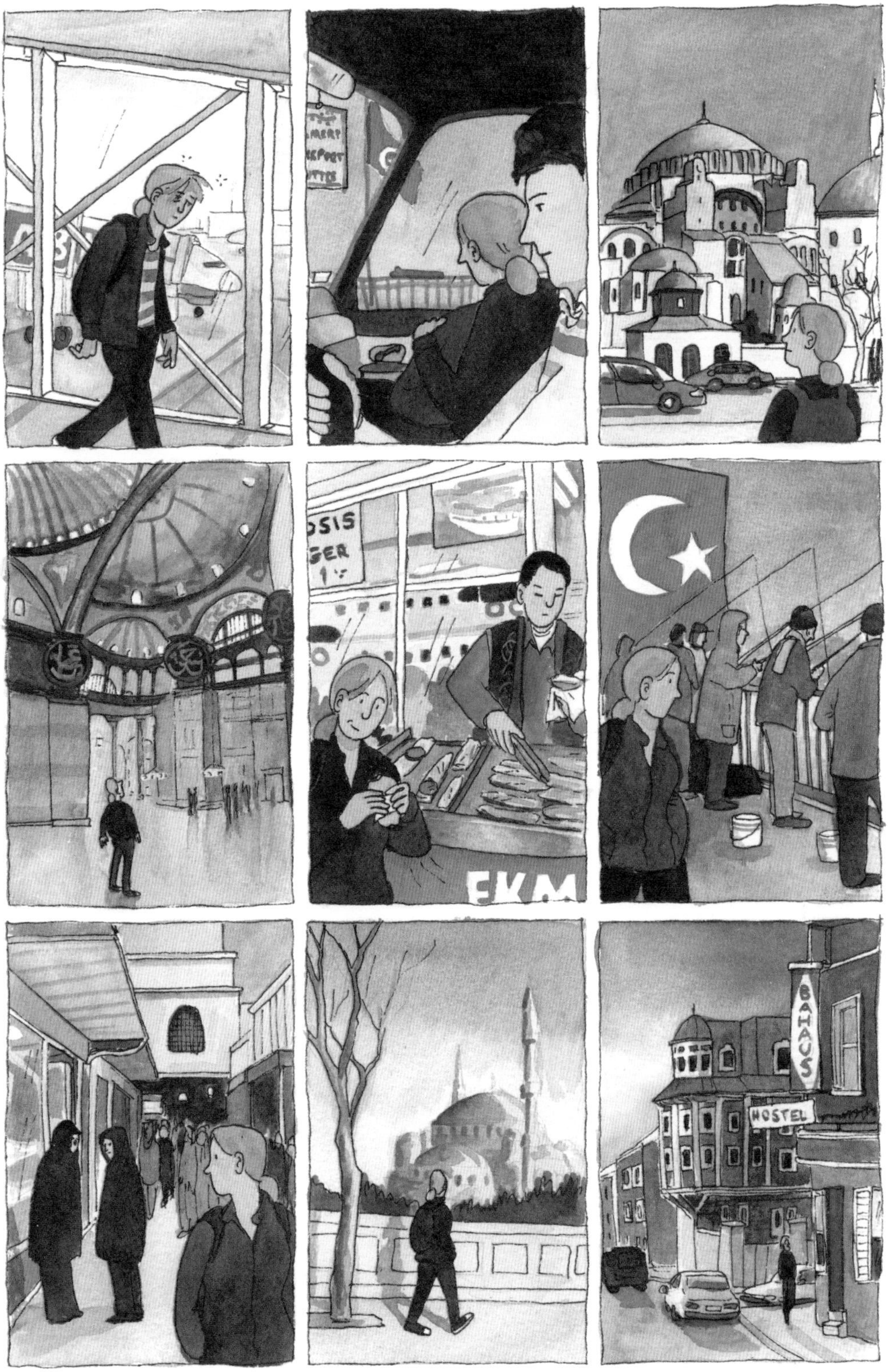
BAHAUS
HOSTEL

ALIYAH: A Hebrew word that translates to "going up" or "ascent" and refers to the emigration of a Jew to Israel. Israel's "Law of Return" states that any Jew may be granted Israeli citizenship. Aliyah also refers to several waves of emigration to Israel, the first aliyah taking place at the tail end of the nineteenth century.

BRITISH MANDATED PALESTINE: After the First World War the Ottoman Empire was dissolved and its territories split up by the Allied European forces. Britain took control over the areas then known as Palestine and Transjordan (now Jordan) and remained in control until 1948.

DREYFUS AFFAIR: A political scandal that took place at the end of the nineteenth century in which a young French Jewish military officer was accused of spying even after evidence of his innocence surfaced. This signaled to many Western European Jews that they were not as accepted by the rest of society as they had previously believed.

GREEN LINE: The armistice line agreed upon by Israel, Syria, Jordan, and Egypt after the 1949 Armistice in which Israel gained its independence. This line separates Israel from the Gaza Strip, the Golan Heights, the West Bank, and the Sinai Peninsula, territory that Israel later captured in the war of 1967.

HAMAS: Palestinian Islamist group and political party that now governs the Gaza Strip. The original Hamas charter called for eradicating Israel as a Jewish state, and encourages suicide bombings and other means of violent action. Although Hamas still refuses to recognize Israel as a Jewish state, there were two successive reconciliation agreements and the formation of a national unity government that took place in 2014 between Fatah and Hamas.

HASIDIC JUDAISM: An ultra-Orthodox sect of Judaism with origins in the shtetls ("small towns" in Yiddish) of Eastern Europe.

HEZBOLLAH: Shi'a Islamist organization based in Lebanon classified by many Western countries, the United States, and Israel as a terrorist organization. Hezbollah's mission statement includes the erasure of the state of Israel through violent means.

INTIFADA: An Arabic word that translates to "uprising" and refers to a mass uprising of the Palestinian population against Israeli occupation. The second Intifada, much more violent than the first, is said to have taken place between 2000 and 2010. While these dates are not agreed upon by all (some sources claim it ended as early as 2003), the Israeli Information Center for Human Rights in the Occupied Territories (B'Tselem), approximates a death toll of 6,400 Palestinians and 1,100 Isralis during that period.

KIBBUTZ: A collective community started in Israel in the early twentieth century with roots in Zionism and Socialism. A kibbutznik is a member of a kibbutz.

KOENIG MEMORANDUM: An internal Israeli report that was leaked to an Israeli newspaper in 1976 and sparked outrage among the Palestinian population. The report suggested ways to reduce the influence of Arab citizens of Israel.

KNESSET: Israeli legislative body that operates out of Jerusalem.

T. E. LAWRENCE: (Made famous by the film *Lawrence of Arabia*.) British officer who acted as a liaison and fought alongside those involved in the Arab Revolt against the Ottoman Empire in the years 1916–1918.

MOSHE DAYAN: Israeli military figure who played a large role in the 1948 war and went on to become Defense Minister during the wars in 1967 and 1973.

PALESTINIAN AUTHORITY (PA): Administrative body responsible for the West Bank, and until 2006, the Gaza Strip. Hamas has controlled Gaza since 2007.

PURIM: This Jewish holiday commemorates a biblical event in which the Jews living in Persia were saved from an extermination plot by Esther, wife of the King of Persia, who kept her identity as a Jew a secret, and her cousin Mordecai. Purim is celebrated in a carnivalesque fashion that includes costumes. For this reason Americans consider Purim to be "Jewish Halloween."

YITZHAK RABIN: Israeli military commander during the 1948 war who went on to serve two nonconsecutive terms as Prime Minister. He was awarded the Nobel Peace Prize along with Yasser Arafat and Shimon Peres for his role in the signing of the Oslo Accords, and was assassinated in 1995 by Yigal Amir, an Orthodox Jew who was opposed to the peace process.

RACHEL THE POET: Also known as Rachel Bluwstein Sela, one of Israel's most famous poets. She was born in Russia and was part of the first wave of Zionist immigrants in the early twentieth century.

SHABBAT: A weekly ritual practiced by all sects of Judaism that welcomes a day of rest, beginning at sundown on Friday night. Work is forbidden, and this includes driving and the lighting of fire, which means cooking is forbidden. Many Israelis are secular, but hotels and other businesses often keep Shabbat in deference to religious law.

SHIVA: A Hebrew word that translates to "seven" and refers to the seven-day mourning ritual. When the family of the deceased is "sitting shiva," they stay at home and follow a variety of bereavement rituals. Friends and relatives visit and bring food to the grieving family.

THE WHITE PAPER: British policy instituted in 1939 that put limits on how many Jewish immigrants were allowed into British-mandated Palestine.

A VERY INCOMPLETE TIMELINE OF THE HISTORY OF ISRAEL

1880s: Over 200 anti-Jewish pogroms take place in Russia and Ukraine.

1894: Dreyfus Affair.

1897: First Zionist National Conference held in Switzerland, led by Theodor Herzl, and states goal to return Jews to Palestine or "Eretz Yisrael" (Land of Israel).

1882–1903: First aliyah. About 35,000 Jews immigrate to Palestine.

1904–1914: Second aliyah. About 40,000 Jews immigrate to Palestine.

1917: Balfour Declaration states British government's support for an "establishment of a national home for the Jewish people in Palestine."

1923: British Mandate of Palestine begins after post-World War I breakup of the Ottoman Empire. The British will remain in control of Palestine until 1948.

1936–1939: Arabs in Palestine revolt against British rulers and Jewish immigrants.

1939: British White Paper restricts Jewish immigrants to 75,000 over the following five years.

1939–1945: World War II. During this time, approximately 100,000 Jewish refugees secretly entered Palestine to escape Nazis in Europe.

1947: After decades of friction between Jews and Arabs in Palestine, the British announce that they will end their mandate. The UN agrees on a partition plan splitting the land into Jewish and Palestinian states, but this is rejected by Arab leaders. Fighting intensifies between the groups.

1948: Israel declares its independence on the night before the British are set to end their mandate.

1948–1949: War between the Jews and Arabs, called the War of Independence by the Jews and the Nakba (Arabic for "catastrophe") by the Arabs. According to a United Nations estimate, 750,000 Arabs became refugees as a result of the war.

1967: Six-Day War in which Israel captures territory now known as the Gaza Strip, the Golan Heights, the Sinai Peninsula, and the West Bank, including East Jerusalem.

1973: Yom Kippur War in which Syria and Egypt launch attack on Israel.

1974: Israel begins withdrawal from Sinai Peninsula.

1979: Israel and Egypt sign peace treaty.

1982: Lebanon War in which Israel invades Lebanon to expel Palestine Liberation Organization. Most Israeli troops are withdrawn by 1985 with Israel Defense Forces troops remaining in the south until the year 2000.

1987: First Intifada begins.

1991: Peace process begins with Madrid Conference in October.

1993: Palestine Liberation Organization Chairman Yasser Arafat and Israel Prime Minister Yitzhak Rabin agree to Declaration of Principles on Interim Self-Government, also known as the Oslo Accords.

1994: Israel and Jordan sign peace treaty.

1995: Assassination of Yitzhak Rabin.

2000–2010: Second Intifada.

2005: Israel withdraws unilaterally from the Gaza Strip.

2006: Hamas wins in first democratic Palestinian election and assumes political control of Gaza. Hamas not recognized as legitimate government by Israel, the United States, or the European Union.

2006: Second Lebanon war, sparked when Hezbollah kills three IDF soldiers and kidnaps two others.

BIBLIOGRAPHY

Agule, Rebecca. "Israel's Bedouin Villages Struggle for Existence." Harvard Law Record. 19 Nov 2009. hlrecord.org/2009/11/israels-bedouin-villages-struggle-for-existence

Armstrong, Karen. *A Short History of Myth.* New York: Canongate, 2006.

Ben-Yehuda, Nachman. *The Masada Myth.* Madison: University of Wisconsin Press, 1995.

Human Rights Watch. *Off The Map: Land and Housing Rights Violations in Israel's Unrecognized Bedouin Villages.* March, 2008. hrw.org/reports/2008/iopt0308

Josephus, Flavius, translated by Geoffrey Williamson, revised by E. Mary Smallwood. *The Jewish War.* London: Penguin, 1981.

Kushner, Tony, and Alisa Solomon, eds. *Wrestling with Zion: Progressive Jewish-American Responses to the Israeli-Palestinian Conflict.* New York: Grove Press, 2003. (Melanie Kaye essay referenced from this book, Kaye anecdote attributed to Larry Bush.)

McGreal, Chris. "Bedouin Feel the Squeeze as Israel Resettles the Negev Desert." Guardian UK. 27 Feb, 2003. guardian.co.uk/world/2003/feb/27/israel

Tessler, Mark. *A History of the Israeli-Palestinian Conflict* Bloomington and Indianapolis: Indiana University Press, 1994.

David Ben-Gurion quotations can be found at: palestineremembered.com/Acre/Famous-Zionist-Quotes/Story638.html Posted Oct 23, 2001.

SARAH GLIDDEN was born in 1980 in Massachusetts and earned a BFA in painting at Boston University. While living in NYC, she was a member of the Flux Factory and Pizza Island artist collectives where she made comics and created her first graphic novel *How to Understand Israel in 60 Days or Less*. In 2010, Glidden shadowed journalists from the *Seattle Globalist* as they reported from Turkey, Iraq, Lebanon, and Syria. Their interviews with refugees and internally displaced people form her second graphic novel, *Rolling Blackouts: Dispatches from Turkey, Syria, and Iraq*. She currently lives in Seattle.

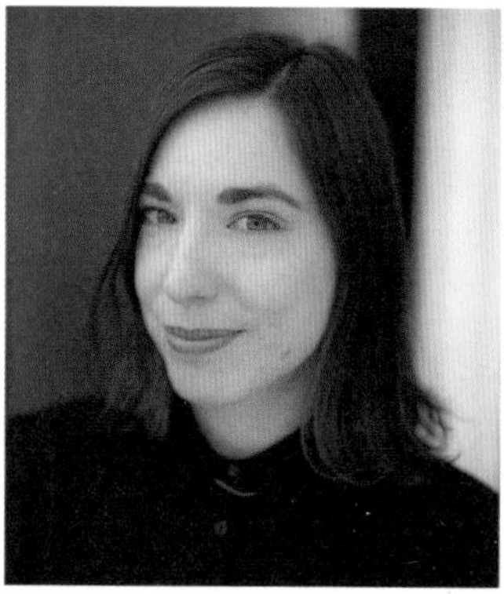

AUTHOR'S NOTE

The reader should be aware that this is a memoir. Certain conversations and timelines have been altered either due to the decay of memory or in order to suit the narrative but always in keeping with an earnest intent to honestly describe the author's experience of events as they occurred.

ACKNOWLEDGEMENTS

Thank-yous go out to Julia Wertz, Tom Hart, Tim Kreider, Jason Little, Nadan Feldman, Emily Brandt, Dylan Williams, Alec Longstreth, AWP, Pizza Island, Chen Tamir, Bob Mecoy, Jonathan Vankin, Bill Frankel, L'Entreprise Culturelle, WOAH Gallery Berlin, and my family. And very special thanks to Jamil Zaki.—Sarah Glidden

Font design: Clem Robins.

sarahglidden.com
drawnandquarterly.com

First Drawn & Quarterly edition: September 2016
Printed in China. 10 9 8 7 6 5 4 3 2 1

Library and Archives Canada Cataloguing in Publication: Glidden, Sarah, author, illustrator. *How to Understand Israel in 60 Days or Less* / Sarah Glidden. Originally published: New York: Vertigo/DC Comics, © 2010. ISBN 978-1-77046-253-3 (paperback) 1. Glidden, Sarah–Travel–Israel–Comic books, strips, etc. 2. Americans–Travel–Israel–Comic books, strips, etc. 3. Jews–United States–Biography–Comic books, strips, etc. 4. Arab-Israeli conflict–Comic books, strips, etc. 5. Israel–History–Comic books, strips, etc. 6. Israel–Description and travel–Comic books, strips, etc. 7. Graphic novels. I. Title. DS128.2.G65 2016 956.94 C2016-900978-5. Published in the USA by Drawn & Quarterly, a client publisher of Farrar, Straus and Giroux. Orders: 888.330.8477. Published in Canada by Drawn & Quarterly, a client publisher of Raincoast Books. Orders: 800.663.5714.